One-Room Country Schools
History and Recollections from Wisconsin

by Jerry Apps

Amherst Press
A Division of Palmer Publications, Inc.
318 N. Main Street
Amherst, Wisconsin 54406

Library of Congress Cataloging-in-Publication Data

Apps, Jerold W., 1934-
    One-room country schools : history and recollections
from Wisconsin /by Jerry Apps. — 1st ed.
        p. cm.
    Includes bibliographical references and index.
    ISBN 0-942495-53-5
    1. Rural schools—Wisconsin—History. I. Title.
LC5147.W6A67 1996
370.19'346'09775—dc20   96-7046
                                            CIP

Printed in the United States of America at Palmer Publications, Inc.

Dedicated to my country school teachers:
Theresa Piechowski, Maty Murty, Violet Lovejoy, Blanche Swett,
Maxine Thompson, and Faith Jenks.

Table of Contents

Preface vii

1   Memories 1

2   Early History 9

3   The Teachers 25

4   Preparing And Supporting Teachers 41

5   All In A Day 57

6   Lessons That Were Learned 69

7   School Of The Air 89

8   Here Comes Santa Claus 99

9   Recess 111

10   Softball 121

11   Up Hill Both Ways 129

12   Beyond The School Room 139

13   Selected Schools 147

14   Modern Day One-Room Schools 165

15   Consolidation 175

16   Learning From The Past 191

Appendix A: Recess Games 201

Appendix B: School Museums 209

Preface

After graduating from a one-room country school in 1947, I took my elementary education for granted, until rather recently. For the last couple of decades, people throughout the United States have been discussing the shortcomings of public education and how it could be improved. As I became acquainted with these discussions, it occurred to me that my elementary education had been excellent, particularly in such basics as reading, spelling, arithmetic, writing, geography, and public speaking. This foundation has served me well over the years, and I gained it in an extremely modest building with all eight grades working together under the direction of one teacher.

A couple of years ago I set out to record what went on in these little one-room schools that were scattered throughout Wisconsin as well as in many other states. How did these schools provide an excellent education for most of the students who attended them? And, likewise, what were their shortcomings?

To begin, I looked at my eight years as a pupil in a one-room school in Waushara County, Wisconsin. But I wanted this book to be more than my own experience. Working with the Wisconsin Retired Educators Association, I asked former teachers and students of one-room schools to send me their stories, and their photos. I gave a talk to the retired teachers at their annual meeting, and asked for information. At the School of The Arts in Rhinelander, where I teach each summer, I mentioned my interest. I discovered several former teachers and students of one-room schools attending the School of Arts, and I interviewed several of them.

The weekly newspaper, The Country Today, printed my request for country school information. The Council for Local History, of the State Historical Society of Wisconsin, ran a notice saying that I wanted information on schools. The word was out.

The letters and photos began pouring in. In many instances, I followed up with interviews and received yet further information. At one point I was nearly overwhelmed with material. I spoke at a rural historical society meeting and asked who in the group had attended or taught at a one-room country school. Three-quarters of the hands went up. Everyone, it seemed, had information for me, and a story about the school they attended.

Early in the development of this book, I decided I couldn't list all the one-room country schools in Wisconsin—there were more than 6,000 of them. Thus some readers will be disappointed when they do not find the name of their school on these pages. Many people sent me information about their schools. I've included much of it, but much more I had to leave out. As I dove into the research, I looked for old textbooks, recess games, history of the earliest schools, Arbor Day, Christmas programs, and the School of The Air. I also searched for, and found, considerable material criticizing the one-room school. A groundswell of opposition to the small school districts and the often very low enrollment of country schools led to legislation that eventually caused the consolidation of rural school districts, and the busing of children to larger schools, often located in villages and cities.

At the end of chapters, I have included notes that list published materials I used. But much of the quoted material in the book comes from interviews and personal correspondence. Several hundred people were ultimately involved in the project, and I owe each of them a special thanks. I have tried as diligently as possible to make sure the source of all material is noted, both published and unpublished.

Many of the photos in this book came from the closets and dressers of former teachers and students. In most instances the photographer is unknown, so I have attributed the photos to those who contributed them. Steve Apps, my son, and a photographer for the Post Crescent newspaper in Appleton, took most of the contemporary photos used in the book. A few photos were also obtained from the University of Wisconsin Archives, and from the State Historical Society of Wisconsin.

Several people went to extraordinary efforts to help me with this project and I want to especially thank them: Larry Behlen, Green Lake; Kathy Berigan, Madison; Lelah Bruso, Rhinelander; Jean Elefson, River Falls; Jane Elmer, Wisconsin Retired Educator's Association, Middleton; Betty Epstein, Black River Falls; Wilmer Gorske, Markesan; the late Dorothy Guilday, Rhinelander; Randy Jablonic, Madison; Kathy Klein, LaPointe Elementary School, LaPoint, Wisconsin; George Klingbeil, Madison; Burton Kreitlow, Grand Marais, Minnesota; Roland Krogstad, Madison; Helen Long, Wild Rose; Elmer Marth, Madison; Esther Niewzwiecki, Owen; Ruth Plautz, Kingston; Jane Rahn, Delavan; William Schuette, Reedsburg; Joseph Sveda, Antigo; Ruth

Vaughn, Superior; Nora Walnoha, Sharon; and Carolyn Wedin, Whitewater.

Many more people sent me materials, or took time for me to interview them. I owe each a debt of gratitude.

Several people read various sections of the manuscript and offered excellent suggestions for revision. I especially want to thank Naomi Flugstad and Marie Draeger, former teachers and Dr. Steven Landfried, currently a teacher, and a researcher of one-room schools. My daughter, Susan Horman, a first grade teacher, read much of the manuscript. Not only did she raise interesting and useful questions about what I was saying, but often suggested I could say more clearly what I intended.

Roberta Spanbauer and her staff at Amherst Press offered excellent suggestions, not only for what to title this book, but how to organize some eighteen different topics into something that flowed and made sense.

My wife, Ruth, was involved with this project from the beginning and deserves my profound thanks. She, too, attended a one-room country school for eight years so offered many of her memories. She transcribed all of the taped interviews (a horrendous task), and read all of the chapters, some several times. She was always ready to offer a fresh perspective, constructive help, and a word of encouragement during those times when the project didn't want to come together.

Jerry Apps
October, 1995

Memories

Today, as I stand by my old country school, long since closed and converted into a home, the memories flow. I close my eyes and focus on a time long ago when I, as a five-year-old farm boy, began my schooling in this building located west of Wild Rose, Wisconsin. I remember that late August morning well. It dawned warm and hazy, like so many other mornings that hot and dry summer of 1939.

Although the morning was quiet with scarcely a breath of wind, great expectancy hung in the air. I waited at the end of the sandy driveway that led to our farmstead. I wore a new pair of bib overalls, a blue denim shirt, and new brown shoes that pinched my feet. New bib overalls were special. I dreaded the day they were washed, for in the washing their newness disappeared, and their specialness. So I would try to keep them clean for as many days as possible to avoid the inevitable washing.

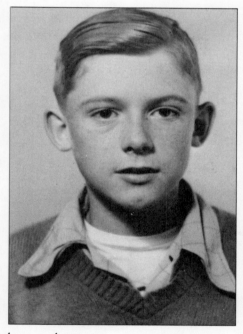

I remember my mother sitting on the porch of our faded white, two-story farm house, husking sweet corn, and occasionally glancing my way as I waited.

Mother insisted that I comb my hair, which I reluctantly did before clamping on my cap. A cap was wonderful for little boys who hated combing their hair, but now I had to comb mine before I could wear my cap. This simple event signaled great changes that were about to occur in my life.

Jerry Apps, 1946

I watched for Mike Korleski, a sixth grade neighbor boy. Earlier my mother had reminded Mike's mother that I would start school today. After what seemed like too long, Mike came into view. He motioned for me, with my lard pail lunch bucket, two new yellow pencils and a five-cent pad of writing paper, to join him. Elderberries hung heavy alongside the dusty dirt road shaded with elm, oak, aspen, and wild cherry trees. As we walked along, we stopped to look at a squirrel scampering in an oak tree. We saw a goldenrod's yellow head hanging over the road, an orange butterfly flitting from flower to flower. We looked for awhile at a striped caterpillar crawling in the dust. But I wasn't as interested in these things this morning. My thoughts were all about school. What would it be like? What other kids would I meet? Would I be able to learn all that kids have to learn?

I stumbled along, walking fast to keep up with long-legged Mike. Impatiently I waited when he explored something or other in the dusty fence rows.

In the distance we heard the eight-thirty school bell, echoing down the valley where the schoolhouse stood and rolling up the hills that surrounded. The school bell's sound alerted those who lived in the Chain O' Lake School District Number Four that school for the fall term was beginning. Children trudged along dirt roads from the east, and from the south, and from the west, as we came from the north.

The bell's sound echoed past Miller's farm and McKinley Jenks' place. Jesse Dewitt heard the bell ring, and although he no longer had children in school, he stopped cutting corn and listened to the clear tones, memories of his school days flooding his mind. The bell's sound rolled over Floyd Jeffers' farm and past Vilas Olson's place. We, too, heard the school bell as Mike stopped to watch Miller's cows grazing in the pasture alongside the road. I waited, but had more important things on my mind than watching Miller's Holsteins, besides I could always watch our own cows. Finally, Mike decided that we must hurry a little, to make sure we got to school on time.

Topping Miller's hill, we saw the white schoolhouse snuggled among the oak trees, the bell tower standing proudly above the front door. I glimpsed the teeter-totter. Some kids were already putting it to use. Coming into the school yard, other children greeted us.

Mike Korleski led me up the steps and into the vast expanse of school room. The pungent smell of freshly oiled floor rolled over me. It was a foreign smell, like nothing I had come across on our farm, and farms have many smells. In the front of the room, behind a huge wooden desk, sat a black-haired woman. Mike Korleski said, "This here is Jerry Apps and he's in first grade this year."

Theresa Piechowski stood up and thrust out her hand to shake mine. "Let's find a place for your lunch bucket," she said, as she led me to the entry way in back of the school.

With the ringing of the nine o'clock bell (an eighth grader had that envious task) I eased into my assigned seat, in a corner of the front of

SCHOOL DAYS
John Greenleaf Whittier
(1869)

Still sits the school-
house by the road,
A ragged beggar
sunning;
Around it still the
sumacs grow,
And blackberry vines
are running.

Within the master's
desk is seen,
Deep scarred by raps
official;
The warping floor,
the battered seats,
The jack-knife's
carved initial;

The charcoal frescoes
on its wall;
Its door's worn sill,
betraying
The feet that, creeping
slow to school,
Went storming out
to playing!

Chain O' Lake School, Waushara County, 1945. Author in second row, first person on the left, in seventh grade.

the room and not far from the teacher's desk. The little desks were in the front and they gradually became larger toward the back, near the huge old black stove that we all came to alternately love and hate as the school days passed.

In the left front of the school room I glimpsed a large white structure, filled with sand. Later I learned it was a sand box, and we'd use it for many projects, from nature to history. A blackboard stretched across the entire front of the school room, not far from my desk. The alphabet, was written across the top of the blackboard, in what I learned later was cursive writing. I just called it writing, because I had seen my mother doing it many times.

A picture of Abraham Lincoln hung on the left front wall, and a print of George Washington was to Lincoln's right, although on this day the pictures were mysteries to me. I had never seen these men before and I wondered who they were and why they were so important that their pictures hang in the front of our school. On the north wall, between the long tall windows, was a windup clock. I could tell by the winding key I spotted. On quiet days, when everyone was busy working, "tick-tock, tick-tock" would be the only sound in the room, except during the winter when the crackling of the wood in the stove punctuated the silence,

Author's first grade report card, 1940. Grades were given for reading, art, language, spelling & phonics, and deportment.

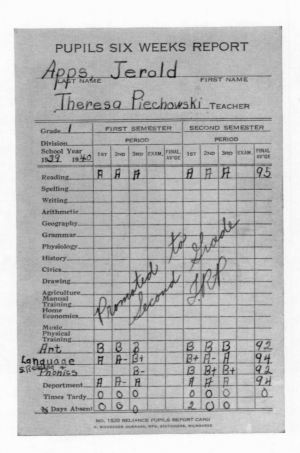

or the wind whistled around the corners of the building and rattled the windows.

An old brown upright piano stood in the northwest corner of the room. Teachers who knew how played it everyday, but it stood silent those years when teachers didn't. During the years it was not used, it became a nesting place for mice, and the only time we heard it was during Christmas programs and other events when someone other than the teacher played the instrument. Because of the mouse damage, the piano alternately sounded like a bar room honky tonk, or a regular piano, depending on which keys were struck.

A table model, battery-powered Philco radio stood on a corner of the teacher's desk, our link to the outside world, and our tie to the Wisconsin School of the Air which was a regular part of our weekly learning. It was absolutely taboo to listen to the radio at any other time than when we were receiving public radio programs for fear of running down the battery.

Just under Lincoln's picture I spotted the map case, organized so the teacher could pull down a map like one would pull down a shade over a window. There was a map of the United States. I believed then that the states were actually different colors. It must have been by second or third grade before I realized that Ohio really wasn't yellow, and that Minnesota wasn't orange. Somehow, I had assumed that if you traveled outside of Wisconsin the color the state you visited would be the color represented on the map.

In the back of the school room, to the left of the stove, I saw a bookshelf with row upon row of books. The book shelves stood taller than I, and they stretched maybe ten feet to the north side of the room. I had never seen so many books in one place before. At home we had only five or six books: the Holy Bible, some kind of religious book written in German, Uncle Wigley books that my mother read to me, and a book about what to do when a horse came up lame, or a cow took sick. That was about it for books at our house. Now there were shelves of them, holding mysteries of every sort, with stories about places in the world I had never known, and situations I had never experienced.

A book is a garden.
A book is an orchard.
A book is a storehouse.
A book is a party.
It is company by the
way; it is a counselor;
it is a multitude of
counselors.
—Beecher

A cupboard with closed doors stood on the right side of the stove. Later I learned that the chocolate flavored goiter pills were stored there, along with an extra box of chalk, paper of various colors, construction paper the teacher called it, and a couple of box games that we would play during recess on rainy days.

A gray porcelain water cooler stood on a little shelf by a sink in the southeast corner of the building. I quickly learned that a daily duty for older students was to carry water from the pump house and fill the water cooler each morning, and on warm days, again at noon.

The water cooler had a silver pipe that came out the side near the bottom and was curved upward at the end. By pushing a button, the water shot up in a little stream that I could catch in my mouth. Underneath the end of the pipe was a little shiny cup with a hole in the bottom that kept the water from splattering.

I learned I could walk back to the water cooler anytime I wanted for a drink of water; the teacher said so. And I must admit, I did it fairly often because I had never seen such a wonderful little device, that with merely a push of a button, water bubbled up for me to drink. At home we got our water from a pail. If we wanted a drink, we used a dipper that hung on a nearby nail. At school we had neither water pail nor dipper, but this ingenious water cooler with its clever little button.

As I stand with my eyes closed, I can see every detail of the school room, and the school yard, too. The girl's outhouse in the northwest corner of the acre school yard, the boy's toilet in the southwest corner. The red woodshed-pump house building just south of the school building. In the pump house was a pump handle pump and a few week's supply of kindling wood for the school's wood stove. Enough wood to last most of the winter was stored in the woodshed part of the building. School board members made sure the woodshed was filled each fall, and replenished again in the late winter if the weather was especially harsh.

Long two-inch planks were stored in the upper reaches of the woodshed, pulled down after Thanksgiving each year, to become a part of the stage that stretched across the front of the school. Shortly after Thanksgiving we would begin practicing for the highlight of the year, the Christmas program.

A woven wire fence stretched around the school grounds. To the south, lilac bushes obscured the wire and would provide the most wonderful smells in spring, when the purple flowers opened. My father disliked lilacs, so this was my first introduction to this wonderful sturdy shrub.

The flag pole stood near the front gate to the school yard, an American flag always fluttered in the breeze when school was in session. Opening exercises included raising the flag. An especially well-behaved student had the privilege of actually running the flag up the pole, and then taking it down again in the late afternoon, always being especially careful to never, ever, let the flag touch the ground.

Now as I stand in front of the old building, I recall not only the building and what it contained, and the outbuildings and their uses, but I recall my classmates and the good times and bad that were associated with my eight years of schooling there.

I recall with fond memories recess time when the schoolhouse door burst open and the laughing children rushed to the wooden plank teeter-totter, and climbed aboard, a child on each end of the plank. The teeter-totter's squeak echoed throughout the school yard as other children organized a special ball game on either side of the red woodshed. The yell of "anti-I-over" was heard over the rhythmic squeaking of the teeter-totter, and the muffled laughter of the little first and second grade girls, too small yet to play anti-I-over, and content to play with their simple, homemade dolls.

The red rubber ball, not so red anymore from almost daily use, came bouncing over the roof and was caught by one of the seventh grade boys. He, together with all the other children on his side of the wood-

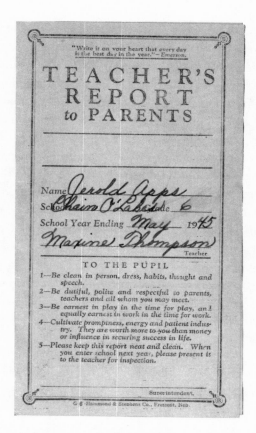

1945 report card.

shed, ran around the west end of the building, hoping to surprise and touch one or more of the children with the ball so that they became a part of his team.

There are other recollections. Country schools illicit memories of fall days waiting for the first snow, of winter days and longing for spring, of spring days anticipating summer vacation. There are memories of long division and the embarrassment of standing at the blackboard with chalk in hand, not knowing what to do with the numbers scrawled in front of you. Memories of the frigid days of winter when everyone gathered around the mammoth wood stove, with the appetite creating smells of homemade soup warming in a pan blending with the pungent smell of drying mittens.

There are memories of teachers, dedicated servants who received scant pay for their work which included building fires, tending to cuts and scrapes, planning programs for the entire community and teaching all eight grades in one room, without electricity, indoor plumbing, or central heating.

There are memories of consolidation, and the fiery community splitting debates. And then the country schools closed, nearly everyone one of them, in a period of a few years. The country kids, accustomed to walking a mile or two one-way to school climbed on buses and bounced around the countryside, sometimes for an hour or more, on their way to school. It was called progress. The new way. The modern approach.

Some of the closed school buildings became storage sheds and cattle barns. Many became homes, town halls, community centers, and museums. Some just stood alone, on their little parcel of land—abandoned. No sounds of children laughing while they played softball, or pom-pom-pull-way, or run sheep run, or fox-in-geese after a fresh snow fall in winter. No squeaky chalk on freshly washed blackboards. No smell of oak smoke from a cranky wood stove. No aroma of fresh paste, or drying mittens. No twisty shoveled paths through the snow to the outhouses.

The passing of an era. The closing of a page in history. Now there are memories, many memories in the heads of former teachers and students who walked the dusty roads, sat in the hard desks, recited, read, studied, listened, helped each other to read and write, and do long division—helped each other learn.

Early History

To begin understanding one-room country schools in Wisconsin, we must go back to some of the early history of the state and its attempts at providing education for its young people. Wisconsin had one-room country schools for nearly 200 years, from French trading days to the 1960s. Early one-room schools were crude structures, generally constructed of logs and heated with a wood stove. Rudely constructed outdoor privies served as toilets. A school was considered advanced if it had separate toilets for boys and girls. Later, the log buildings were replaced with wood frame structures; a few were constructed of brick or stone. In 1934, Martha Riley, an educator researching one-room country school history, wrote her graduate thesis on the topic. In her thesis she explained that the early schools had no grades and few books. The teacher taught any way he or she wanted, with or without the help of books. There were no maps and no blackboards and each pupil was called to recite his lessons each day.

In her research, Riley discovered that in winter the schools often enrolled from thirty to eighty pupils. There was also a two-month sum-

Quarry School children, Waukesha County, 1892-1893.

From Joy Buslaff.

mer school. A teacher in Waukesha County, in the 1860s, was known to teach a school of 112 pupils. She learned that during the 1800s, men teachers were in great demand during winter months when the older boys attended. Teachers who could handle disorderly pupils were wanted in many districts. Young women received $1.25 to $2.00 per week for teaching. Men received up to $20.00 per month. Board and room was often provided by the community.[1]

When rural electric lines marched across the state just before and immediately following World War II, the schools replaced kerosene and gas lamps with electric bulbs. But for most of them, the rusty wood stoves and smelly outhouses remained until the school closed.

All eight grades, from timid five or six year olds to those fourteen or older, gathered in one room, with one teacher, often a teenager, and she or he with extremely limited educational training. In the earliest one-room schools the teacher may have only completed eight grades before becoming a teacher. In later years, teachers completed high school plus two years of normal school.

Fernside School, Sauk County, 1900.

From Sauk County Rural Schools History Project, William C. Schuette.

Thousands of these little buildings dotted the northern regions of the United States. When school consolidation was underway in the 1950s and 1960s, they closed and rural children were bused to nearby village and city schools. Today, only a handful remain as operating schools, although many of the buildings stand as quiet reminders of an earlier day when elementary education held a very special place in the hearts and minds of the people who lived in each school district.

In The Early Years

Wisconsin's earliest schools were constructed at the French trading posts. Jean Nicolet stepped ashore at Red Banks, north of Green Bay, in 1634, and lands that were to later become Wisconsin were soon immersed in fur trading. It was a time of small trading posts and missionary priests.

Fur trading was a nomadic occupation, and only when the traders got too old to travel did they build cabins and live in one place, usually near a trading post. By the middle 1700s a few families lived at Prairie du Chien, Portage, and at La Baye (later Green Bay). These settlements were on the historic travel route formed by the Fox River, with a brief overland trip at Portage to the Wisconsin River, and then on to the mighty Mississippi.[2]

The first organized school in the region opened in 1791, when Jacques Porlier, considered Wisconsin's first schoolmaster, was hired to teach Pierre Grignon's children in Green Bay.[3] He soon left teaching to devote full time to his employer's fur trading business.

By 1817, schools were quite common in Green Bay and Prairie du Chien. They were supported by religious organizations as well as by the community. Legislation creating the Michigan Territory, of which Wisconsin was a part from 1818 to 1836, provided for schools in the territory and that tax money, at least in part, ought to support them. The Michigan law stipulated:

✐ The township should have responsibility for examining teachers and visiting schools.

✐ The cost of building a school building was to come from district taxes on property, but it could be paid in labor or materials instead of money.

✐ If other money was insufficient, a rate-bill tax could be levied on the parents in proportion to the number of children they had in school.

🖋 Parents, additionally, were required to contribute wood for fuel, again based on the number of children in school.

🖋 The cost of teaching indigent children was to come from general property tax.[4]

By 1839, Mineral Point and the citizens of Grant County had petitioned the legislature for help in supporting their schools. Money from the stipulations of Michigan law were plainly inadequate.

Most schools, during the years before Wisconsin became a state, were subscription-type schools, popular during colonial times in New England. Students attending subscription schools paid for their schooling. For example, in Green Bay in 1817 Thomas S. Johnson was hired to teach reading, writing, arithmetic and the English language to children in the area. Nine men in the community signed the agreement with Johnson, and they agreed to pay his salary of $6.00 per student. The parents of the children who subscribed to the school provided the teacher's salary, a "suitable house for the reception of the scholars, and the necessary wood. . . ."[5]

Train up a child in the way he should go; and when he is old he will not depart from it.

—*Webster's American Spelling Book, 1831*

The first known school in Iowa County began in Mineral Point in 1829, seven years before Wisconsin became a territory. The school was a small cabin made of poles and sod, built to house pupils for only a few months of the year. The first teacher was a Mrs. Harker.[6]

New England Schools

To understand the foundation for Wisconsin's one-room schools, we must look to New England and examine colonial schools.

In 1647, the Massachusetts Bay Colony passed a law establishing a school system. The schools were called petty schools and became the forerunner of grammar schools. The law stated that "The General Court of Massachusetts, 'taking into consideration the great neglect of many parents and guardians in training up their children,' required that the selectman in each township make provision for building schools."[7] The support for these schools came from a combination of taxes, land rental, and parents who contributed a few pennies a week.

Most formal education was in the hands of the church. The basic purpose for the schools was to teach young people how to read the Bible, and, if they continued their education, to become preachers. In the 17th and 18th centuries, parents believed their children were doomed for damnation unless they were saved through religion. The school's purpose was to help with the children's salvation. The curriculum in these church sponsored schools focused mostly on scripture, Biblical teaching, and rudimentary Latin. Secondarily, these schools taught reading, writing, and arithmetic.

Beyond religious purposes, early colonial schools throughout New England focused on developing national patriotism. Noah Webster's "blue backed speller," as it was popularly called, included many moral and patriotic essays.

When the United States Constitution was drafted in 1787, no provision was made for schools and education. Article Ten of the Bill of Rights, adopted in 1791, stated that all powers not specifically delegated to the federal government became the responsibility of the states. Thus public education became each state's obligation. Responsibility for schooling was further decentralized by state laws to the townships, the smallest form of organized government. Within the townships school districts were formed, an even smaller unit of local government. A local school district often was no larger than four miles square with the school located in the center of the district. The reason for the district's small size was so no child would have to walk farther than two miles to school. There were, of course, many exceptions to this.

Before paper and pencils, slates were commonly used in schools.

Photo by Steve Apps.

The colonial school model, with township schools under the control of township government, became widely adopted, with many adjustments to be sure, in the Northeast, Middle West, and later in the West. In the South, however, a different educational structure emerged. For those families with money, private schools at home and abroad, plus private tutors became popular. For the poor, educational opportunities were sparse.

School Legislation

Thomas Jefferson believed in free public education as an essential ingredient for a strong democracy. The Northwest Ordinances of 1785 and 1787 encompassed land which later become Ohio, Illinois, Indiana, Wisconsin and Michigan, and included providing public lands for

*1892 plans for
one-room schools.*

ARCHITECTURE

VENTILATION

AND

FURNISHING

OF

School Houses

BY

OLIVER E. WELLS

STATE SUPERINTENDENT

———

MADISON, WISCONSIN
1892

ONE ROOM SCHOOL HOUSES　　19

One Room School Houses.

These plans are designed to aid those country and village districts that can ill-afford to employ an architect. It is hoped that they offer valuable suggestions, and will help districts to furnish schoolhouses that are better lighted, better warmed and ventilated, and that will furnish better conveniences for pupils and teachers than are ordinarily found in one-room school buildings.

They will accommodate from 35 to 75 pupils, and may be built at a cost varying from $500 to $1,200. The first cut, from designs by J. Bruess, of Milwaukee, gives the front elevation, a perspective view, and the floor plan of a plain building, designed for country districts. The style is simple and inexpensive. A small fireplace, designed to aid in ventilating the room, and a sash door, giving egress to the boys' play ground, are shown in the floor plan. The room should be warmed by a ventilating stove which is supplied with pure air by a flue leading from the outside under the floor, and through an opening in the floor under the stove to a hot air chamber. Blackboards of suitable width should extend along the entire end opposite the entrance, and along either side to the first window. They may be extended across all the spaces between windows. The teacher's table is at the rear of the room, and the pupils sit with their backs to the entrance.

FRONT ELEVATION

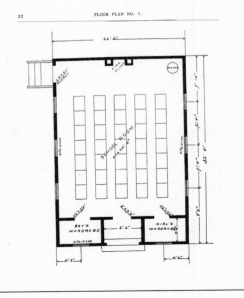

establishing local schools. As each new state was formed, the ordinance stipulated that the sixteenth section of every township of thirty-six sections be sold for the support of schools. The money received was generally used for constructing a school building. However, with so much land available, land prices were often low, and not enough money could be raised to build school buildings.

An 1840 Wisconsin territorial law laid out a plan for townships to organize local schools including examining and certifying teachers, and electing trustees. It also gave county commissioners the right to levy a one-fourth percent tax for building schools and paying teachers. The tax money was to be divided among the various school districts based on the number of students per district. There was no mention of a rate-bill (parents providing some direct monetary support to the school) in this law. Discussions about the power of counties and about taxes in general were heated. How much, if any, county taxes should go toward schools?

The discussions resulted in a new Wisconsin Territorial law passed in 1841, which was a considerable set back for those interested in promoting free public education. The 1841 law essentially threw out the mandatory county tax, and severely restricted the taxing power of the local districts. That law allowed the school districts to tax, but no more than $200 could be used for building purposes. Before taxes could be levied for teachers' salaries, three-fourths of the legal voters in the district had to agree. Rate-bills could be used if not enough money could be raised from other sources.

Most Wisconsin citizens did not like the rate-bill idea, but they disliked property taxes for school purposes even more.[8] Meanwhile, bills to appoint a state superintendent of schools were introduced as early as 1839, but the bills consistently failed. In the last session of the territorial legislature, in 1848, a general school act was passed which lifted restrictions on how much tax money districts could use for building purposes. During the debates over statehood, the matter of schools came up often. The first constitutional convention met in Madison on October 5, 1846 and education was high on its agenda. Wisconsin's new constitution was adopted by the constitutional convention on February 1, 1848 and by the voters of the territory on March 13. Congress ratified the action on May 29, 1848, the official beginning for the state of Wisconsin. Article X of Wisconsin's constitution included several provisions about education. These became known as the School Law of 1848, although some revisions were made in 1849. In brief, the school law said:

It is easier to pull down than to build up.

—Anonymous

✐ Elementary school education should be free to everyone between the ages of four and twenty. Financing for schools should come from the sale of sixteenth section lands, and from interest from sale of federal land grant money originally earmarked for internal improvements. Other funding sources could be state, township and district taxes.

✐ Provided for the election of a state superintendent of schools.

✐ Authorized township boards of supervisors to organize school districts within their respective townships. The local school district would administer the school in its district, and, in most respects, was accountable to no higher government authority. Many claimed later that this provision led to excessive localism, and resulted in substantial differences among school districts. If a district wished to hold down its taxes by contributing minimally to its school and its teacher, it could. If it wanted to support its school well, it did. Some of these disparities continued until the 1960s when the country schools closed with school consolidation.

✐ Provided for a township school superintendent who would examine and certify teachers, and who had the power to consolidate township school districts. The township superintendent did not have the power to create districts. Because the township school superintendent certified teachers, teaching certificates were only valid in the township that issued them. In 1861, the legislature established the office of county superintendent with responsibility for examining and certifying teachers. Eventually teachers were examined by a state board so their certificates would be valid in any school in the state.

✐ District taxes for school buildings should be limited to $300, unless the town superintendent deemed that more was needed.

✐ Districts could vote a tax "of not more than twenty dollars for globes and similar instructional equipment, and a tax of thirty dollars for building a library."

✐ Schools must be open at least three months during the year, winter or summer term, or both.

The following subjects should be offered: reading, writing, arithmetic, geography, English grammar, orthography, and whatever other subjects the board wanted to add.

The state superintendent of schools had general supervisory authority over the state's schools. The state superintendent should try to secure textbook uniformity and discourage sectarian teaching, and the use of sectarian materials. Salary for state superintendent: $1,000 annually.[9]

Francis Creek School, Manitowoc County, c.1920.

From Clarence Rezek.

Wisconsin a Leader in Free Education

With the authority of the state's constitution, Wisconsin's public schools were free to all children, no matter what their economic, religious, or ethnic background. Wisconsin became a leader in the country in providing free education. As of 1846, states such as New York, Pennsylvania, Michigan, Rhode Island, and New Jersey continued using rate-bills to support their schools, some until the Civil War. Free public schools were not widely available in the United States until after 1865.

First Free Public Schools in Wisconsin

Kenosha, earlier known as Southport, claims the first "free public school in Wisconsin, and one of the first in the United States outside of New England." Michael Frank came to Southport from New York State and was interested in free public schools. He was a member of the Wisconsin territorial legislature, and a strong advocate of free public education. On June 16, 1845, a free public school opened in the Catholic church basement in Southport as there was yet no school-house.[10]

Kindergarten

The first kindergarten in the United States began in Watertown, Wisconsin, in 1856. Margarethe Meyer Schurz began this new form of early childhood education which she called her "garden whose plants are human." Schurz was a student of German education leader, Fredrich Froebel. Schurz, a German immigrant and wife of diplomat Carl Schurz, taught kindergarten classes in German.

The kindergarten idea spread across the country, but it had little influence in country schools. Few one-room country schools saw fit to offer more than grades one through eight. In most instances, the teacher had plenty of work with eight grades. She did not want the added responsibility of caring for pre-first grade youngsters who often required considerable looking after. Some country schools had a kind of kinder-garten when they invited children who would be attending first grade in fall to attend for a few weeks during the spring term, to get acquainted with the routine of school.

Home Credits

In some country schools, students were given special credit for work at home. There was a strong belief that home and school should be closely associated, with each playing a part in the child's development. To encourage, and to recognize work done at home, pupils kept a record of home tasks. When a student had earned 500 credits, he or she was given a special diploma to recognize their "at home work." Here are examples of credits that could be earned:

Building fire in the morning	1
Milking a cow	1
Currying a horse	2

Gathering eggs	2
Feeding the hogs	2
Churning butter	2
Mixing and baking bread	10
Getting a meal	6
Washing and wiping the dishes	6
Scrubbing the floor	4
Washing and ironing own clothes	20
Bathing	6
Practicing a music lesson 30 min	6
Carrying in wood for day	4
Brushing teeth	1
Sleeping with window open	1
Retiring before nine o'clock	1
Cleaning a lamp	1 [11]

Home credits accomplished several things. They recognized tasks that many children were already required to do such as carrying in wood or milking cows. But they also encouraged several practices such as brushing teeth, bathing, and going to bed early.

New Directions

By the time settlers began pouring into Wisconsin in the middle and late 1800s, various national school reforms were already under way. In the beginning of the 19th century, religion and patriotism were still major school themes. The assumption that children were destined to eternal damnation without Bible study in the schools was questioned by such philosophers as John Locke. Locke argued that children were more blank slates than creatures doomed to Hell. Locke and others said pupils should learn a variety of skills and subjects beyond Biblical guidelines. [12]

Two educational leaders, Horace Mann and Henry Barnard influenced the direction for schools in Wisconsin and in the entire nation. Horace Mann, who was born in 1796, argued that every child ought have a free and comprehensive education as a birthright. He believed that education should be publicly supported, publicly controlled, and that there should be mandatory attendance.

Henry Barnard was credited with reorganizing both the Connecticut and Rhode Island educational systems in the early 1800s. In 1846 he was asked to speak at Wisconsin's first constitutional convention. In his two addresses, Barnard outlined a comprehensive approach to education, from district schools to a university. He argued for improved school buildings, better teaching approaches, and normal schools for the preparation of country school teachers. Barnard also said, "Schools should be good enough for the best and cheap enough for the poorest."[13] Later, he moved to Wisconsin and became chancellor of the University of Wisconsin from 1858 to 1860.

Truancy Problems

In 1870, more than seventeen percent of Wisconsin's adult males were illiterate. Between forty and fifty thousand Wisconsin children did not attend school at all in 1870. Thousands of others attended a few weeks during the year, generally when their parents did not need them for work on the farm.

Lost, yesterday, somewhere between sunrise and sunset, two golden hours, each set with sixty diamond minutes. No reward is offered, for they are gone forever.

—Horace Mann

In 1873, Wisconsin's assembly adopted a resolution directing the state superintendent of schools to examine the truancy problem and offer suggestions for a compulsory school attendance law. But it wasn't until 1879 when a modest compulsory attendance law was passed. It stipulated that children between the ages of seven and fifteen should attend a public or private school for at least twelve weeks of the year. Unfortunately, the weakest of excuses allowed parents to keep their children home from school, and local districts, who had the authority to enforce the law, seldom did.

The Bennett Law of 1889 was a somewhat stronger law. It directed parents to send their children age seven to fourteen to a public or private school for at least twelve weeks each school year. It also stipulated what was an appropriate school, which angered many private and parochial school interests.

It wasn't until 1907 that a more stringent compulsory attendance law was passed. This law said children seven to fourteen, who lived in first class cities, must attend school during the time that school is in session. The only excuse was if they were "regularly and legally employed." Students living in smaller cities must attend not less than eight months, and those living in townships and attending one-room schools, and those living in villages must attend not less than six months in each school year.[14]

Purposes for Schools

Should schools pass on the culture, focus on training children for useful and employable skills, or some of both? Prior to 1900, in

Wisconsin, and throughout much of the country, it was assumed that most children would follow the occupations of their parents. This was particularly so for children attending country schools where nearly all of them came from the farm and were expected to return to the land.

After World War II farm children by the thousands began leaving the farms where they grew up. Now the question became, are these children prepared to work off the farm, to move to the cities and work in factories?

Fifty years earlier, in the late 1800s, it was generally agreed that the public schools should: transmit an inherited body of culture; teach practical work skills; classify students for future occupations; and teach skills for living, such as health, morals, and how to treat one another.

Other purposes for the schools emerged as debates over organizing, reorganizing, and funding schools took place. Many people argued that education would improve a person, both economically and socially, and, with more educated persons, society would be changed for the better. Thomas Mann, in the 1800s, said that schools should provide a "moral uplifting for students."

Practically speaking, many saw the public schools as the place where thousands of immigrants would learn the English language and become Americanized. In the early days of Wisconsin's history, land speculators saw schools as enhancing the value of land; thus they encouraged and supported building them. Some believed that education would end crime. Others saw schools, in the most narrow terms, as a place to send their children and get them out of their homes.

At a higher level of purpose, many people argued that the school was an early opportunity for rich and poor, religious and non-religious, immigrants and non-immigrants to learn how to work, study, and play together.

1908 "End of School" Souvenir. Note that 56 pupils attended this one-room school. Waushara County.

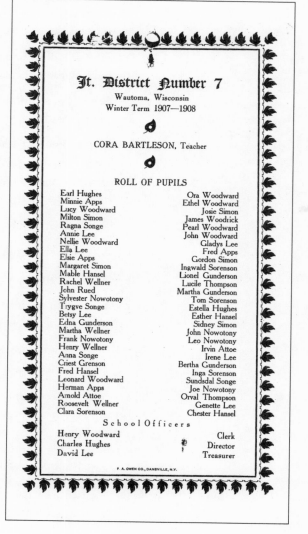

Jt. District Number 7
Wautoma, Wisconsin
Winter Term 1907—1908

CORA BARTLESON, Teacher

ROLL OF PUPILS

Earl Hughes	Ora Woodward
Minnie Apps	Ethel Woodward
Lucy Woodward	Josie Simon
Milton Simon	James Woodrick
Ragna Songe	Pearl Woodward
Annie Lee	John Woodward
Nellie Woodward	Gladys Lee
Ella Lee	Fred Apps
Elsie Apps	Gordon Simon
Margaret Simon	Ingwald Sorenson
Mable Hansel	Lionel Gunderson
Rachel Wellner	Lucile Thompson
John Rued	Martha Gunderson
Sylvester Nowotony	Tom Sorenson
Trygve Songe	Estella Hughes
Betsy Lee	Esther Hansel
Edna Gunderson	Sidney Simon
Martha Wellner	John Nowotony
Frank Nowotony	Leo Nowotony
Henry Wellner	Irvin Attoe
Anna Songe	Irene Lee
Criest Grenson	Bertha Gunderson
Fred Hansel	Inga Sorenson
Leonard Woodward	Sundsdal Songe
Herman Apps	Joe Nowotony
Arnold Attoe	Orval Thompson
Roosevelt Wellner	Genette Lee
Clara Sorenson	Chester Hansel

School Officers

Henry Woodward	Clerk
Charles Hughes	Director
David Lee	Treasurer

F. A. OWEN CO., DANSVILLE, N.Y.

Summary of Dates Important for Wisconsin One-Room Schools

1634   Jean Nicolet stopped at Red Banks, north of Green Bay. Soon French traders established a vast fur trading business in what was later to become Wisconsin.

1647   Massachusetts Bay Colony passed a law establishing a school system from which one-room schools emerged.

1785 and 1787   Northwest Ordinances, which included what was later to become Wisconsin and several other midwestern states included a provision for establishing local schools as states were formed.

1791   First school in Green Bay. Taught by Jacques Porlier who was paid by the father of the children who attended.

1817   Schools common in Green Bay and Prairie du Chien. Supported by religious organizations.

1818-1836   Wisconsin became a part of Michigan Territory and subject to its school laws. Michigan law said that if there was insufficient tax money for schools, parents of students could be assessed to make up the difference. This was called a rate-bill tax.

1829   First known school in Iowa County, in Mineral Point.

1830   Mission school opened on Madeline Island in Lake Superior.

1836-1848   Wisconsin a separate territory.

1840   Wisconsin territorial law laid out a plan for townships to organize schools, including examining and certifying teachers.

1845   First free public school in Wisconsin, in Southport, later to become Kenosha.

1848   Wisconsin became a state, and in its constitution was a provision for free education for everyone between the ages of four and twenty. Wisconsin became a leader for free public education. Constitution also provided for the election of a state superintendent of schools.

1861   Legislature passed legislation establishing the office of county superintendent of schools.

1879   First compulsory attendance law passed. Said that parents of children ages seven to fifteen must attend a public or private school for at least twelve weeks of the year. Law poorly enforced.

1907   A strong compulsory attendance law passed.

1937-1938   Wisconsin reaches its peak of 7,777 school districts and 6,181 one-room schools.

1947   Wisconsin legislature directed each county board in the state to form a committee and develop a plan for the consolidation of the county's school districts.

1949   Modified school consolidation law passed. A master plan for consolidation of each county's schools must be submitted to the state superintendent of schools by 1951.

1962   Nearly all of Wisconsin's one-room schools were closed, with the small districts consolidating into larger ones.

1995   A one-room school with students in kindergarten through seventh grade operates on Madeline Island. Wisconsin has about 420 school districts, which is 7,357 less districts than it had in 1939.

Chapter Notes

1. Martha Riley. *Social and Economic History of Lafayette County.* Milwaukee, WI: Marquette University Graduate School, 1934. Quoted in Lucile Bisegger, Marjean Bondele, and Harriet Halloran. *Wiota: William S. Hamilton's Diggings—1828-1993.* Gratiot, WI: Privately published, 1993.

2. See Alice E. Smith. *The History of Wisconsin: From Exploration to Statehood.* (Vol. 2). Madison: State Historical Society of Wisconsin, 1973, and Robert C. Nesbit and William F. Thompson. *Wisconsin: A History* (2nd Ed.). Madison: The University of Wisconsin Press, 1989.

3. Lloyd P. Jorgenson. *The Founding of Public Education in Wisconsin.* Madison, WI: State Historical Society of Wisconsin, 1956, p.5.

4. *Ibid.,* p. 17.

5. *Ibid.,* p. 7.

6. Margaret Metcalf, Violet Williams, and Marion Pustina. *Schools of Iowa County.* Blanchardville: Iowa County Bicentennial Education Committee, 1976, p. 95, 191.

7. Andrew Gulliford. *America's Public Schools.* Washington, D.C.: The Preservation Press, 1984, pp. 36-37.

8. See Jorgenson, pp.18-24 for a discussion of this issue.

9. Jorgenson, pp. 68-100.

10. Conrad E. Patzer. *Public Education in Wisconsin.* Madison, WI: State Superintendent's Office, 1924, pp. 13-14.

11. Metcalf, Williams, and Pustina, 1976, p. 133.

12. Gulliford, pp. 37-38.

13. Story Moorefield in U.S. Department of Health, Education, and Welfare. *A Nation of Learners.* Washington, D.C.: U.S. Dept. of Health, Education and Welfare, 1976, p. 119.

14. Patzer, pp. 76-78.

The Teachers

Inez Thompson Hawley sits at the teacher's desk in the Progressive School (Waushara County) where she once taught. The Progressive School, also known as the Swamp School, is now a school museum in Wild Rose.

Photo by Steve Apps.

Teachers were essential to the success of country schools. They were mostly women, primarily young, and generally poorly paid. Many began teaching when they were eighteen or nineteen, or sometimes, seventeen. It was not at all uncommon, in some country schools, for a few students to be older than their teacher. In most instances, the country school teachers had, themselves, been students of the country school. They knew about rural communities, about isolation, and about teacher expectations before they were hired. They were immediately put in charge of a room full of young minds who were a few steps away from their farms, but destined, most of them, to leave the country for work in the city, particularly after the 1930s.

Country school teachers were idealists. They believed they could make a difference—and they did, most of the time. Following is an example of the idealism that was prevalent in the late 1800s and the early and middle 1900s when country schools were found throughout the upper Midwest. One kind of idealism was expressed this way:

Teacher's Creed

"I believe in boys and girls, the men and women of the great tomorrow; that whatsoever the boy soweth the man shall reap. I believe in the Curse of ignorance, in the efficacy of schools, in the dignity of teaching and the joy of serving another. I believe in wisdom as revealed in human lives, as well as in the pages of a printed book; in lessons taught not so much by precept as by example; in ability to work with the hands as well as to think with the head; in everything that makes life large and lovely. I believe in beauty in the school room, in the home, in daily life and out of doors. I believe in laughter and love, in all ideals and distant hopes that lure us on. I believe that every hour of every day we receive a just reward for all we are and all we do. I believe in the present and its opportunities, in the future and its promises, and in the divine joy of living." 1

*Stone School,
Sauk County.*

*From Sauk County
Rural Schools History
Project, William C.
Schuette.*

There was another side, too. One Wisconsin educational historian wrote, "Many, indeed most, of the teachers who pledged undying loyalty to the cause of education deserted it as soon as more attractive prospects beckoned." The average teachers' tenure in the middle 1800s was two years. Only a handful had more than five years experience.2 Because young women couldn't continue teaching when they married, this became the main reason for short teacher tenure.

Teacher Duties and Expectations

Marcia Staton attended country school near Bruce, in Rusk County, during the late 1930s and early 1940s. She said this about her teacher, "It was her responsibility to teach all eight grades including music and art, keep the schoolhouse clean and the fires burning, fix a snack at lunch to supplement what we brought in our lunch pails, bring out books from the county library in Ladysmith once a month (about twenty-seven miles away), help organize regular PTA meetings, put on a Christmas program, and file all required reports. For that she received the lordly sum of $60 per month. She was a marvelous teacher, very creative and artistic, good with children, and great in imparting knowledge. I will not forget Mrs. Worall."

One teacher responsibility was to leave an accurate report for the teacher who would follow come the next year. At the end of the 1933-1934 school year, teacher Raymond Nelson, who taught in the Kaminski School, Waushara County, left this report for his successor:

Dear Madam,

The following is a report which may be used to an advantage. No. 1 is ready for the second grade. You will find him a very good pupil. No. 17 is very weak in phonics. Here promotion may be possible with extra drill in phonics. No. 18 is ready for second grade and is a very good worker. No. 2 is ready for fourth grade. An excellent pupil. Nos. 3 and 4 are ready for the fifth grade. No. 3 finds it hard to learn, but tries very hard. Nos. 9 and 10 are ready for seventh grade. No. 9 is bright, but is inclined to waste time. No. 10 is a very good worker. No. 12 was very weak in his grade. I think it advisable to take the grade over. No. 13 is ready for the eighth grade. An excellent pupil. No. 15 and 16 graduated. No. 14, 5, 6, 7, and 8 moved from the district. All pupils above the second grade have Reading Circle Diplomas. All pupils had a literary Society which met every two weeks. The course of study has been completed in all grades.

I wish you the best of success.

Raymond Nelson

Phyllis Uminski taught in several Grant County schools. One year the school was able to get some ham and beans for their school lunch program. But she had never made bean soup before. Phyllis recalled that her mother had said to soak the beans the night before, and then put the beans with the ham on the stove. How many beans should she soak? This she hadn't remembered from her mother's teaching. She decided one cup of beans for each child in the school seemed about right. She dumped the beans into a pot of water and went home for the night. The next morning when she arrived at school there were beans everywhere. An eruption of beans. They had expanded beyond anything she had expected.

Kateri Dupuis attended Roosevelt School in Marinette County in the 1940s. She recalled her first day of school and her teacher: "A small, old, four-seat car came to our farm to pick me up for my first day at school. About a quarter mile down the road I began to whimper. It was the first time I had ever been away from my mother and sister. When I arrived at school, Mrs. Georgia Siedenglanz welcomed all of us, especially me because by then I was sobbing. This teacher was a miracle worker. My tears were soon turned off when the teacher said she needed help. Within a week this wonder woman had me talking in class."

Elta Mantor, Rhinelander area, recalled some of the rules for teachers. She said the rules were not quite as strict in the 1920s and 1930s as they were in the early 1900s, but there were still plenty of rules. For instance, women teachers couldn't marry. If a woman married, she had to resign. Visiting a tavern was forbidden, so was smoking and living in an apartment. Women had to wear long hair. Teachers must stand before their students and should never be seen sitting. Elta Mantor continued, "The school room must be kept neat and clean, with the floor and blackboard cleaned each day. The fire must be built in time to have the room warm by 9:00 a.m., at the time that the school bell would be rung. A good Christmas program must be prepared for the community, the evening before the winter vacation began. Arbor Day must be recognized, and a picnic held at the end of the school year. The teacher should not wear bright clothing in the classroom, and skirts must be near the ankle in length. Any teachers who smoked, used liquor in any form, frequented pool or public halls, were required to give reason to the superintendent as to why he should not suspect the teacher's worth, intention, integrity, and honesty."

Elta Mantor said that when the Prohibition law was removed (1933), a few teachers joined other citizens in enjoying a glass of beer in the dining room of the local hotel. These teachers were reminded that they should not let that happen again.

Teacher Characteristics

As long as there have been teachers, someone has been more than willing to list the characteristics a teacher ought to have. For instance,

Housework is a breeze. Cooking is a pleasant diversion. Putting up a retaining wall is a lark. But teaching is like climbing a mountain.

—Fawn M. Brodie, 1977

the authors of the book, *The Rural School: Its Methods and Management* wrote that someone who is considering becoming a teacher must be concerned about **Physical ability** ("The person that stands from day to day before the boys and girls should be physically whole."), **Health** ("The young man or woman who starts out in life to be a teacher needs a good constitution."), **Nerves** ("The work of the school room is a constant drain upon the nervous system."), **Disposition** ("In order to succeed, the teacher should be kindly disposed toward children."), **Knowledge of subject matter**, and professional training. This book further stated that the country teacher must have legible hand writing, ability to express thoughts in passable English, know principles of arithmetic, and be aware of the events of American History. [3]

Many others have written about the characteristics of the ideal teacher. In 1924, Conrad Patzer, a Wisconsin Educator, wrote this, "A teacher of children and particularly a teacher of young children should have a pleasing personality. She should have an attractive personal appearance but this should not necessarily imply physical attractiveness. Children are more impressed by the earnestness and interest clothed in the vestment of love and happiness than by any other quality the teacher may possess. It is the **inner life of the teacher** which appeals to children. **It is her soul that speaks to them....She influences her pupils more by what she is than by what she knows and teaches.**" [4]

Homer Seerley, writing in 1913, said this about the country school teacher: "He is supposed to have the necessary scholarship, the real personality, the acquired training, the magnanimity of spirit, the knowledge of human nature, the qualities of self-control, and the capability of instruction that such a calling as teaching exacts. All the other things are preliminary to the contact of the teacher with the pupils, all the other factors are cooperators, the teacher is the constructor and the creator of what is regarded as success in educational

Rules for teachers, 1915. Polk County Historical Society.

From "Memories of The Round Lake School," Frederic, WI, 1995.

Rules For The Teacher ... 1915

You will not marry during the term of your contract.
You are not to keep company with men.
You must be home between the hours of 8 p.m. and 6 a.m. unless attending a school function.
You may not loiter downtown in any ice cream stores.
You may not travel beyond the city limits unless you have permission of the chairman of the board.
You may not smoke cigarettes.
You may not under any circumstances dye your hair.
You may not dress in bright colors.
You may not ride in a carriage or automobile with any man unless he be your father or brother.
You must wear at least two petticoats.
Your dresses must not be any shorter than 2 inches above the ankles.
To keep the schoolhouse neat and clean, you must: sweep the floor at least once daily; scrub the floor at least once a week with hot, soapy water; clean the blackboards at least once a day; and start the fire at 7 a.m. so the room will be warm by 8 a.m.

Polk County, Wis. Historical Society

work. He is the living personality that inspires enthusiasm, that compels love to be given, and that arouses activity of intellect and emotion to succeed in the joint undertaking that pupils and teachers are united in accomplishing."[5]

Former country school students enjoyed describing their teachers. Judy Lee Tarbox attended a country school near Gays Mills in Crawford County where Mrs. Miriam Hayes was teacher. Judy described her this way, "She was a wonderful, caring, kind person, very knowledgeable, and she made school fun. She had a very kind face, was soft spoken—everybody listened to her. She got respect just by the way she treated us. I suppose she seemed old to me. She had light brown hair when I was in first grade, but it was gray by the time I finished eight years later. She always wore her hair pulled back, but it had a nice wave in the front."

Not all former country school students had polite things to say about their teachers. Bonnie Trudell, who attended the Squaw Lake School in St. Croix county, talked about Miss Jones (not her real name). "Miss Jones, she was strange. She lived with my grandmother. She came from Elk Mound and had this bright red hair, and she was very heavy and she wore thick glasses. I remember my friend and I would have overnights with each other, and we'd get into bed and we'd say, 'What are we going to talk about?' And one of us would say, 'I really hate Miss Jones.' It seemed that Miss Jones was getting heavier and heavier, and then she had this little vacation. It turned out she was pregnant. Nobody knew. Then she left the community and it was after that people found out."

Hiring Procedures

Teachers remember well when they were first hired.

Mildred Larsen Knoff graduated from the Outagamie County Normal School, one year program, in 1936 and began looking for a teaching job. "At that time there was an over abundance of teachers, so it wasn't the best time to find a teaching job. I went to the Waupaca County Superintendent of Schools for the names of districts needing teachers. I chose to go for an interview with the school board at Pioneer School, Marion. On an April morning I went for an interview with the school clerk who told me I must also interview with the other two board members. They both lived on a side road that was impassable and closed to all traffic. I parked my car on the highway and began my half-mile trek to the treasurer's home. I had to walk on the side of the road to avoid the deep ruts and mud puddles. After a brief interview with the treasurer, I trudged another half-mile to the end of the road where the school board director lived.

"He was plowing in a back field. I had no choice but to walk over the freshly plowed furrows to speak with him. My shoes, at this point, were heavy with clay mud. The director was a man of very few words who seemed more intent to get on with his plowing then to talk to me about a job.

"At this point, I was beginning to feel somewhat discouraged. However, I trudged back the mile of road to the highway, sidestepping the ruts and puddles. I returned to the clerk's home to find out that there would be a board meeting soon to decide on a teacher. I was informed that there were several applicants for the position.

"I arrived at the appointed meeting along with the other applicants. We were parked in the clerk's yard waiting for the board's decision. After a short wait, the clerk's wife appeared at the doorway and called out my name. She went to the other applicants who then drove away after finding out that the position was filled.

"I was elated beyond words. I went into the dimly lit kitchen where the board was gathered around the table. The clerk congratulated me on how 'lucky' I was to get the job. I knew that, but then I found out what he really meant. As there were several applicants for the job, the board decided to put all the names in a straw hat and shake them up. The clerk's little daughter drew out my name—I became a teacher because of a 'straw hat lottery.'"

Robert Erickson was in his second year at the Vernon County Normal School in 1948. In the spring, various school boards came to the Normal School to hire teachers for the coming fall term. Erickson met with the School Board from the South Natwick School, located west of Westby. They asked him how much money he expected. He said they should make him an offer. They suggested $260.00 per month, but with the stipulation that he must haul water to the school each day because the well was broken.

A few minutes later he saw the president of the Normal School, J. H. Wheelock. "How much did they offer you?" Wheelock inquired.

"$260 a month," replied Erickson.

"That's way too much," said Wheelock. "No beginning teacher is worth that kind of money. You go back and tell that school board you want less money."

So Erickson went back into the room with the school board.

"I've thought it over," said Erickson. "And I'm willing to accept a lot

All mankind lives on the fruits of the earth— the first and most necessary employment, therefore, is the tillage of the ground, called agriculture, husbandry, or farming.

—*Webster's American Spelling Book, 1831*

1907 Teachers' Contract. Washington County. Note that the salary was $55 5/9 per month.

TEACHERS' COMMON SCHOOL CONTRACT

(State of Wisconsin)

IT IS HEREBY AGREED, by and between the District Board of School District No. _10_, of the Town of _Addison_, for and in the name of said School District, and _John J. Hess_, a duly qualified Teacher legally licensed in the County of _Washington_ and State of Wisconsin, (a copy of said License being attached hereto;) that the said _John J. Hess_ is to teach the Common School of said District for the term of _9_ months, for the sum of _55 5/9_ Dollars per month, commencing on the _9_ day of _September_, 1907, it being expressly understood and agreed by the parties hereto, that _20_ days shall constitute, in this case, a School month, and that on Saturday, ther shall be no School taught;

And for such services properly rendered, the said District Board, for and in the name of said District, is to pay the said _John J. Hess_ on or before the _first_ day of _July 1908_, the amount that may be due him according to this contract.

Witness our hands,   _J. A. Wirstnacht_ Director.
this _2_ day of _July_,   _M. Stoffel_ Clerk.
A. D. 1907   _J. S. Muller_ Treas.

Signed in Duplicate,   _John J. Hess_ Teacher.

less money than you offered me."

The school board, unaccustomed to such a response, talked it over for a little awhile. The board chair said, "How about $225 a month, then?" The board consisted of Ella Olson, Selmer Haugen, and Arnold Kjelland.

"That sounds better," answered Erickson.

"But you still have to haul water each day," the board chair reminded him.

So Robert Erickson began teaching in the fall of 1948 for $225. The following year the board increased his salary to $260 per month, which had been its original offer.

Other would-be teachers didn't fare as well during their interviews. Elizabeth Rooney attended the Blue Mounds School in Dane County. Her father was on the school board and once interviewed a prospective teacher who said that he didn't approve of capital punishment for children, when he probably meant corporal punishment. He didn't get the job.

First Year Teaching

Linde Lee Priem was nineteen when she graduated from the Rusk County Normal at Ladysmith in June, 1930. She signed a contract with the Maple Valley School, which was located seven miles north of Weyerhauser, for $90.00 per month. Different from most country schools, this one had an adjacent annex where the teacher lived. Two of her pupils lived with her through the winter. There were eleven students, ranging in age from six to fourteen years.

Living in a remote area, Priem was advised to have some protection. She had a German Shepherd dog, "Pal," who was her constant companion. Previous teachers also had rifles, but Priem owned an automatic pistol. The county sheriff gave her permission to carry it, and she attended classes on how to care for and use it. On Friday nights she often had to walk from her school to Weyerhauser, plus an additional mile and a half to her home, her pistol in her pocket and her dog by her side.

During the fall, a "friend" visited the school each night. It was a brown bear who came and sat on the top step, against the door, searching for crumbs the children left when they ate their lunches. Toward morning the bear would get up and amble off the porch and into the woods.

One winter night the dog was barking and she peered out the window, but saw nothing. She heard a "crunch crunch" on the snow. She slid open the window and yelled "Who's there?" No reply. So she shot into the snow. This time she heard fast crunches as something or someone left the area. Later she learned that Carl Larsen had been walking by the school on his way to his cousin's place. A World War I veteran, he told Priem, "I have been chased and shot at by Germans; but when a school marm starts shooting, I run!"

Alva Mott remembers her first year of teaching at Popular Grove School, near Solon Springs, in Douglas County, this way. The year was 1941. "There were about fifteen children, but I found I had to teach thirty-three classes a day, so it kept me up most of the night. I was usually tired by recess, so if I put my head down, people would think I was sick. I just had to struggle through. I was nineteen then.

"I wanted each child to learn, but there just wasn't enough time. It was such a struggle. I also had learned about grading on the curve when I was studying to be a teacher. I learned that there are always the lowest and the highest and those in between. Sometimes it works out, but lots of times it doesn't. I had a couple of boys in fifth grade that weren't very

Here I stand with a stiff-stand collar. I wouldn't kiss a school marm for a half a dollar.

good, so I flunked one of them. I thought that somebody had to be on the bottom. Long afterwards I thought, "That was a stupid thing to do. That boy was all right. He would have done all right," but I had been taught that somebody has got to be on the bottom, no matter what grade he'd go into. Keeping him back wouldn't make him brighter. But I didn't know that then. I seem to remember my own weaknesses the best."

Ray Schueffner signed his first contract to teach in the spring of 1935 for $65.00 dollars a month. Rural school boards consisted of a director, a clerk, and a treasurer.

"At the end of each month no one delivered a check to you. Rather,

Fond du Lac County country school Teacher's Contract for 1950. Note that the contract required the teacher to "carry water daily for school use."

Fond du Lac School Supply Co., Fond du Lac, Wis.

Teacher's Contract

It is Hereby Agreed by and between School District No. __2__ in the Town of Springvale, County of Fond du Lac, State of Wisconsin, and Aileen Madigan a legally qualified teacher, that said teacher is to teach, govern and conduct the common school of said district to the best of h ability; keep a register of the daily attendance and studies of each pupil belonging to the school, and such other records as the District Board may require, make such reports as are required by law, and endeavor to preserve in good condition and order the School-house, grounds, furniture, apparatus, and such other district property as may come under the immediate supervision of said teacher, for the term of __9__ school months, commencing on the __1st or about__ day of __Sept__ A. D. 19 , for the sum of __Two Hundred Sixty__ Dollars per school month, to be paid at the end of each month, it being understood and agreed that __20__ days teaching shall constitute a month and that on Saturday there shall be __no school unless otherwise agreed__

__* Carry water daily for school use__

And the said School District hereby agrees to keep the school-house in repair, to provide the necessary fuel and school register, and for the services of said teacher as prescribed above, well and truly performed, to pay said teacher the sum of __Two Hundred Sixty__ Dollars per school month, at the end of each month, during a term of __9__ school months, commencing on the __1st or about__ day of __Sept__ A. D. 19__50__.

Provided, That in case said teacher shall be legally dismissed from school, or shall have h certificate legally annulled, by expiration or otherwise, then said teacher shall not be entitled to compensation from and after such dismissal or annulment; provided further, that the wages of said teacher for the last month of school term shall not be paid unless said teacher shall have made the report for the school term as required by law.

In Witness Whereof, we have hereunto subscribed our names this __17th__ day of __April__ A. D. 19__50__

Frank Limiese Director

_____ Treasurer

Lloyd H. Pinch Clerk

Aileen Madigan Teacher

(Over)

REMARKS:—This contract should be made out in duplicate, and one copy given to the teacher. No Board should allow a teacher to commence school, until a written contract is properly signed by both parties.

you would go to the clerk who would issue the order, and then to the director who would sign the order. After that you would take the order to the treasurer who would issue the check. The treasurer's usual comment was, 'You back again! Seems like you were just here!' If any one of the three was working in the field or was not at home, it would be necessary to wait, often over a weekend to get paid."

Wilmer Gorske taught at the Mt. Moriah School, in Green Lake County, beginning in 1931. His starting salary was $90.00 a month. But as he said, "This was the height of the Great Depression, and staying in this position for three years, the salary was lowered to $75.00 a month. My fourth and fifth years of teaching were at $65.00 a month and I was just pleased to have a position. Salaries began moving upward after World War II." Mr. Gorske went on to become Superintendent of Schools for Green Lake County.

The first year of teaching wasn't always pleasant. Pearl Johnson's first year teaching was at the Linrud School in Vernon County, beginning in 1942. She had about twenty-five students, and received $70.00 per month salary. She recalls, "Some of the older boys knew I was a beginner; they liked to make things difficult for me by misbehaving. One of the older boys I didn't trust. I didn't want to be in the schoolhouse when he was there. I don't know what it was, his leer maybe. He frightened me. I finally got through the year, and moved to another school in Holman, La Crosse County."

Challenges

The country school teacher was challenged inside the classroom and outside. Sometimes she faced thirty or forty or even fifty children, all in one room with ages ranging from five to sixteen or seventeen, and in eight grades. They represented Protestants, Catholics, and those with no religion. They sometimes were all of one ethnic background, true in some German, Polish, Norwegian or Swedish communities. Shirley Bennett Madden taught at the Woodrow Wilson School in the southern end of Marinette County. "All of my students were of Polish descent and one family, at least, did not speak English yet."

More likely there was a mixture of ethnic groups. In my country school in Waushara County, we had children of Polish, Czech, English, German, Norwegian, and Welch backgrounds. Agnes Lynch Greene, who taught at Wisconsin Point School near Superior, said she had "white Americans (the government lighthouse keepers), Canadian

French, one Belgian, and an extended family of Chippewa Indians."

Personal hygiene for some pupils was a problem as well. A well-circulated story illustrated the problem. It seems the teacher sent a note home with a little boy asking his mother to give him a bath because he was not only dirty but smelly. The next day the little boy handed the teacher a note from his mother. "Learn Jimmy, don't smell him. Jimmy ain't no rose."

Ruby Schultz began teaching country school in 1944, in Door County. She had between twenty-five and fifty students in eight grades. "In one school, I wound up with fifty kids. I had fifteen first graders, with fifteen minutes for a reading class—a minute a student. The day was hectic. I taught reading, writing, arithmetic—there was a list that you followed. Ten minutes for this class, fifteen minutes for that. I managed to get through it."

Ruby had some trying moments as well. "During my first year of teaching, I had a seventh grader who lived with his grandparents. He was always disruptive and I kept after him. One day I was sitting and talking with him and he hauled off and hit me and my glasses flew off and under the piano."

Looking back now, some of what happened in Ruby Schultz's classroom was exceedingly humorous. At the time no one considered what was going on as funny. "During the year when I taught fifty students, I expelled the entire fifth and sixth grades. There was one girl who did not behave. She made me so angry, so I said to the whole class, 'You are expelled!' One of the school board members lived right across the street, right across the road from the school. So I talked to her and we notified the parents. They came with their children to the school that night. Every child had to get up in front and individually apologize to me for misbehaving. Their parents sat in the back of the room. These kids had to publicly apologize, and their parents supported me. The kids came back to school the next day, and I didn't have any trouble from that group anymore."

Inside the classroom, the challenges went well beyond trying to teach eight subjects to a room full of energetic young people. For instance, it was not unusual for children to come to school and not be able to speak English.

Joe Sveda from Antigo recalled when he started at Badger School, located north of Antigo, in Langlade County. The year was 1938. "I couldn't speak a word of English when I started school," Joe said. "I spoke Czech." His family had come from Czechoslovakia. The teacher

The teacher affects eternity; he can never know where his influence stops.

—Henry B. Adams, 1907

couldn't understand Czech.

So Joe had a double problem: trying to learn English and at the same time, learn to read, write and all the rest.

"I was ashamed that I couldn't speak English," Joe said. "So I didn't try. I'd just rattle something off in Czech when I had something to say."

Joe learned later that the County Superintendent had told his teacher that unless he could speak English by the end of the school year there was no way he could be promoted to second grade. "At Christmas time, my teacher let me know that I must begin learning English," Joe said. One of his favorite little songs, which he sang in Czech, was, translated "Annie in the Cabbage Patch."

The teacher said she would make little Joe a deal. If he would learn how to recite "Little Boy Blue" in English, she would learn how to sing "Annie in the Cabbage Patch" in the Czech language.

Little Joe came back the next day and recited "Little Boy Blue." It took the teacher two weeks to learn one verse of "Annie in the Cabbage Patch" in Czech. After that Joe Sveda spoke English. He went on to become a teacher and later an administrator in the Antigo School system.

Some children were so shy that they wouldn't talk when they got to school, even when they knew English. Aileen Straseski taught at the Dodd School in Fond du Lac County, starting in 1949. She said, "One little girl, Cheryl, was in the first grade and very shy. She wouldn't talk so I had no idea what she was learning. One day I decided to have the children make monkey dolls out of work socks, for an art project. Some of the older children had a hard time threading a needle and sewing. Cheryl's mother had taught her to sew so she was showing some of the others how to do it. All of a sudden one of the older boys said, 'Cheryl is talking.' Cheryl did well the rest of the year."

Some of the challenges left the teacher not knowing what to do. "Not too many years ago a young teacher attempted to gain the attention of a language class of primary graders. She was way ahead of her time and so was one eager little first grade boy. According to the version of the story the teacher read, Little Red Riding Hood was devoured by the wolf, in a violent climax. This was too much for the bugeyed listener in the front row who expressed his reaction to this horrible situation with, 'Why, the son of a _____' ".6

A few teachers had quite pleasant surroundings in which to teach, without the challenge of starting early morning fires, toting in wood from the woodshed, or pumping water from a reluctant outside pump.

Hazel Udelhoven taught at Rock School Joint Number eight, South Lancaster Township in Grant County from 1944-1955. "The new brick building where I taught was erected in 1922 at a cost of $7,837. Rock was one of the most modern one-room rural schools in Grant County. It was equipped with modern furniture, central automatic heating, a water system, indoor plumbing, electricity, electric range, piano, radio, phonograph, strip film projector and steel filing cases as well as an extensive library and a huge cupboard full of all the books listed on the County Superintendent's textbook list.

"Rock School also had young, progressive and interested parents. There was an active community club and a mother's club. Mother's club members took turns providing a hot lunch for the school children at noon. A public bingo party held each year to make money for the school was a gala affair which brought people from Lancaster and miles around.

"Spelling bees, speaking contests, ball playing, sleigh-riding among schools of South Lancaster Townships were highlights. Two board members owned and piloted airplanes so contour and strip-crop farming could be studied from the air as well as viewing the Mississippi River, Dubuque, Iowa Lock and dam, city of Lancaster, the airport and so on."

The pupils apparently learned well at Rock School. One year the high school valedictorians at Lancaster and Potosi High Schools had both attended the Rock School for eight years.

The teacher's out-of-school life was equally challenging.

Diederich Luening taught at the Hillside School in Sauk County beginning in 1870. When Mr. Luening began teaching, he couldn't find a boarding place in the school district. He did find an unused log cabin with a stove, table and two chairs. From his parent's home in Sauk City, he brought a fifty pound sack of flour, some coffee and other staples and settled into his one-room cabin. During the school year, the children brought their teacher eggs, milk, molasses and pork, so he was to save most of the $37.50 he received each month as wages.[7]

Ruby Mabon, a teacher in the early 1900s, in the Louisville School in Dunn County, had a different challenge; "It was customary in those days for the teacher to be entertained in the homes of her pupils, usually overnight and I was no exception. I well remember being bedded down in the spare bedroom which was usually off the parlor where no fire was ordinarily kept. To say it was cold was putting it mildly. I dare say there are still those in the neighborhood who can remember, as I do, the long confidential visits we used to have. I learned to be thankful and prolong the visit as long as possible for I knew the longer we stayed up, the less time I'd have to freeze in a cold bed."

Getting to school each day, no matter what the weather, was always a challenge. Lelah Bruso taught in the Ferndale School, in Oneida County in the late 1930s. She traveled back and forth to school each day on the train. One day the engineer forgot to stop the train to let her off. They traveled all the way to Monico, so they had to back up four miles to drop her off by her school.

Agnes Lynch Greene taught at the Wisconsin Point School, across the bay from Superior, starting in September 1914. She got to and from school each day with a row boat, when the bay wasn't frozen. She said, "Throughout the year, the biggest problems were concerned not with running the school, nor with the pupils, but with getting to the school and back home on the other side of the bay. I lived with my parents in the east end of Superior. I kept my boat at Pittsburgh Coal Dock No. 5, which was a short one-mile row from school. Of course this row was made in all sorts of weather. We had rain, sleet, snow, and some howling winds with mountainous waves piling down the nine-mile length of Superior Bay. Three mothers living closest to the school took turns inviting me to lunch at their homes and insisted that I should not cross the bay on stormy days. They made storms an excuse for me to stay overnight, and I was very happy to do so because we had so much fun."

"I never owned a boat all the time I taught on the Point. All my boats were borrowed. I marvel now at how kind everyone was. Will Elliott, Superintendent of Pittsburgh No. 5, invited me to keep my boat in the coal dock slip near his office. One day I arrived at the dock and found that someone had stolen my oar locks. This was no problem at all when I told Mr. Elliott. He had his blacksmith make me a new pair. I wasn't even late for school."

Once the bay was frozen, Agnes skated all the way to school. Then she recalls the big snows coming in February and everyday after that she skied to school, right from her back door in Superior, across the bay to her school. When the ice went out in the spring, it was back to the row boat.

These were quite unusual cases, to be sure. Most teachers walked to school, as did their students. In most instances the teacher boarded with a nearby family, so the distance to school wasn't quite as great as it was for many of the students. Hazel Udelhoven who taught at the Dyer School in Grant County (1931-1932) paid two dollars a week to board at a neighbor's house. Teachers' salary was then $65 per month.

We teachers can only help the work going on, as servants wait upon a master.

—Maria Montessori, 1949

Pleasant Surprises

Teachers were forever being surprised. I don't know the source of the following story, or where it happened, but the message rings true.

A first grade teacher asked her little ones to draw something for which they were thankful, in preparation for a discussion of Thanksgiving. She expected to see pictures of turkeys and tables heavily laden with food, of mothers and fathers, of clothing items and pets.

Little David's picture surprised her. He was a child of particularly poor circumstances, coming from a large family that scarcely had enough to eat. David had drawn a hand, but whose hand?

When David held up his picture during the sharing time, the pupils guessed whose hand it might be. One said, "It must be the hand of God that brings us food." Another offered that it was all the hands that help us, but David had room to draw only one.

Later, when the children were working on something else, the teacher walked by David's desk. She bent over him and asked whose hand it was. David whispered, "It's yours, Teacher."

Chapter Notes

1. Edwin Osgood Grover. *The Price County Training School Annual Catalog, 1910-11.* Reprinted in *Country School Recollections II*, Price County Historical Society, 1990.

2. Lloyd P. Jorgenson. *The Founding of Public Education in Wisconsin.* Madison, WI: State Historical Society of Wisconsin, 1956, p. 132.

3. Horace M. Culter and Julia M. Stone. *The Rural School: Its Methods and Management.* Boston: Silver, Burdett and Company, 1913, pp. 45-48.

4. Conrad E. Patzer. *Public Education in Wisconsin.* Madison, WI: State Superintendent of Public Instruction, 1924, pp. 389-390.

5. Homer H. Seerley, *The Country School.* New York: Charles Scribner's Sons, 1913, pp. 8-9.

6. Elta Mantor and others. *A History of The School District of Rhinelander.* Rhinelander, WI: Rhinelander Area Retired Teachers Association, 1982, p. 184.

7. Erhart Mueller. *Always in Sumpter.* Stevens Point, WI: Worzalla Publishing Co., 1983, p. 119.

Preparing and Supporting Teachers

In the early days of public schooling in Wisconsin, teacher preparation was minimal and often nonexistent. A few teachers were well prepared, some even college graduates, but this was clearly not the standard. More often a teacher might be someone who had done well as a student in a country school and became a teacher upon leaving it, with no further training. Unfortunately, one state superintendent said, "An illiterate teacher is best for a school of beginners; that a teacher who knows but little is better adapted to scholars who know still less."[1]

Teachers, themselves, recognized the need for further training. Many of them organized into teacher associations. In Kenosha, earlier known as Southport, a teacher's association was organized in 1847. A Mining Region Teacher's Association, in southwestern Wisconsin, began in 1848, and the Wisconsin State Teachers' Association started in 1853.

Even though some saw no need for teacher preparation, many state leaders did. In 1849, when the state of Wisconsin was only a year old, the legislature made plans to create a normal department for teacher training within the state university. The thinking then was that a normal

Stevenson Training School, later renamed Marinette County Normal School, 1941. Two of the men in the photo were killed in World War II, never having the chance to teach. Thirty-three students graduated. Three were men. Most of the young women taught in rural schools in Marinette and Oconto Counties.

From Shirley Bennett Madden (middle of the front row).

department at the university, plus a series of teacher in-service institutes would meet teacher training requirements. But the legislature didn't make funds available for such a normal department. Finally, university regents, in 1855, found $500. This normal department was to focus on "professional instruction in the art of teaching," and be available for five months each year.

Normal Schools

Tis education forms the common mind, just as the twig is bent the tree's inclin'd.

—*1911 School Souvenir*

Slowly, state legislators began to see the need for a more comprehensive system of normal instruction. A bill creating a system of normal schools passed in 1857; it included a system for raising money to support them. The law was broadly interpreted, and soon colleges, academies, and even high schools began receiving state aids to support teacher training. Unfortunately, many of these so called normal departments were poorly focused for the preparation of school teachers. In 1865, the legislature passed a new law creating a system of state normal schools. 2 This legislation encouraged cities and villages to bid for a normal school. Initially, bids were received from sixteen cities, mostly in the southern half of the state. The bids from Platteville and Whitewater were the first accepted, and the first normal school in the state opened in the old academy building in Platteville on October 9, 1866. The Whitewater Normal School opened in September, 1868. The following subjects were part of the Platteville normal school curriculum: penmanship, English grammar, arithmetic, spelling, reading, physical geography, algebra, Latin, German, trigonometry, surveying, U.S. History, drawing, geometry, rhetoric, criticism, physiology, philosophy of natural history, vocal music, and theory and practice of teaching. Anyone examining the curriculum could clearly see that subject matter knowledge was far more important than preparation to teach it. In 1867, the Wisconsin legislature authorized $5,000 for teachers' institutes, particularly for those areas of the state that received least benefit from the state normal school legislation.3

State normal schools did not begin to meet the demand for teachers in Wisconsin, particularly in the rural areas. A movement began to authorize county boards to establish normal schools within their counties for preparing rural school teachers. In 1899 the legislature passed an act which "declared that the county board in any county in which a state normal school is not located was authorized to appropriate money for the organization, equipment, and maintenance of a county training

Sauk County Training School, Reedsburg, Wis.

school for teachers of the common schools." The first county training school opened in Wausau in 1899. Their names were changed to County Rural Normal Schools in 1923. By 1924, thirty-two such schools were scattered across Wisconsin.4

In many Wisconsin counties, new rural school teachers were desperately needed. For instance, in 1908, in Price County, eighty-six schools required one hundred twenty teachers. As County School Superintendent, May McNely wrote in her report to the Price County Board, "The day is gone by when the teacher of limited education and without training can do well enough for a primary or small district school." The Price County Board voted to establish a training school on the second floor of the Phillips Elementary school, and appropriated $1500 for maintenance and equipment. Steam heat and electric lights were provided by the City of Phillips. The first principal of the school, D.O. Swartz was hired for $150 per month.

The Price County Training School offered two courses of study. If a prospective teacher had a high school diploma, she would study for a year at the training school, pass a test, and then apply for a license to teach at a rural or a state graded school. If she had completed only

Sauk County Training School, Reedsburg.

From Sauk County Rural Schools History Project, William C. Schuette.

eighth grade, she could pursue a two-year program at the training school, and then be eligible to teach in the rural schools. Because of the great need for teachers, and because many young people needed to find employment as soon as possible, the second alternative was the most popular.

Sigrid Jensen Hansen attended the Price County Training School in 1914. "When I went to Training School my sister and I roomed at Walter Coop's farm just on the western outskirts of Phillips on the way to the Danish Settlement where we lived. My mom made food for us, nothing elaborate, and we would heat whatever it was or else make sandwiches. We ate at the table with the Coop's, but ate only our own food.

"My dad would take us in on Monday morning, driving five miles with the horse. When Friday night came, we walked home. Sometimes we were mighty cold when we got home."

In 1915, the course of study for the Price County Training School included the following:

Two-Year courses (For eighth grade graduates, high school graduates were exempt from these courses)

✐ Composition, political geography, physical geography, writing, spelling, elementary science, English and American history.

One- and Two-Year Courses (One-year students were high school graduates)

✐ Orthoepy (Pronunciation, needed with non-English speaking students), professional arithmetic, cooking, psychology, music, gymnastics, professional English, methods and observation, school management and rural economics, agriculture, story telling, grammar, arithmetic, practice, professional history, professional reading, civics*, drawing, construction, sewing, physiology*, library methods, professional geography.

*High school graduates may be exempt in these subjects upon showing satisfactory standings.[5]

The two pronged curriculum offered at the Price County Training School was followed in other normal schools as well. Inez Thompson Hawley remembered fondly her days attending the Waushara County Normal School from which she graduated in 1937: "There must have been twenty to twenty-five in my class. I went to the normal school for one year because I had gone to high school."

Naomi Flugstad taught at the Vernon County Normal School from

1952 to 1965. She taught music, art, and library science. "One of the things we did in the art class was to make our own clay, with clay soil we got from an area farm. We met in the dining area, so we always had quite a bit of clean-up when we were working with clay mud. I wanted to show the students that there were many things they could do in the arts that didn't require a lot of money. We made our own paste, did a lot of clay work, and we wrote on paper sacks. When new teachers graduated and were hired in a rural school, they couldn't say, 'well the school board won't give us the money, so we can't do anything in art.' I felt it was very important for them to get the children interested in art, and that the children use inexpensive things for art work, things the children may have at home."

The demonstration room was an important feature of normal schools. Naomi Flugstad talks about the demonstration room at the Vernon County Normal School. "We had a demonstration room with up to thirty-five students in grades one through eight. First year normal students were required to observe the demonstration room teacher and the other normal school teachers working with the children. By the end

*1933
Oneida County
Normal School
Diploma.*

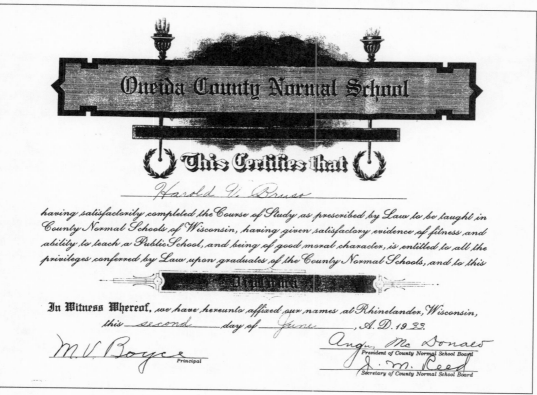

*Waushara County
Normal School.
Wautoma.*

Photo by Steve Apps.

of their first year, the normal school students went out to visit the rural schools and spent time there. They observed and helped the rural school teacher by taking care of recess, helping with spelling lessons—a variety of things that weren't too difficult to do. In their sophomore year, the normal school students went out to the rural schools in the fall and in the spring, and they continued working with the children in the demonstration room. They were working with the children all the time. A strength of the normal schools was the time spent with children. Unfortunately, there was not enough time in a year-program to devote to history, literature and other academic subjects. But the students did learn how to handle a classroom." The demonstration room was run as a replica of a one-room country school, except it was a part of the normal school and the children were from the village or city in which the normal school was located.

In addition to the academic subjects that were taught, and the time spent working directly with children, the normal schools also tried to help the normal school teachers-in-training see a world beyond the area where they grew up. In many instances, normal school students knew little beyond their own rural neighborhoods. Taking trips was one way to do this. Naomi Flugstad recalled a trip where she accompanied the

Vernon County Normal students. "I remember the first trip I took them on, traveling to La Crosse, crossing the river, and heading for Colorado. I heard one of the students say she'd never seen such a big bridge. She was referring to the Mississippi River bridge in La Crosse, which crossed into Minnesota and was less than fifty miles from Viroqua. So these teachers-in-training were getting out and seeing some things. This gave them something to feel that they had accomplished."

High School Teacher Training

High schools, growing in prominence as the years passed, offered some teacher training. In 1913, the legislature passed a law authorizing any school board with responsibility for a high school, and in a county where there was no normal school, to offer a teacher training course. By 1924, twenty-nine high schools offered organized teacher training courses.6

In a continual effort to upgrade teacher training, soon high schools were no longer allowed to offer teacher training programs. And during the 1960s, all of the county normal schools closed when elementary school teachers were required to have four years of preparation rather than the two years which had become the normal school standard. Many one-room school teachers with two-year preparation attended summer schools at four-year colleges and universities to complete their bachelor's degrees and meet the four years of preparation requirement.

Supervisory Teachers

After the creation of the office of county superintendent of schools in 1861, the county superintendent had responsibility for visiting the country schools and supervising the country school teachers in his county. It quickly became apparent that the county superintendent didn't have time to make the rounds of often over 100 schools in a county. Not until 1915 was the county supervising teacher position established to assist the superintendents. The county supervising teacher was to encourage good teaching, support the teachers, and work with the local school boards. When the teacher knew the date for a supervising teacher visit, she made sure the school was in the best shape possible. The students and teacher together cleaned the inside of the building, made sure the outhouses were especially clean, and that the students knew their lessons well. Sometimes the supervising teacher came unannounced, and then the teacher made do, hoping that the supervising teacher had selected a day when the students were well behaved and had done their home work.

How well supervising was received by the local teachers often depended on the personality of the supervisory teacher. Elizabeth Dunn was a supervising teacher in Price County from 1923 to 1943. Teachers said this about her, "Miss Dunn provided an open door even on Saturdays for teachers to visit her at the Normal School for books, advice or just a listening ear. She was described as attentive and perceptive, noticing problems and difficult situations before teachers could even point them out, remembering every child's name in every classroom she visited two or three times a year. Her warm manner and quick sense of humor endeared her to students and teachers alike. Some students recall how they held Miss Dunn in awe as their teachers anticipated her visits with some trepidation, but also respect and appreciation."7

1917 Common School Diploma. Burnett County. Mrs. August Dahlberg, teacher. Walter Erickson, pupil.

Other country school teachers didn't have such kind things to say about their supervising teachers. Ruby Schultz, who taught in several Door County schools starting in the 1940s, recalled the year she had 50 students and the supervising teacher came to visit. "She said to me,

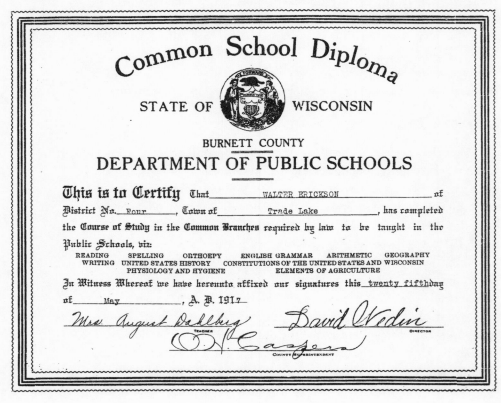

Common School Diploma

STATE OF   WISCONSIN

BURNETT COUNTY

DEPARTMENT OF PUBLIC SCHOOLS

This is to Certify That ___WALTER ERICKSON___ of

District No. __Four__, Town of ___Trade Lake___, has completed

the Course of Study in the Common Branches required by law to be taught in the

Public Schools, viz:

READING   SPELLING   ORTHOEPY   ENGLISH GRAMMAR   ARITHMETIC   GEOGRAPHY
WRITING   UNITED STATES HISTORY   CONSTITUTIONS OF THE UNITED STATES AND WISCONSIN
PHYSIOLOGY AND HYGIENE   ELEMENTS OF AGRICULTURE

In Witness Whereof we have hereunto affixed our signatures this __twenty fifth__ day

of ___May___, A. D. 191_7_

Mrs. August Dahlberg
TEACHER

David Wedin
DIRECTOR

O. H. Caspers
COUNTY SUPERINTENDENT

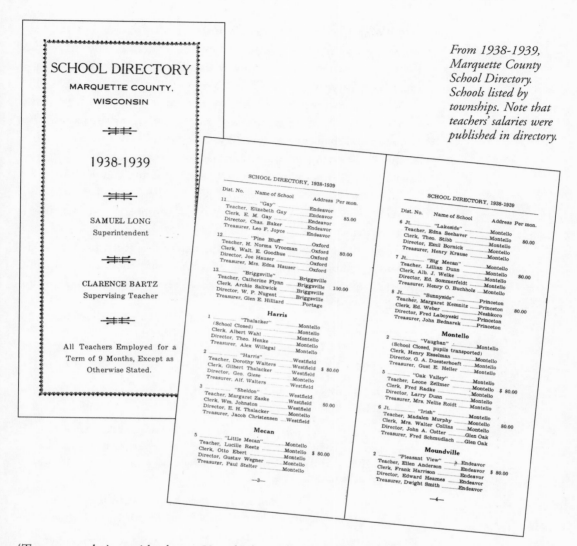

From 1938-1939, Marquette County School Directory. Schools listed by townships. Note that teachers' salaries were published in directory.

'Turn your chair upside down. You don't sit down when you teach a class.' This same supervising teacher also said to me one time, 'Go visit this young teacher, go to his school and watch him teach. He does such a good job.' This guy turned out to be a bum, never amounted to anything. Another time she said, 'You watch that clock and when it's time for a class to end, end! and go to the next class.' I asked her what I should do if I'm giving a spelling test and it runs over. 'You quit right there.' I didn't get along with my supervising teacher."

Aileen Straseski, who taught in Fond du Lac County, recalled a visit from her supervisory teacher. "My first experience with a supervisory teacher was on a warm fall day. It was cool in the morning so my father had stoked up the heater. Then the sun came out and it got really warm, got over ninety degrees in the classroom. All the while the supervising teacher was watching me teach. She finally told me we should have a recess.

"This supervising teacher would not only watch me teach, but sometimes she would judge how well I was teaching by the page in the book the pupils had progressed to. I later learned I had some slow learners, and I was trying to move them along at their pace. She told me, 'Teachers in the other schools are a lot further along than you are.'

"She would also look in the corners of the school for dust, and how well I had cleaned the room. I was not impressed with my supervising teacher."

Other country teachers found their supervising teachers more helpful. George Klingbeil, who taught in Oak Dale School in Marquette County in the 1930s, received this written report from his supervising teacher:

September 23, 1937   George Klingbeil
Enrolled 13--12 present
Decorations--Good
Assignments--Good, well written
Recitations--Good
Discipline--Very good

Suggestions. When using flash cards, hold card so pupils can see it for just a few seconds. Just long enough for him to see what is wanted. You will find that all children need lots of drill in arithmetic and in the mastery of difficult words.

I am pleased to see that you are getting such a fine start. Keep up the good work and do not be discouraged if things do not always go right.

Look up records of Gerhardt Henke. You have a fine school and I feel that the children will like to come to school. Best wishes for a successful year. S. Long, Supervising Teacher

In the spring of 1939, Mr. Klingbeil received this written report after another supervisory teacher visit.

Oak Dale School

April 14, 1939

The room is well kept and has been made attractive by the use of posters, charts, and pictures. The pupils have a fine attitude toward their work and toward you. They seem interested in their work and are kept busy at well worked out assignments. I saw many good study questions and vocabulary helps on the board.

I saw no signs of any discipline problems and the class recitations were well conducted.

You have done much to interest your pupils in conservation, through pictures, magazines, and feeding stations.

Work on the reading skills that your pupils need help with; this should help some of your upper grade pupils to better understand the material in their content subject textbooks.

I would not use the study questions as a basis for the class discussions in the upper grade classes. The study questions have their place in the preparation, but in class we should try to get the pupils to carry on informal discussions around larger units of thought. Clarence Bartz, Supervising Teacher.

After several years of country school teaching, Mr. Klingbeil went on to become a Professor in the College of Agriculture at the University of Wisconsin-Madison.

County Superintendent of Schools

In the 1840s, schools were under the jurisdiction of township superintendents who often had few qualifications for selecting teachers, and supervising classroom activities. The inadequacy of the town superintendent system became increasingly evident, leading to the Wisconsin legislature passing a law in 1861 creating the position of County Superintendent of Schools with a minimum salary set at $400 per year. The county superintendent's primary duties were examining and certifying teachers, inspecting schools in their counties, condemning unfit schoolhouses, ordering new schools built, encouraging formation of teachers' associations, organizing and conducting at least one institute annually, introducing best methods of instruction in the schools, and ad-vising school boards on various legal matters such as ventilation of school buildings. A few years later, teachers were certified by a state board of examiners, so once approved they could teach in any school in the state. 8

In later years, the County Superintendent of Schools also served on the County Board's Agricultural and Conservation, County Health, and County School Committees. The Agriculture and Conservation committee had responsibility for hiring and receiving reports from the County Extension Agents in the County (4-H Agents, Home Economists, Agricultural Agents).

There is no real teacher who in practice does not believe in the existence of the soul, or in a magic that acts on it through speech.

—Allan Bloom, 1987

27

TEACHERS' COMMON SCHOOL CONTRACT

(State of Wisconsin)

IT IS HEREBY AGREED, by and between the District Board of School District No. *10*, of the Town of *Addison*, for and in the name of said School District, and *Mary A. Foote*, a duly qualified Teacher legally & licensed in the County of *Washington*, and State of Wisconsin, (a copy of said License being attached hereto;) that the said *Mary A. Foote* is to teach the Common School of said District for the term of *Five &* months, for the sum of *Seventy* Dollars per month, commencing on the *6th* day of *January*, 1913, it being expressly understood and agreed by the parties hereto, that *20* days shall constitute, in this case, a School month, and that on Saturday, there shall be no School taught;

And for such services properly rendered, the said District Board, for and in the name of said District, is to pay the said *Mary A. Foote* on or before the *last* day of *the month*, the amount that may be due *her* according to this contract.

Witness our hands
this *31st* day of
December A. D. 19*12*

J. S. Mueller ~~Treas.~~ Director.

Math Stoffel Clerk.

Geo. Sherman Director ~~Treas.~~

Mary A. Foote Teacher.

One-room school teacher's contract for 1913. Mary A. Foote, teacher, Washington County. Salary: $70 per month, for five and 5/20 months.

There were other duties as well. Hazel Leicht served as La Crosse County Superintendent of Schools from 1938 to 1962. She said, "I assisted with sugar rationing during the war. When the Sauk polio vaccine was available, I distributed all the parent consent slips to all the rural schools. The work in connection with the consolidation of schools required hours of extra work. When petitions were received I spent hours at the court house checking property descriptions, and preparing notices in various districts affected by the petition."9

Richard Berger, was County Superintendent of Schools in Ozaukee County (1900-1949). He died in office and at the time was the oldest superintendent both in age and in years of service. His son, Ken Berger, recalls when his father was in office:

"State Superintendent Callahan often came to Port Washington to speak at Dad's annual County Teacher's Institutes. There were no restaurants as such then, so speakers would always come to our house for lunch, and I, the kid, had to be on my best behavior.

"The superintendent's job was an elected office and the term was for two years, later changed to four. Dad had opposition twice in all those years. However after each spring's election results were noted he always had a big party at our house in Fredonia for all his loyal supporters from the various townships. The pay was $75 per month. Dad ran the farm, where we now live, on the side.

"One year, when the issue of pay raises was discussed at the County Board meeting, Ray Blank from the Town of Grafton got up and said, 'All the county workers always want a raise. Rick Berger has been working here for forty years and never once asked for a raise. I propose we double his salary to $150 per month.' It passed unanimously. So for the last nine years Dad was, as they said in those days, 'well off.'"

Until 1875, only men held the office of County Superintendent. In Price County, the first woman superintendent was Anna Brosnan who served from 1887-1890. She came from upper New York state, home to many Wisconsin settlers. She apparently did very well for The Phillips Times reported on September 17, 1887, "Miss Brosnan is making a splendid record as Supt. of Schools. Her conduct of this important position will do much toward removing any prejudice that might exist among the people of Price County in relation to women holding public office."10 Visiting country schools in Price County, in the late 1800s, was an onerous task. Transportation was primitive or nearly nonexistent. The County Superintendent took the train to one of the villages on the rail line. There she rented a room, hired a carriage and a horse driver, and spent two or more days visiting the outlying schools.

In the first place God made idiots. This was for practice. Then He made School Boards.

—Mark Twain, 1897

In 1965, with school consolidation, and the formation of Cooperative Educational Agencies, there was no longer a need for County Superintendents of school and the position was discontinued.

County Nurses

In addition to the county superintendent and the supervising teacher, the county nurse also made the rounds of the country schools. Palma Gorhn was the first Sauk County visiting nurse. It's not known exactly when she started, but she worked at least part of the 1919-1920 school year and in 1920-1921. Mrs. Norma Acott became visiting nurse in 1921. In her 1924-25 report to the County Board, she wrote: "116 schools inspected, 3,187 children with 2,631 having defects. Health

1947 Teacher's Contract.

VOID IF NOT RETURNED BEFORE APRIL 15, 1947

TEACHERS' CONTRACT FORM   Rhinelander Office Supply Co.

TEACHERS' CONTRACT

It is hereby agreed by and between School District No. ......one..... in the Town

of ..Arbor Vitae-Woodruff County of ....Vilas.and.Oneida............, State of Wisconsin, and

..Harold.Bruso........................ a legally qualified teacher, that said teacher is to teach,

govern, and conduct the xxxxxxxxxxxxxxxxxxxxxxxxxxxxxxxxxxxxxxxxx Upper.Grade

department of the graded school of said district, (strike out one) to the best of h.is ability; keep a
register of the daily attendance and transportation and a record of the classes of each pupil belonging
to the school, and such other records as the District Board may require, make such reports as are required by law, and endeavor to preserve in good condition and order the school house, grounds, furniture, apparatus, and such other district property as may come under the immediate supervision of said

teacher, for the term of ...nine................ school months, commencing on the ..1st.... day

of ....September............... A. D. 19.47. for the sum of .....244.44.............Dollars
per school month, to be paid at the end of each month, it being understood and agreed that twenty
days teaching shall constitute a month.
Addenda clauses 1,2,3, and 4 are part of this contract.
      And the said School District hereby agrees to keep the school house in repair, to provide the
necessary supplies to maintain the school, and for the services of said teacher, as prescribed above, well

and truly performed, to pay said teacher the sum of two hundred forty four and 44/100 Dollars per school

month, at the end of each school month during a term of ...9...school months commencing as above.
Teachers are to report for work on Monday, August 25th, 1947 and are to receive
one week's additional pay at the rate of their regular 9 month's contract.
      Provided. That in case said teacher shall be legally dismissed from school or shall have h.is
certificate legally annulled, by expiration or otherwise, then said teacher shall not be entitled to compensation from and after such dismissal or annulment; provided further, that the wages of said teacher for the last month shall not be paid until the teacher shall have made the report for the school term
as required by law and it be approved by the County Superintendent of Schools.

      Provided further.   That it is hereby agreed and understood that this contract shall not be-
come active and in force until the above named applicant for the position provided for in this agreement has filed with the school clerk an affidavit signed by a physician licensed to practice medicine
and surgery as provided in the Wisconsin Statutes. Said affidavit shall state that the physician, signing the affidavit, has given the applicant a skin test for tuberculosis and shall state whether the reaction was positive or negative. If the reaction is positive the applicant shall file with the clerk a second
affidavit following a physical examination and X-ray and whether the applicant's physical condition
is a health hazard to the pupils of the school.

      The School Board also reserves the right to require an examination and X-ray of the applicant
at any future time during the life of this contract, provided that such examination and X-ray shall be at
the expense of the school district.

      In Witness whereof, We have here unto subscribed our names this 23. day of April., 19.47

      Fred J. Schmidt Director. *James W. Whitman* .... Clerk
      Mildred Brown Treasurer..... *Harold Bruso* . Teacher

      This contract provides for sick leave according to 40.87 (4) (B); Wis. Statutes 1943; Chap. 37,
Laws, 1943.

      IT IS FURTHER understood that this contract is entered into subject to the provisions of the
Wisconsin "State Retirement Law" for Teachers and the blank spaces below are filled for the purpose
of enabling the Retirement Board officials to certainly identify the reports and payments in behalf of
any teacher coming within the provisions of the statute.

Name in full: School address this year

....

Home Address   School address last year

....

Date of Birth

....

TEACHER'S CERTIFICATE
Copy*

Clause 1: This teacher will be given one school visitation day
during the school year. This day to be spent in a school or
department of another school which has been approved by the
principal of this school and the County Superintendent's office.
The purpose of this day is to observe teaching technique.

Clause 2: An additional $50 will be apid said teacher as a
part of the final payment of this contract if said teacher has
fulfilled all the terms of this contract.

Clause 3: $10.00 per week for each week of regular summer
school attended. This sum to be paid just before Christman
Holidays, 1947. Said teacher shall have a certified statement
filed with the school clerk from the teacher training school
attended verfying such summer school attendance.

Clause 4: Said teacher to meet the requirements of the State
Department of Public Instruction in meeting the requirements
of certification for this school year to teach the subjects
or grade covered by this contract. The principal is to be
consulted in regards to anticipated summer school courses taken
at summer school if such attendance is required for certification.

talks to children and parents and articles written for newspapers. Twenty-two people were taken to institutions or I was instrumental in getting them there. Examples of such institutions were the County Farm, Mendota, various tuberculosis sanitariums, children's homes, Salvation Army, etc. Four days of chest clinics at 3 locations. Clothing relief to 45 families, 344 home calls, 16 cases of neglected children, 4 days at county fair—1000 children weighed and measured." 11

In Price County the first county nurse, Teresa Gardner, was hired sometime after 1910 with the first records available in 1919. She had some difficult times in the early years of her work.

"Miss Gardner, always somberly dressed and conscientious with a no nonsense attitude, is still recalled by some former students. At times, messages conveyed in the classroom met at home with less than enthusiasm. The admonition to sleep with the windows open prompted one mother to exclaim, 'Enough cold air gets in through the cracks around our windows to let us get sufficient fresh air!' Miss Gardner also emphasized the importance of regular bathing. She said to the students, 'Enjoy your bath, splash around and have fun." One child found this did not sit well with her mother who had just scrubbed the kitchen floor for Sunday, and the big round wash tub placed before the open door of the wood stove oven was not the place to have fun." 12

Miss Gardner and other county nurses like her regularly visited the schools, measured children, checked teeth, eyes, hair and skin. They gave instructions for brushing teeth, and sometimes even gave children toothbrushes and sample toothpaste, a real gift to a youngster who had never seen them before. Nurses talked with students about drinking milk, eating fruits and vegetables, and getting a good night's sleep. She often dispensed cod liver oil, and handed out iodine pills (to prevent goiters) until iodized salt was available. When immunizations for whooping cough, diphtheria, and smallpox became available in the 1940s the county nurses helped to organize clinics to immunize all the school children. In the 1950s, nurses also helped dispense Sauk polio vaccine.

*When you've work to do,
Do it with a will;
They who reach the top,
First must climb the hill.*

—1904 speller

Although the rural school teacher is often viewed as someone working alone with no support, support was available in several ways. The school board and the parents were the first line of support, then the county supervising teachers and the county superintendent of schools, and the county nurse. Of course the supervising teacher might only visit once a year, and likewise the nurse may not visit anymore often, yet, they were available and committed to helping the rural school teacher with her job.

Chapter Notes

1. Lloyd P. Jorgenson. *The Founding of Public Education in Wisconsin.* Madison: State Historical Society of Wisconsin, 1956.

2. *Ibid.*, pp. 167-168, 170-173.

3. Conrad E. Patzer. *Public Education in Wisconsin.* Madison: State Superintendent's Office, 1924, pp. 145-157.

4. *Ibid.*, p. 176.

5. Committee for Research on Price County Schools. *Country School Recollections II.* Phillips, WI: Price County Historical Society, 1990, pp. 4-5, 8.

6. *Ibid.*, p. 177.

7. *Ibid.*, p. 22.

8. Jorgenson, pp. 104-105.

9. Estella Krohn Bryhn. *Early Schools of La Crosse County.* West Salem, WI: Block Printing, 1985, p. 180.

10. Committee for Research on Price County Schools, p. 2.

11. Rural Schools Research Committee. *Good Old Golden Rule Days: A History of Sauk County Wisconsin Country Schools.* Baraboo, WI: Sauk County Historical Society, 1994, p. 31.

12. Committee for Research on Price County Schools, pp. 23-24.

All In A Day

When I attended Chain O' Lake, I tried to finish my barn chores a little early, so after walking the mile to school there would be time for play, a kind of before school recess. Also, those children with particular assigned duties, such as pumping and carrying water, toting wood, and sweeping out the outhouses arrived a little earlier to finish their tasks before the nine o'clock bell announced the start of another school day.

The teacher had arrived much earlier. In almost every school the teacher had responsibility for starting the fire in the stove, and making sure the school room was clean—some of the tasks were delegated to students. She also wrote the assignments for the day on the blackboard, and generally made ready for the arrival of the pupils. Different from today's modern schools, the teacher and the students had complete responsibility for the operation of the school, in all respects.

Union No. 1 School, Pierce County, 1893. School built for $600. Closed in 1944 and is now a home.

From Edna Runquist.

57

Early Morning Duties

Bonnie Trudell, who attended the Squaw Lake School (St. Croix County) in the late 1940s and early 1950s, recalled, "We all had duties. Putting coal in the furnace, taking out the clinkers—these jobs rotated among the sixth, seventh, and eighth graders. Someone was responsible for erasing and washing the chalkboards, cleaning the erasers, sweeping the floor, putting up the flag, and bringing in the mail. We were in charge of keeping the building running. There were no custodians—we were it."

Water proved a problem at many schools. Isabel Clark Thompson, a student at Prairie View School in Green Lake County, said, "Our school did not have a well. Each day two students took a tall pail, a cream pail with a cover, and walked to the nearest farm (Rader's) and pumped the pail full of water. Then they carried it back to school and put the water into an earthen water cooler. This was our drinking water for the day."

Beneath the hill you may see the mill, Of wasting wood and crumbling stone; The wheel is dripping and clattering still, But Jerry, the miller, is dead and gone.

—John Saxe 1888 Reader

Mabel Grundahl Larsen attended Meadow View School (Dane County) in the late 1920s. "A bucket of fresh drinking water was brought into the hallway at the beginning of each day. It had a common dipper from which we all drank. There was a pump outside with a cup hanging beside it. The voice of the pump chortled and creaked as it gushed forth cold fresh water. When we see such a pump today, it stands a wistful monument of the past. I have seen them decorated with vines and flowers, but no longer gushing forth fresh water."

The Polk Dairy School in Washington County, where Elmer Marth attended, was another school without a well. "Daily, two of the older boys who walked past the cheese factory on their way to school picked up a large can of water, carried it to school and dumped the water into a stoneware crock. The well at the cheese factory was the source of water because it was tested regularly and was known to be pure. Sometimes water in the school was gone before the school day ended; however we all survived nicely."

Robert Erickson, a nineteen-year-old teacher at South Natwick School in Vernon County in the late 1940s, brought a ten gallon milk can of water each day to school with him. He strapped the can on the back of his Model A Ford car, fastening the strap to his spare tire.

There were other tasks shared by various pupils. For most of the tasks it was thought an honor to be selected to perform them. Passing out the chocolate flavored goiter pills (iodine pills to combat goiter problems) was one of those special tasks.

At the Bryon School in Fond du Lac County, carrying out and burning the waste paper was an honored task. Charles Rhern attended this school in the middle 1950s. "Some of the jobs at our school were of higher responsibility. You had to be older. Burning the waste paper was one of these jobs. You had to be in fourth grade before you were eligible to get one safety match and two waste paper baskets. You carried the baskets out to the burn barrel stuck behind the school, and struck the match. I had been waiting four years to have this job. I can't believe that anything could be more exciting. I was very, very excited to have my opportunity."

Proudly, Charles carried the waste paper to the burn barrel, knowing that the young students were eying him and waiting for the day when they would have this highly important and responsible task thrust on them. But then the worst possible thing occurred.

"I really don't know what I did, but the grass near the barrel caught fire. It was very dry, I remember that. Before it was over, I had acres of dry grass burning next to the quarry at Byron. It took two or three fire departments to put out the fire, and that was the last time I got to burn waste paper. I lost my privilege to burn paper."

A globe, flag, maps and lessons on the blackboard were common in country schools.

Photo by Steve Apps.

There were other tasks. At my country school we had a safety patrol, complete with badges and white belts with a strap going over the shoulder. One day the whole kit of materials, including badges, belts and instructions, arrived at the school. Our teacher appointed an older student captain of the safety patrol, she appointed another lieutenant, and two or three more were appointed patrol officers. The captain's badge was gold, the lieutenant's was red, and the rest were silver.

The instruction book was clear about the duties of the safety patrol. When children were crossing streets going to and from school, a safety patrol officer was to watch to make sure no car hit them. There was one small problem at my country school. No more than two or three cars a day passed the school on the sandy, dusty road. No one had bothered to check if every school needed a safety patrol, which our school clearly didn't. Nevertheless, we had the equipment, and the teacher appointed children to the positions, as per her instructions. Although we had nothing officially to do, it was fun to wear our badges and white belts.

Opening Exercises

After the sounding of the final morning bell, at most schools students gathered around the flag pole and watched two older students raise the flag. One was in charge of the rope, and the other made certain that the flag would not touch the ground. With the flag fluttering from the top of its pole, they recited the pledge of allegiance and sang "America." On bitter cold or stormy days, they recited the pledge and sang "America" inside the school building.

After the opening exercise, students filed inside the building and spent the first fifteen minutes singing, often songs from *The Golden Book of Favorite Songs.* In my school, singing was much more fun when our teacher could play the piano, which was not always the case. My eighth grade teacher, Faith Jenks, was a particularly good piano player. She could make the old upright piano spill out music no one believed was in it.

Even on the coldest days of winter, we always sang for the first several minutes each day. Sometimes, on below zero mornings, the school room was so cold that we all huddled around the wood stove, wearing our coats and mittens, but we still sang songs. Mrs. Jenks always played the piano, too, even though it was located at the front of the freezing room. On the most frigid days she played while still wearing her brown cloth gloves.

Randy Jablonic, currently the University of Wisconsin-Madison's Crew Coach, attended the South Bright and the North Bright schools in Clark County. At the South Bright School, the teacher had made an arrangement for a neighbor to come in early on cold winter days to start the fire. But this didn't always happen as regularly as expected. As Jablonic explained, "On very cold mornings in winter, especially when the fellow who was supposed to have started the fire in the morning didn't because he was nursing a severe hangover, the students and teacher put on WHA radio and marched around and around the inside of the school-house to warm up."

One year, at my school, our teacher couldn't play the piano. We listened to records on our windup Victrola record player—Sousa's "Stars and Stripes Forever" was one of our favorites.

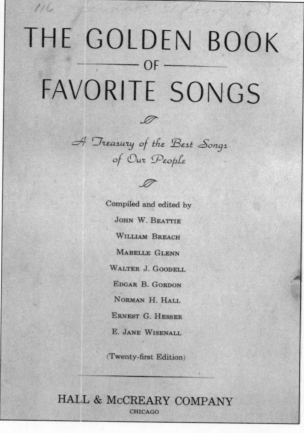

THE GOLDEN BOOK
— OF —
FAVORITE SONGS

A Treasury of the Best Songs of Our People

Compiled and edited by
JOHN W. BEATTIE
WILLIAM BREACH
MABELLE GLENN
WALTER J. GOODELL
EDGAR B. GORDON
NORMAN H. HALL
ERNEST G. HESSER
E. JANE WISENALL

(Twenty-first Edition)

HALL & McCREARY COMPANY
CHICAGO

The Golden Book of Favorite Songs. A popular song book in country schools.

The Classes

At 9:15 the day's classes began. Classes were called to the front of the room, to sit with the teacher, and recite. The number of classes depended on the number of students in the school, and whether there were students in each grade. Most of the time, but not always, the classes were small with only three or four students in a grade, sometimes only one or two.

Often classes were combined. Reading four and five, or reading seven and eight met together. A typical day's schedule began with first grade reading for fifteen minutes, followed by second grade reading. Classes for arithmetic, spelling, language, and social studies, grade by grade, came to the front of the room for recitation. There was a fifteen minute recess in mid-morning and again in mid-afternoon. Noon included a full hour for lunch and outdoor activities.

Looking back at this system of schooling, today's teachers and stu-

Typical one-room country school schedule. Dalton School, Green Lake County, 1936-37. Vera Lawson, teacher.

RECITATION PROGRAM
School Year 19 *36* to 19 *37*

1936/37   THIS PROGRAM TO BE LEFT AT SCHOOL HOUSE TO ASSIST NEXT YEAR'S TEACHER

FORENOON PROGRAM			AFTERNOON PROGRAM		
RECITATION BEGINS	CLASS RECITING		RECITATION BEGINS	CLASS RECITING	
	GRADE	SUBJECT		GRADE	SUBJECT
9:00	All	Music	1:00	1	Reading
9:15	1	Reading	1:25	2 A	Reading
9:40	2 A	Reading	1:35	2 B	Reading
9:55	2 B	Reading	1:45	4	Reading
10:10	4	Reading	2:05		Art Writing Folk Dances
10:30		Recess	2:30		Recess
10:45	2	Arithmetic	2:45		Games
11:00	1	Reading	3:00	1-2	Language
11:15	4	Arithmetic	3:15		Free Activity
11:30	2	Spelling	3:30	4	Spelling
11:45	4	Language	3:40	4	Social Studies
12:00		Noon Recess	4:00		Dismissal Recess

Dalton School - Vera Lawson, teacher

dents wonder how it could work, and how anything good could come of it. The teacher was nearly always in class, and everyone in the room could overhear what was going on during each of the recitation periods. Some students, no doubt, found this distracting, but for many others listening to the recitations was a definite advantage.

Pupils had the advantage of reviewing what they had previously studied, and were introduced to what they would soon be studying. For instance, Ellouise Halstead, who had attended a one-room school said, "I learned by osmosis—I did my own seat work, but I couldn't help but hear the other classes up in front, on the benches, or at the board. I found that much more interesting than my own assignments, so I listened to them and I learned before I needed to learn it."

Ada McKnight, who started teaching in 1929 at the Reynald School near Boscobel in Crawford County said, "The little ones learned from the older ones. I had a little first grade girl who could spell everything that was on the board. She picked if off the blackboard; they got so much that way. Pupils went through each grade two or three times. In this school, most of the work was done on the blackboards. We didn't have many books; we didn't even have a library in that school. I had a very stingy school board. If I requested twelve text books, they would buy me six."

School leaders believed coming to the front of the room to recite served many functions. In the early days, recitation was emphasized because there were few textbooks and little paper. Also, educators knew that reading out loud was important for learning how to read. And as Andrew Gulliford pointed out, "the prevailing education belief during the 19th century was that the mind was like a muscle: If not continually flexed, it might atrophy or lose all of its knowledge."[1]

If students were doing exceptionally well in a particular subject, they were allowed to sit in with the next highest class. Likewise, if a student was having difficulty with a subject, he or she might sit with a lower class. For example, a student in the fifth year of school might sit with the sixth grade reading group, and with the fourth grade arithmetic group. Thus students moved around, based on how well they were doing, and what additional help they required.

The secret of education lies in respecting the pupil.

—Emerson

Bonnie Trudell said it this way. "I was the only person in my grade, and that gave me a lot of latitude. For those things I was really good at I could keep on pushing. I got encouraged to do that. When I was in the lower grades, I got assigned an older student to go to. Like in reading, if you didn't know how to pronounce a word, or needed help in spelling or in looking something up, we had assigned mentors to help us."

The mentor system was common in the country schools. It was expected that older students would help the younger students, and as is commonly known, when an older student faced trying to explain something to a younger student, the older pupil generally learned the material more deeply as well.

Lunch Time

Lunch time was special. In the early days of country schools, and in most instances right up to the time the schools closed, pupils carried their lunches. Most families could not afford fancy lunch buckets, so children carried their lunches in metal lard pails or syrup pails. A typical lunch consisted of a couple of jelly sandwiches, perhaps a sugar cookie

Children attending Reynald School, Crawford County, 1929.

From Ada McKnight, teacher.

or two, and in the fall of the year, an apple. Rare indeed were oranges, and even more rare, bananas.

Sometimes lunch also included a pint jar of chocolate milk—everyone had cows so a little chocolate syrup was poured into the jar of milk. Sometimes it was dark chocolate milk, sometimes only tan, but it was always enjoyed. When there was snow on the ground, and the weather wasn't too terribly cold, those with chocolate milk placed the jars in snow during the morning recess. By noon the milk was properly chilled, as good as if it had been in a refrigerator—a convenience that many students did not know.

In the winter, lunch often included a pint jar of soup or chili. A pan of water always steamed on the top of the stove, for the purpose of adding humidity to the always too dry room. Those with soup jars placed them in the pan of water during morning recess, and by noon time the soup was warm and deliciously ready to eat. For many of the students, the smell of soup wafting around the room made it nearly impossible to concentrate on anything but lunch those minutes before noon, when every thing seemed to drag and take forever.

Some children had little in their lunch pails, and some sharing took place. Occasionally a child would come to school without lunch. Paul Nagel, shared this story. "An eighth grade girl excused herself from the building each day to presumably go home for lunch. It was discovered that she walked the roads an appropriate time, and then returned to school. She didn't want to reveal to the teacher, and especially to her peers, the abject poverty of the family which could not send a lunch for her."

School lunch programs, of one kind or another, were available in some of the schools. Sally Smith attended a country school in Wood County, during the 1940s. She enjoyed arriving at school each day because the room was warm and it smelled so good. "We had a cook who made bread for us. She was an old-fashioned cook. There was a small kitchen behind the blackboard. This was one of the first schools to start an orange juice program with concentrated orange juice. Back then nobody knew about concentrated orange juice, and we were the first ones to start that. Some of us girls would get the assignment to help the cook. We'd go down in the basement and run water in these big buckets, and add the concentrate that came in cans. It was during World War II."

Mischief

The school day was not as orderly and planned as it might appear. From time-to-time, students, as they were and are sometimes still prone to do, played little tricks on their teacher. Common ones were putting thumbtacks on the teacher's chair, or stuffing a live frog or snake in the teacher's desk drawer.

Otto Festge, former mayor of Madison, attended the Union Valley School in Dane County from 1926 to 1934. "In elementary school I participated in my first protest. We had a teacher who insisted that in winter, no matter how cold, or how bitter the weather, we had to go outside for fresh air during recess. This particular day it was below zero, cold, snowy, blizzard conditions. We decided we'd had it. We sent somebody into the schoolhouse under the pretext that a student had been injured. The teacher came outside, without a coat. As soon as she stepped outside, the biggest kid stood in front of the door. We said, OK, now you either stay outside with us, or if you go in, then we all go in. She thought for a minute and said, "Fine, we'll all go in."

The students weren't too concerned about punishment because the biggest kid was taller than the teacher. As Festge said, "We had power on our side."

The most necessary part of learning is to unlearn our errors.

—Webster's American Spelling Book, 1831

Carolyn Wedin, currently a professor at the University of Wisconsin-Whitewater, and a former student at Round Lake School in Burnett County, was party to a larger protest. The protest became a full blown student strike, unheard of in country schools in those days, or in any school for that matter.

The problem was with the teacher, a tyrant, as Carolyn described her. By March of the school year the students had enough. An eighth grade boy suggested that all of the students should go outside the school and cross the fence, off the school grounds, and not return to the school room until the teacher was fired. Off the school grounds, the students reasoned, the teacher had no jurisdiction.

When everyone was safely on the other side of the fence, one of the seventh graders ran across the pasture to her parents to inform them that the students were on strike and wouldn't go back to school until they got a new teacher. The telephone lines were soon buzzing as parents called each other with the rather shocking news. Within a short time, parents began arriving at the school, and before the end of the afternoon the teacher was fired. A replacement was found to complete the school year. The strike had been successful.[2]

Chain O' Lake School, Waushara County, 1943. Author in second row, first person on the left, in fifth grade.

Some student mischief probably wasn't intended. Judy Nelson, a student in Bryon School, Dodge County, told this about her little brother, Charles. "I remember when he was in first grade. He was punished by having to sit under the pigeon hole of the teacher's desk. While there, he bit the teacher on the leg. It was a terrible embarrassment for my sister and me." (Incidently, Charles is the same little boy who started the grass fire when he was in fourth grade, while burning the school's waste paper.)

Loren Lewis, now a retired pastor, attended a country school in the 1920s, in Leota, Indiana. He recalled this event. "In the midst of

December, our teacher told us that he was not going to give us a treat that year for Christmas. So the next morning, we came to school a little early. We found the place all locked up, so we crawled in a window and started the fire for ourselves. And we locked the door from the inside. When the teacher came, we wouldn't let him in. We were all cozy inside and having a great time while he sat outside in his car, trying to keep warm by running his engine." Everything seemed on hold for the moment, until the students thought of a strategy.

"One of us sneaked out the window and stuffed an old glove in his exhaust pipe. He couldn't understand why his car wouldn't run. He finally negotiated, and we got our treats for Christmas."

Ruby Waldon Mabon taught at the Louisville School, Dunn County, from 1912-1913. She told, "I remember the bell rope hanging just to the left of the teacher's desk. I would wrap my arm up in the rope when I rang the bell. One morning, when I did as usual, to my surprise, I felt the rope tighten and my feet leaving the floor. It was over in less time than it takes to tell it, and I was lowered back to a standing position, no doubt because the boys who had climbed up into the belfry found my weight a little more than they had counted on."

Of course not all of the mischief was against the teacher. Kids commonly pulled all kinds of stunts on each other. In my school, bats roosted behind the window shutters. A common trick was to take a bat by its wing tips, and then chase the girls around the schoolhouse, listening to them scream and threaten to tell the teacher on us.

Joe Sveda, retired school administrator in Antigo, attended the Badger School, north of Antigo. He said he was always small, and that the older boys often picked on him. "There was a huge woodpile piled up against the shed, but open in the middle. The older boys would pick me up and drop me in the center of the woodpile, and I was so little I couldn't crawl out by myself. Thank God for the girls. They rescued me many times, but I would never tattle to the teacher. That's something we wouldn't do."

And so the school days began and ended, one after the other, year after year. All of the school age children from a family, and all of the children from the community learning together, helping each other, discovering how to get along, younger with older, Catholics with Protestants, Germans with Norwegians. The school was the community, in miniature. What was learned in the classroom and outside was important to the future of the community and how it shared and cared for the people in it.

Chapter Notes

1. Andrew Gulliford. *America's Country Schools.* Washington, D.C.: Preservation Press, National Trust for Historic Preservation, 1984, p.55.

2. Carolyn Wedin Sylvander. *Wisconsin: A Year.* Whitewater, WI: 1985, pp. 27-28.

6

Lessons That Were Learned

Mention country schools, and you often hear the ditty, "Reading and 'riting, and 'rithmetic, taught to the tune of the hickory stick." There were no hickory sticks when I attended country school in the 1930s and 1940s, or in many rural schools, but there was clearly an emphasis on reading, arithmetic, and writing including spelling and proper use of English in speaking and in writing. My fifth grade report card included number grades for: arithmetic, geography, grammar and composition, reading, spelling, and writing. By the time I was in seventh grade, American history and science were added to these subjects. Along the way some attention was also given to art and music. Starting in the 1930s, in many Wisconsin schools, art, music, nature study, and literature were supplemented by radio courses from the Wisconsin School of the Air (WHA radio in Madison).

1910 spelling book.

Reading and Arithmetic

Of all the subjects, reading was emphasized the most of all. I remember first grade, when my teacher, Theresa Piechowski, devised an interesting reading game for us. She had little metal cars on a long sheet of paper that she placed on the floor in the front of the room. As we learned a new word, we could move our car a space on the paper highway that she had mapped out for each car. There must have been three or four of us doing this activity, although there were only two of us in first grade. Perhaps a couple of second graders were included in the game for remedial practice. I remember being excited about each new word I learned. My love for words continues to this day, and it all started in first grade at the age of five. Of course my mother had read to me since I was a baby so the idea of words and the wonderful meanings they could convey were not new to me. But the idea that I could identify words by myself was such a marvelous thing. I've never gotten over the wonder of it.

In some schools, arithmetic was emphasized almost as much as reading. Wilmer Gorske, who taught at the Mt. Moriah School in Green Lake County, recalled the county-wide math contest for rural school children. "Harley Horne was pretty good in math, so we entered him in the math contest which was usually held at Thrasher's Hall in Green Lake. Each school or classroom was allowed to enter two students. A month before the contest was held, we held practice and speed sessions at school. The day the contest arrived we drove to Green Lake. The math contest included all phases of addition, subtraction, multiplication, division in plain numbers and so on. It was a written examination. Before the contest began, participants were issued a warning: 'The first one finished never wins.' After fifteen or twenty minutes of work time, Harley Horne was the first one finished. And, in spite of the earlier warning about early finishing, Harley went home with the championship math banner for Mt. Moriah School. What an honor!"

Textbooks

Before the 1800s, public school teachers had few classroom materials to work with, and few instructions about what they should teach, or how they should teach it. Many of them had to find their own books—the Holy Bible was a popular choice for many—for there were no textbooks available.

Personally, I am always ready to learn, although I do not always like being taught.

—Winston Churchill

The *New England Primer* became available in 1760. Primers were designed to help students learn the basics of reading. From primers, pupils advanced to readers.

In 1783, Noah Webster published one of the first textbooks for common school use. His *American Spelling Book*, which became popularly known as "Webster's Blue Back Speller," became instantly popular, even though the publisher who printed the book insisted that Webster pay the publishing costs because it seemed like a risky publishing project. The publishing history of this little book marked a special place in American publishing history. By 1807 the book sold 200,000 copies, by 1837, fifteen million copies had been sold. In 1855 another publisher took over the book and by 1880 could say that Webster's Speller was the biggest selling book in the world except for the Bible. By the beginning of the 1900s, it was still selling a million copies a year. The book was republished as late as 1958, more as a curiosity than as a textbook that students would use.

Noah Webster's American Spelling Book was more than a speller. It included a section titled "Analysis of Sounds," later known as phonics. The 1958 facsimile contained sixty-one pages devoted to an "Easy

1936, Second level reader.

OUT OF DOORS

Good Morning

Good morning, sky,
Good morning, sun,
Good morning, little winds that run!
Good morning, birds,
Good morning, trees,
And creeping grass, and brownie bees!
How did you find out it was day?
Who told you night had gone away?
I'm wide awake;
I'm up now, too.
I'll be right out to play with you!

47

Standard of Pronunciation." Following this section, the book contained a series of lessons encouraging students to practice pronunciation and spelling. Nearly all the lessons contained a moral message. Statements like this were sprinkled throughout the book:

"He that speaks loud in school will not learn his own book well, nor let the rest learn theirs; but those that make no noise will soon be wise, and gain much love and good will."

The speller also contained poetry and fables. One of the fables was about a boy, up a tree, who was about to steal apples. The owner of the apple tree discovered him and instructed the boy to come down. When he didn't, the man pulled up some grass and threw it at the boy. The boy laughed at the old man. The old man then said that if neither words nor grass will bring you down, perhaps stones will, and he began lobbing stones at the boy. The would-be apple thief quickly climbed down. At the end of the fable, these words appear under the title, "Moral": "If good words and gentle means will not reclaim the wicked, they must be dealt with in a more severe manner." Following each statement, fable, or poem are lists of the words used in the piece, and instructions on how to pronounce them.

In the early schools, great emphasis was placed on recitation and reading aloud. Indeed, that is how students were tested on whether they were learning the material. The idea of written tests came later.

The famous *McGuffey Reader* built on Webster's work. William Holmes McGuffey was born in 1800, and by 1836 was President of Cincinnati College. In 1836 the first two volumes of the McGuffey's Eclectic Readers were published. They sold more than 122 million copies between 1836 and 1920. Like Webster's Speller, the McGuffey readers contained inspirational material, rules for living, poetry, short stories and factual material. According to Andrew Gulliford, "Before 1870 children who attended school regularly in the primary grades achieved the reading level of *McGuffey's Third Eclectic Reader*. After the 1870s education standards were raised throughout the United States, and a system of eight grade levels was instituted. Eighth-grade country school graduates were expected to complete McGuffey's fourth or fifth reader or a book of similar difficulty. Even for high school graduates today, mastering *McGuffey's Sixth Eclectic Reader* would be a formidable task."[1]

The McGuffey reader not only provided exercises for reading, but introduced students to some eighty-seven authors who represented much of English literature of the time. It was also a challenging book. The fifth reader was well beyond the capabilities of most students in the fifth grade.

South Bright School, Clark County, c.1916.

From Esther Luke Niedzwiecki.

South Bright School, Clark County, 1952.

From Esther Luke Niedzwiecki.

The 1879 edition of *McGuffey's Fifth Eclectic Reader* included material from Louisa May Alcott, John James Audubon, James Fenimore Cooper, Charles Dickens, Washington Irving, Henry Wadsworth Longfellow, William Shakespeare, John Greenleaf Whittier and many more. A short biography of each author preceded the writing selection. After each piece was a short list of definitions for those words which students might find new. For instance, the Audubon piece was about the passenger pigeon. At the end of the article definitions for "aerial," "mast" (fruit of oak, beech or other forest trees), "rendezvous," "subsequent," and "perambulate" were offered.

Other books attempted to compete with McGuffey including Harper's Educational Series. *Harper's Fourth Reader*, published in 1888, included this information in the publishers' introduction: "In entering upon the publication of a new series of School Readers the publishers desire to call attention to some of the features which distinguish these books from others of their kind, and which they believe will commend them to all progressive educators."

Ten features were then listed including: practical work of the classroom, cultivating taste for the best style of literature, attention to moral truths, "some of the finest gems of poetry in our language," and "illustrations of a high order of merit." The publishers concluded by saying, "These readers are not the result of haphazard methods or of untried theories, but are the outgrowth of the experience of practical teachers thoroughly acquainted with the most approved methods of instruction and understanding the present demands and needs of the schools."[2]

As the introduction promised, many of the pieces had a moral bent. This poem, by an unknown author, is an example:

Some write for pleasure,
Some write for fame.
But I simply write
To sign my name.

—Anonymous

The Noblest Men

The noblest men that live on earth
Are men whose hands are brown with toil;
Who, backed by no ancestral graves,
Hew down the woods and till the soil;
And win thereby a prouder name
Than follows king's or warrior's fame.

The working men, what'er their task,
Who carve the stone or bear the hod,
They wear upon their honest brows
The royal stamp and seal of God;
And worthier are their drops of sweat
Than diamonds in a coronet.
God bless the noble working men,
Who rear the cities on the plain;
Who dig the mines, who build the ships,
And drive the commerce of the main!
God bless them! for their toiling hands
Have wrought the glory of all lands.[3]

The *Fourth Reader* is comparable to *McGuffey's Fifth Eclectic Reader* in level of difficulty. It clearly challenged country school children to reach high levels of reading ability.

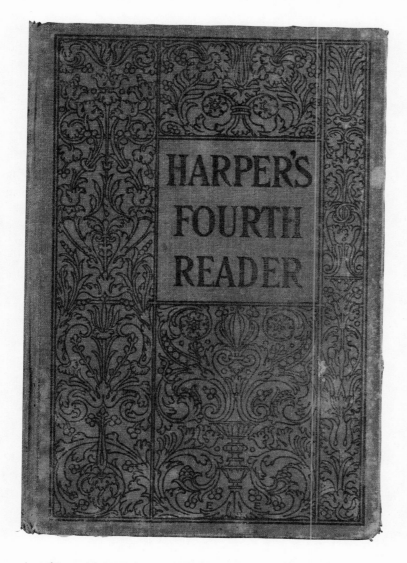

1888 Fourth Reader.

Another reader used in country schools at the turn of the century was *The Progressive Course in Reading*. The Preface to the third book states: this "is something more than a book of selections which pupils may read—it is a textbook in reading. In preparing and arranging its lessons, the present and the future needs of the pupil have been considered."[4] The *Third Book* in the series included short stories about animals, verses about the seasons, old and new fables, a section on riddles, another on nature, and seven stories by Hans Christian Andersen.

Many of the readings in the *Progressive Course in Reading* also contained a moral lesson. Here is another anonymous fable:

The Oxen and the Lion

A lion used to prowl about a field in which four oxen were kept. Many a time he had tried to capture one of them, but all in vain.

Whenever the lion came near, the four oxen turned their tails together, so that he met a pair of horns on every side.

But at last the oxen began to quarrel among themselves. They became so angry that each went off to a corner of the field and grazed alone.

When the lion came back, he seized the oxen one by one, and soon made an end of all four.

In union there is strength. United we stand, divided we fall.[5]

Memorizing poetry was common in the country schools. Rural school children could all recite Longfellow's "The Village Blacksmith," which begins:

> Under a spreading chestnut-tree
> The village smithy stands;
> The smith, a mighty man is he,
> With large and sinewy hands;
> And the muscles of his brawny arms
> Are strong as iron bands.

In 1939, when I began school, we did not use McGuffey readers, or Webster spellers. The first reader I remember was called, simply *Elson-Gray Basic Reader, Book Two*. It was a wonderful book. It included stories and colored pictures. I can still recall how it smelled when I first opened it, and the feel of the cover and the pages when they were turned. Nothing in my life at that time was more important than that book I owned and carried back and forth to school, along with my five cent pad of paper, a half dozen Crayolas, and a two-for-a-nickel lead pencil. At my school, we had to buy our books. The Stevens' Drug Store in Wild Rose had a supply of textbooks for the schools in the area, plus paper, pencils, paste and other school supplies. The cost for my new, hardcover reader was twenty-five cents. I vividly remember its cover with a little girl skipping rope surrounded by a squirrel, a rabbit, a cat, a Scotty dog, and a boy and a girl.

My first textbook included illustrated stories, interspersed with little poems—not by name authors, likely, because the source of the writing was not noted. One of the poems was the following:

Good Morning

Good morning, sky,
Good morning, sun,
Good morning, little winds that run!
Good morning, birds,
Good morning, trees,
And creeping grass, and brownie bees!
How did you find out it was day?
Who told you night had gone away?
I'm wide awake;
I'm up now, too.
I'll be right out to play with you![6]

It was a great book. But as I think about it now, it had one short-coming. It didn't say much about farm kids. It was a city kid's book. The children pictured wore clothing that farm kids would have considered dumb. What farm kid would run around wearing shorts—he'd end up with his legs all scratched. And what little girl went outside wearing the one good dress she ordinarily wore to church and other events. At least it looked to me like all the girls in the book were wearing their Sunday best dresses all the time.

The Dick and Jane series of readers became very popular. But now the good stories, even if they mostly included city kids, disappeared. In their place was such exciting material as "See, Dick. See, Jane. See Dick Run. See Jane Run." Very difficult for a kid to avoid staring out the schoolhouse window while reading such griping narration I felt.

In third or fourth grade, I was introduced to another wonderful reading book titled *If I Were Going.*[7] It was a part of the Alice and Jerry Reading Foundation series. This fascinating book included stories about people in different countries of the world: Norway, Lapland, England, Brittany, Spain, and Africa. Along with the stories were colored paintings of trains, and boats and exotic places, lands I had never heard of before. Each page of the book was a new adventure. Learning how to read took care of itself, I was too excited to find out where we were traveling next.

A well educated gentleman may not know many languages, may not be able to speak any but his own, may have read very few books; but whatever language he knows, he knows precisely; whatever word he pronounces, he pronounces rightly.

—John Ruskin

Handwriting

Cursive writing was emphasized in country schools over hand printing or lettering, except for those pupils just beginning to write. Cursive writing, with the letters flowing together, was believed faster than printing where each letter was individually formed. The assumption, often erroneous, was that each child could learn how to write readable cursive handwriting. Country school children spent many hours trying to follow the Spencerian approach, and later the Palmer approach (introduced in 1894) which had fewer flourishes. Palmer's book, *Palmer's Guide to Business Writing*, became the standard text for handwriting. Many country school children vividly remember the alphabet written in perfect cursive style displayed above the blackboard in the front of the room.

Many children also recall the many hours spent forming circles and ovals in an attempt to match Palmer's ideal. Some children developed beautiful handwriting following the Palmer method, and they found it fun to do. Many left handed students had great difficulty mastering the cursive style, and some right handed students had troubles as well. I was one of them.

In many schools, handwriting was graded. Of all grades, my marks for handwriting were always the poorest. This caused my mother to raise her eyebrows before signing my report card. At each signing she said, "Jerold, are you really trying to write better?"

"Yes, Ma," I always replied, but my handwriting never improved.

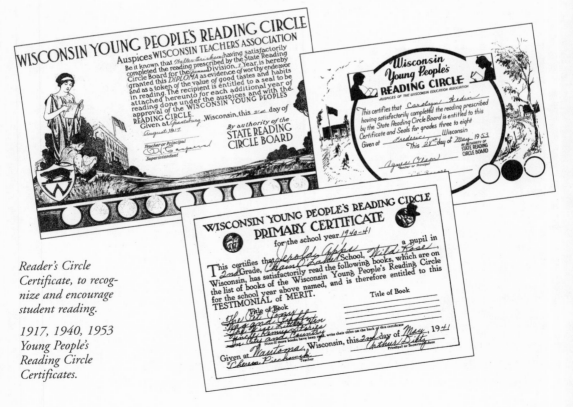

Reader's Circle Certificate, to recognize and encourage student reading.

1917, 1940, 1953 Young People's Reading Circle Certificates.

Spelling

Children attending country schools learned how to spell. Each week, the teacher wrote lists of words for the various grades on the blackboard. Usually on Friday there was a test. In some schools, spelling bees, contests between students to see who was the best speller, were held. In some communities the adults also became involved, and the spelling bees became not only spelling contests but social events as well. Where memorizing how to spell words could be deadly dull, the addition of spelling bees gave new excitement to the learning.

Webster's Speller, mentioned earlier, was an interesting spelling book. Some of the later spellers were less so. In the early 1900s and through the 1930s, many country schools used J.N. Hunt's *Progressive Course in Spelling Complete.*[8]

The book contained page after page of word lists. For instance, there was a list of words containing a silent "i"—pail, mail, sail, paint, saint, and so on. A list of words with silent vowels: great, tired, tried, tread, guide. Words that depicted work on the farm: sow, mow, feed, reap, haul, load, hitch, plow. (The book recognized that some kids lived on farms.) But it was a dull book.

Aside from the dullness of some of the spelling texts, most country school teachers were able to make spelling come alive. Spelling contests helped. So did constant attention to correcting misspelled words. Parents' interest helped, too. I remember the hours my mother spent with my brothers and with me helping us master our spelling words. We had special radio programs we listened to: the Lone Ranger, Terry and the Pirates, and Captain Midnight. We couldn't listen to our programs until our chores were done, and we had a school session with our mother which always included spelling.

With the spelling lists for each grade displayed on the blackboard each Monday morning, students worked at mastering the words for their grade. Many students also mastered the words for the grades ahead of them, a definite advantage to having more than one grade in one room.

Science

Although country schools had no formal laboratories or much in the way of science equipment, science was a part of the curriculum. The school itself was in the middle of a great laboratory. Children, on their

*Bell School,
Fond du Lac County,
1950.*

From Aileen Straseski.

walk to school, could bring plants they had found, insects they had discovered, and observations of the weather and the changing of the seasons. Many schools had a nature corner where all manner of objects was collected and displayed. Those students who could listen to "Afield With Ranger Mac" on the radio each week received specific instructions on how to build a nature corner in their schools. In addition, Ranger Mac described activities, from how to read the clouds to understanding an ant hill, in a way that all students could participate.

Farms kids also brought a vast knowledge of science with them to school. They were present when calves and baby pigs were born. They helped plant corn, oats and other crops, and watched them poke out of the ground and grow. From first hand experience, they learned about the weather, and the importance of rain for the growth of plants.

When these topics were discussed in school, farm kids could quickly relate, and could offer stories about what they had personally experienced. The study of science, in the natural laboratory of the country school was real, and often personal. Such basic understanding of science wove together in a rich tapestry the home life of children with their schooling and made learning easier and natural. School and home became one. The potential for learning was everywhere, and the one-room school simply became a focal point.

Teaching Aids

Country school teachers, no different from teachers today, were extremely resourceful. Because money was always tight, they learned how to make do. Most schools had some standard resources: a pull down set of maps and a chalkboard. Most teachers had access to the Sears Roebuck Catalog. In some schools the Sears catalog served as a reader, a source for arithmetic lessons, and an encyclopedia. When it got a bit dogeared, the catalog graduated to a place of prominence in one of the two outdoor privies. Some schools had globes. My school didn't. Our library was meager. It consisted of four or five shelves of books, in the back corner of the school room, near the wood stove. I don't remember the school receiving one new library book during the eight years I attended. Many country schools had much better library resources than we did, often with a connection to a town library that regularly lent the school new books.

We had a piano in our school as many schools did. Some had organs rather than pianos. This kind of organ required the organist to pump with her feet while she played the keys, quite a workout for someone playing a spirited tune.

To assist with learning arithmetic, country schools had vast sets of flash cards. On one side was the problem, $10 \times 12 =$. On the other side the answer, 120. Students worked in pairs at school with the flash cards; at home parents helped with the flash cards, sometimes making a set out of scrap sheets of paper. Everyone learned the multiplication tables through the twelves. Pupils knew what each combination meant so well they didn't have to think for an instant what eleven times twelve was. Same with spelling. No time to try and sound out the word, which sometimes helped. The idea was to know the spelling of the word without thinking.

Hectographs

There were, of course, no ditto, mimeograph, photocopy or other duplicating equipment that we all take so much for granted today. Most schools had a hectograph machine. It was hardly a machine. Teachers began the operation by creating the surface for the "machine." Doris

Suderland, a former Oneida County teacher, offered the following recipe for making a hectograph machine. You need:

- One package of Knox gelatin (four envelopes, use it all)
- One cup of cold water
- One pint of glycerine (buy at the drugstore)
- Two tablespoons of sugar (for helping to set the concoction)

Mix the sugar and gelatin together, add the water, add the glycerine, and let it all come to a boil. By this time, a foul smell should be coming from the boiling pot. Let it boil for one minute, then pour the mixture into a pan. Take a sheet of paper and draw it across the surface to remove the bubbles.

To use it, wet the surface with a wet cloth (cold water). Make a copy of what you want on a sheet of paper with a hectograph pencil. This becomes your master copy. Place the master copy carefully on the gelatin surface as smoothly as possible. Rub it, and smooth it on, and remove it. Now take clean sheets of paper, place them on the gelatin surface (which has the image from the master copy) and you have a copy. The machine will make fifty copies. In the process you will likely transfer some purple color to your hands, but soap and water quite readily removes the stain.

The following are penmanship exercises:

A poor workman never has good tools.

Hidden fire makes black smoke.

Little strokes fell great oaks.

The sleeping fox catches no chickens.

A little leak will sink a great ship.

Reference Material for Teachers

As a reference for teachers, some schools had the *Public School Methods* series in seven volumes. It was published in 1922, and included supplementary teacher materials for nearly every curriculum area from Kindergarten (not a part of most rural schools) to nature study, spelling, history, geography, language and grammar, civic government, music, agriculture, penmanship, domestic science, and understanding rural life.

These reference materials included not only supplementary curriculum materials, but there were many ideas for visuals, exercises and games. The authors of the series wrote in the introduction, "*Public School Methods* is the most complete professional help that has ever been prepared for the use of elementary teachers. 'It is a normal school in book form.' Every page has been prepared by an educator of acknowledged authority on the subject discussed."[9]

The editorial staff for the seven volume series included thirty-nine educators, and researchers, plus a dozen artists. A major portion of volume two was on nature study. It included paintings, photographs, poetry, stories, and multiple classroom activities. It combined reading, arithmetic, art, and science. The nature study section began with a quotation from John Burroughs that set the tone for how the material was presented.

"I am forced to conclude that my passion for nature and for all open-air life though tinged and stimulated by science, is not a passion for pure science, but for literature and philosophy....I find something akin to poetry and religion... in the shows of day and night, and in my excursions to fields and woods. The love of nature is a different thing from the love of science, though the two may go together." [10]

Another section on rain begins with the L.H. Bailey poem: (Here are the first four lines)

> The soft, gray rain comes slowly down,
> Settling the mists on marshes brown,
> Narrowing the world on wood and hill,
> Drifting the fog down vale and rill. [11]

County Examinations

At the completion of seventh grade, many rural school children were expected to pass a county-wide examination before they were admitted to eighth grade. Usually, this examination was for only two or three subjects such as reading and arithmetic.

To graduate from eighth grade, all country school children had to pass a county-wide standard examination that was given on one long day at the county seat.

I will never forget the frightful day, May 28, 1947, when I took county exams at the Waushara County Normal School. Eighth graders from throughout the county gathered that day, in the same large room in Wautoma, to write examinations on an assortment of subjects: reading, spelling, grammar, arithmetic, geography, U.S. history, civics, and science. Once I got past a bad case of jitters, I worked as hard as I could, all day, taking exam after exam (with a brief rest at noon to eat a sandwich I had brought from home). A couple of weeks later the test scores arrived in the mail. Would I be allowed to graduate and go on to high school? I ripped open the envelope and read the scores. I was near perfect in science, high marks in spelling, reading and civics, but a sad score in handwriting—a mark that brought down my otherwise respectable academic average. A brief note at the bottom of the grade sheet read:

"Your diploma will be granted on Friday, June 6, 1947 at the Court House in Wautoma. Graduate exercises start at 1:15 pm. Arthur Dietz, County Superintendent." I was on my way to high school.

Eighth Grade Graduation

Graduation day in June dawned sunny and warm. I knew that Dad was a little uneasy about taking off a half day from planting corn to traipse off to Wautoma, but there was no word of complaint as we all sat around the kitchen table and ate breakfast. Because graduation exercises didn't begin until afternoon, Dad hitched up the team and planted corn in the morning. My brothers, Donald and Darrel, had their regular chores to do which included feeding the chickens, hauling in wood for the cook stove, and helping our mother around the house. But I was excused from my duties. Mother had said, "This is a special day for you, Jerold. No chores. But don't get too used to it, because there is lots of work for tomorrow." She smiled when she said it.

I spent the morning reading a book and thinking about high school, in a school building with more than a hundred students, and where I would have twenty-five or thirty or more classmates in my grade. Almost my entire time in grade school I was the only student in my year.

After a quick lunch, the entire family piled into our black, 1936 Plymouth and drove the twelve miles to Wautoma where we parked by the court house. Cars were parked everywhere. Eighth grade graduation was a major event in the city. Each of the more than one hundred country schools in Waushara County had one or two, sometimes even three graduates. And each graduate's family came along.

This was the first time I had been in the court house and in the massive courtroom on the second floor. As graduates, we sat in the front rows with our families sitting in the back.

Shortly after I eased into my seat, somewhat uncomfortable in the clothes I usually only wore to church, the graduation exercises began. Arthur Dietz, County Superintendent of Schools, welcomed all of us, thanked our parents, and told each of us what an achievement it was to complete eight years of school and successfully graduate. I can't recall ever feeling more accomplished than I did that June afternoon, sitting in the stuffy courtroom designed for trying criminals rather than recognizing boys and girls for their academic achievements.

After a series of presentations, some from the students, we, in single file, marched across the front of the courtroom where Mr. Dietz handed us our diploma. It was a beautiful piece of paper. My name was written on it, too. I saw that right away. It was hand written, in a large cursive style. Memories of my struggles with cursive writing came to mind, but I pushed them aside. This was a day to feel good.

On the way home from Wautoma my brothers held the diploma and looked at it and I'm sure dreamed of the time four years from then when they would repeat what I had just done. When we arrived back at the farm, Dad parked the Plymouth under the old elm tree that shaded the kitchen and we all went into the house to change clothes and get ready for the afternoon chores.

"Wait here a minute," Dad said as he disappeared into the bedroom. He returned carrying a small package.

"Here, this is for you," he said, holding the package in his large calloused hand.

I quickly tore off the wrapping paper, revealing a pocket watch. My first watch.

"It's a graduation present, and you've earned it," my mother said. I could see the pride in her eyes, and in my father's, too, for neither of them had graduated from eighth grade.

Eighth grade graduations in other counties, and in other years had many similarities to my own graduation.

Elmer Marth, who attended the Polk Dairy School in Washington County, recalled his grade school graduation. "Graduation exercises for 138 graduates from all the rural public schools in Washington County

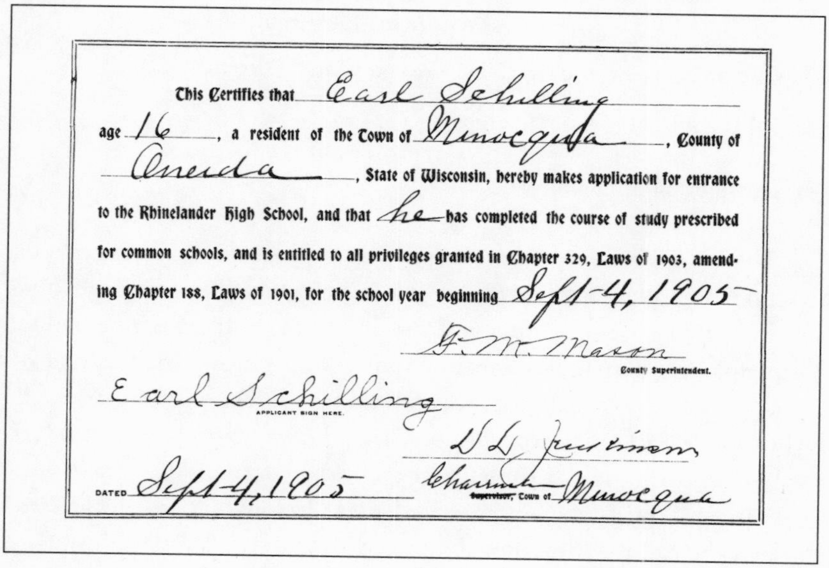

1905
Eighth grade diploma,
Oneida County.

were held in the auditorium of the newly built McLane Grade School in West Bend on May 29, 1940. The entire program consisted of group presentations by the graduates. The six graduates of the Polk Dairy School gave a presentation on the 'gift of artistic expression.' The class of six graduates was unusually large when one considers that the total enrollment of about twenty-five students was distributed among eight grades."

The 1960 Waupaca County Graduation Exercises were held at the Manawa Field House in Manawa. The evening program was as follows:

7:30-8:00 Seating of graduates. (There were 178 graduates from 48 schools. By 1960, many country schools had already closed and been consolidated into larger districts.)

Opening Remarks	Mr. George W. Barber, Superintendent of Schools Waupaca County
Vocal Solo	"Bells of St. Mary" Sandra Servin Jean Woolsey, Accompanist Gard's Corner School
Tap Dance	"Music, Cow, Cow Blues" Jeff Heger Gard's Corner School
Flute Duet	"Gavotte" Nancy Duzynski and Peggy Tarry Mary Keeney, Accompanist Weyauwega Elementary School
Commencement Address	Dr. George Walter, Director, Teacher Education Lawrence College, Appleton

Distribution of Diplomas

The lessons country school pupils learned varied some from school to school, but all focused on a core: reading, writing (including spelling, and the proper use of words) and the ability to do basic mathematics. The emphasis on these fundamental subjects, considered essential to living in the society of the time, was on mastery. When pupils graduated eighth grade from a country school, they knew how to read, how to spell, how to do basic arithmetic, and how to communicate orally and in writing. If they had not mastered these lessons as they progressed through the eight grades, they did remedial work until they did.

Wisconsin Public Schools

Waupaca County

This is to Certify That

Lillie Ann Johnson

has completed the Course of Study prescribed by Law for the Elementary Schools of Wisconsin, and therefore merits this

Diploma

which entitles the holder to admission to any High School in the State.

Given at Waupaca, Wisconsin,

this 31st day of May 1939

County Superintendent

1939
Eighth grade diploma,
Waupaca County.

Perhaps most importantly, by the time most children had completed eight grades of country school they had developed a great love for learning, the fun in doing it, the joy in helping others, and the ability to learn on their own—a skill that would help many of them the rest of their lives.

Chapter Notes

1. Andrew Gulliford. *America's Country Schools.* Washington, D.C.: The Preservation Press, 1984, p.51.

2. Harper and Brothers. *Harper's Fourth Reader.* New York: American Book Company, 1888.

3. *Ibid.*, p. 190.

4. George I. Aldrich and Alexander Forbes. *Third Book: The Progressive Course in Reading.* New York: American Book Company, 1900, p. 3.

5. *Ibid.*, pp. 78-79.

6. William H. Elson and William S. Gray. *Elson-Gray Basic Reader, Book Two.* Chicago: Scott, Foresman, 1931,1936.

7. Mabel O'Donnell and Alice Carey. *If I Were Going.* New York: Row and Peterson, 1936,1941.

8. J. N. Hunt. *The Progressive Course in Spelling.* New York: American Book Company, 1904, 1910.

9. Quarrie Corporation. *Public School Methods.* Chicago: School Methods Publishing Co., Vol. I, 1922, p. vii.

10. *Ibid.*, Vol. II, p. 1.

11. *Ibid.*, Vol. II, p. 20.

School Of The Air

The two second graders huddled in the front of the school room with Miss Murty for their daily reading class. Using their "inside voices" they took turns reading out loud. Others in the room worked on arithmetic problems, read silently, or listened to the reading class. It was approaching 9:25 and everyone was sneaking peeks at the school clock hanging on the north wall, its ticking louder than the quiet activity in the room. Anticipation was growing. Had the teacher forgotten that this was Monday? Shouldn't she be tuning in the radio?

Miss Murty hadn't forgotten. A couple minutes before 9:30 she snapped on the Philco battery operated radio, and tuned it to 900 KC, WLBL, Stevens Point. The radio whistled and crackled a little, and then, promptly at the half hour, The Wisconsin School of the Air came on, with "Afield With Ranger Mac."

Children listening to Wisconsin School of the Air. Notice radio in front of room.

University of Wisconsin-Madison Archives.

89

School of The Air

Radio was in its infancy in the 1920s, but the University of Wisconsin's 9XM, later to become WHA, was an early entrant to broadcasting, and particularly educational broadcasting. In 1917 university physics professors and students successfully transmitted music and voice using handmade vacuum tubes.

By the 1920s WHA was broadcasting a homemakers show, market news and an agricultural program, and Edgar "Pop" Gordon's music appreciation series, which became the foundation for the school of the air, beamed to the country schools scattered throughout the state.

An early technical problem was how to provide access to the entire state with the school of the air programs. In 1947-48, the percentage of schools signed up for the school of the air ranged from ninety-one percent in Columbia County to no schools in Bayfield, Ashland, and Florence counties because the radio signal could not reach that far north. Eighty percent of the schools in Trempealeau County participated, eighty-three percent in Monroe County, seventy-eight percent in Green Lake County, and seventy-one percent in LaFayette County. With the advent of a statewide network for FM stations in the 1940s, programs became more available, but the challenge of providing radio access to all corners of the state was never completely met.

Of course many country schools did not have radios, and most of them, until the 1940s, did not have electricity. The old battery operated radios worked best with a fully charged battery. "Radio time" in the schools was carefully rationed, usually to two or three favorite programs, to conserve the radio battery's energy.

Teachers worked out ingenious ways to expose their students to the School of the Air. Roland Krogstad taught at Fairview School, east of Ellsworth in Pierce County. He had returned from World War II in the fall of 1945 and discovered that because he was a veteran he was fifth on the list to purchase a new car. He bought a green, 1946 Ford, with a radio. His school did not have one, so when it was time to listen to "Afield With Ranger Mac," Krogstad

Wakelin McNeel. On the Wisconsin School of the Air from 1933-1954, with "Afield With Ranger Mac." More than 700,000 school children heard his popular nature program.

University of Wisconsin-Madison Archives.

and his students went outside and gathered around his Ford car and listened on the car radio. "Got a little cold sometimes," Krogstad shared, "but we never missed a program."

Afield With Ranger Mac

In a deep, sometimes mysterious, but always interesting voice, Wakelin McNeel, Ranger Mac, came on the air with his injunction to be "Up and away." The program was only fifteen minutes long, but it was enough to keep pupils enthralled about the outdoors, which they experienced first hand everyday, but were now learning behind the scenes information.

Program Three, October 12, 1942, was about earthworm farming. A guidebook sent to all country school teachers who signed up included this information:

> "Visit a garden in the morning, preferably after a light rain, and notice the wrinkled masses of dirt about the entrance to the burrow of an earthworm. Examine closely to detect how earthworms plug the mouths of their burrows. Go deeper into the burrow, where bits of leaves, grasses, maybe petals of flowers line the upper part."

> The teacher's material included "Listen for these ideas:" "What is meant by a 'lowly-organized creature?' What is meant by nocturnal? Is the earthworm nocturnal?" and so on.

This was followed with a section on "We want to learn more." There were suggested activities students could do at home, and recommendations for related reading material.

Sometimes "Ranger Mac" did his programs from his garden, or at a fish hatchery, but mostly he did them at the WHA Radio Studio on the University of Wisconsin campus.

Affectionately known as Chief of the Junior Forest Rangers, McNeel was also State 4-H Club Leader for Wisconsin, and a Professor of Extension Education. He started his radio program in 1933, and retired from it in 1954. In those twenty-one years, he talked to more than 700,000 Wisconsin school children. The program was designed for those in grades five through eight, but in a one-room school, all of the children listened. About 50,000 school children tuned in each week to hear about nature and the great out-of-doors for fifteen minutes. McNeel ended each program with "May the Great Spirit put sunshine in your hearts, now and forever more. Heap much!"

In his retirement letter to Harold McCarty, WHA program director, McNeel wrote, "I have appeared regularly on Monday mornings, throughout each school year, preparing and rendering over six hundred programs with few duplications of titles and but little in subject matter.

"I have arrived at a point where my judgment tells me it is inadvisable to continue carrying on this program. It is with deep regret that I feel compelled to make this decision. I do it with the fervent hope that the program will be continued with increased effectiveness because the subject of conservation is of great importance in all lives, and of supreme importance in the lives of young people." He signed the letter, "Ranger Mac."

Through his radio programs, and other efforts, McNeel helped to promote the development of school forests and the protection of woodlots throughout the state. And through his "Conservation Corner" he encouraged hundreds of schools to develop a nature corner in the school room where students kept logs of outdoor occurrences, and built conservation exhibits.

McNeel began his career as a school teacher in Tomah and at Fort Atkinson. At age twenty-two he was the youngest superintendent of schools in Wisconsin.

"Afield With Ranger Mac" was recognized nationally. In 1942, McNeel won the George Foster Peabody Radio Award for the outstanding educational program in the United States. The citation read in part, "The award for the outstanding educational program goes to station WHA, Madison, Wisconsin for its splendid series on natural science and conservation entitled 'Afield With Ranger Mac.' Originated by the 'Wisconsin School of the Air, ably and accurately presented by Wakelin McNeel, chief of the Junior Forest Rangers, this series sets an example which should be widely followed." The Peabody award for radio is equivalent to an Oscar for film production.

With McNeel's retirement, Professor Robert Ellarson took over with "Wonderful World of Nature" and it continued for another twenty-five years.

Let's Sing

A clear favorite for thousands of Wisconsin school children was Pop Gordon's "Let's Sing." Gordon, a University of Wisconsin music professor, presented his radio programs for twenty-four years. From a WHA studio in Madison, Gordon had a radio style that entranced young peo-

ple. For many children, it was their first introduction to a music teacher. Like "Afield With Ranger Mac," Gordon's radio programs attracted thousands of school children. In 1939, his beginning course had signed up nearly 19,000 students with another 14,000 signed up for the advanced course called, "Journeys in Music Land II."

In the introduction to the 1943-1944 "Songbook for Children," Gordon wrote, "The children who first sang with me are grown up and out of school now. Probably many of the boys are off fighting in various parts of the world. I like to think of them as singing in their camps and as they march, for I'm sure that they can find in song a source of comfort and relaxation from the strain of the job they must do before they can return home."

Gordon firmly believed in the importance of music to enhance everyone's life. Many country school teachers had limited musical backgrounds, and only a few could play a musical instrument. Likewise, many rural homes had little music of any kind. In the minds of teachers and parents, Gordon's radio programs clearly met a need. Gordon wrote further in the 1943-1944 songbook (which sold for 15 cents), "Music participation can bring you a great deal of pleasure as you grow older. That why it's well to learn how to sing when you're still in school

E.B. Gordon at state-wide music festival, Stock Pavilion, University of Wisconsin-Madison, May 1947. Children who listened throughout the year to Gordon's School of the Air music programs have an opportunity to see and sing with their teacher.

University of Wisconsin-Madison Archives.

and an important part of learning to sing is *learning to read music*. This year we shall devote quite a bit of time to note-reading, and I believe we'll have great fun doing it."

Children were learning how to sing and having a great time doing it. Bonnie Trudell attended the Squaw Lake School in St. Croix County in the late 1940s and early 1950s. She and her schoolmates listened to "Let's Sing." "We'd tune in the radio, all sitting at our desks with our song books, and there would be talk about where these songs came from, and a demonstration of the song. Then we'd all sing along. I remember the theme song, 'Sing, sing the whole day through. The best of things will come to you. A song will always see you through, so sing, just sing.'"

A highlight of Gordon's programs was the regional gatherings, and the state festivals held at the Stock Pavilion on the University of Wisconsin Campus. As many as 4,000 of Pop Gordon's loyal listeners traveled to Madison and joined in a broadcast, singing together the songs they had learned during the year. In the War years, 1943 and 1944, the festivals followed a "stay at home" pattern to conserve rationed gasoline. These were organized school by school, or by groups of schools in an area. In 1943, at least a hundred such "stay at home" festivals were held around the state. Some of them were elaborate, separate programs, others were a part of Mother's Day programs, graduation exercises, and other special events that were supplemented with singing.

Tell me what you like, and I'll tell you what you are.

—*Edgar Gordon in School of the Air study guide, 1945*

Let's Draw

The critics were many. How could anybody teach drawing and art over the radio? Jim Schwalbach, a former high school teacher, who became a university professor, took up the challenge.

In the introduction to the 1939-1940 School of the Air program, "Let's Draw" was described this way. "This year, his fourth on the School of the Air, Mr. Schwalbach will emphasize instruction in basic art principles and the manipulative skill to be developed through craft work. By dramatization, music, story, or poetry, he interests the children in the subject of the program and gives them ideas for pictures. Then, supplementing the stimulation of creative work, he gives them a basic foundation in art."

Exactly how did this over-the-air process work? Here is a portion of a radio script: "We named this week's program 'Paintings in Music.'

Finding paintings in music is a little stunt we enjoy very much at Wisconsin High (the university of Wisconsin high school) and so I thought perhaps you might like it too. I'm going to play on the Victrola for you—Edvard Greig's 'Marche of the Dwarfs;' but before we begin the music I want you to take a speedy little journey with me to the place where Edvard Greig lived and wrote his music. If you are sitting at a desk, I want you to put your head and arms on the desk and close your eyes and if you haven't a desk at hand just bury your two eyes in the palms of your two hands.

"All ready? Eyes closed! Here we go. Up and away from the low, brown and light green hills of Wisconsin—East—over New York,—across the Atlantic Ocean—over England—across the North Sea—to the rugged, deep-green, blue and purple hills and mountains of Norway. Mountains covered with the heather, the juniper, and the birch. High up on the side of one of these thickly wooded mountains, just out in the country from the old fishing city of Bergen, is the old, white, farmhouse where Edvard Greig lived and wrote his music. His studio is down the hillside from the large main house and so we hurry down under the trees, through the grass and flowers to peer into the open door of this tiny brown hut. A window on the North and another to the West, two small chairs, a few small pictures on the wall, and his piano—placed right where he can play and look out through the trees and vines to the distant mountains, fields, and fjords, below. Now I think we are quite ready to see the paintings in his music. Let's imagine we are sitting just outside his doorway—all by ourselves among the grass, flowers, and leaves. Keep your eyes closed and just listen to the music. Look for the pictures that he paints in his 'Marche of the Dwarfs.'"

The script goes on raising several questions with the children, to help them think of pictures they see in the music. Then the music is played again, and the students are instructed to take up their crayons or watercolors and fill in the paper "with quick sketches, notes and ideas that come to you out of the music, and then when the music is finished we will take these sketches—select the best ones and then work them up into paintings and drawings that represent the pictures we saw in our imagination. Work large. Work fast. If you want—just write what you see—and draw afterwards."

As with all of the School of the Air programs, teacher and student aids were available. Schwalbach, in 1939, prepared a 100-page illustrated booklet to aid teachers. It was printed in loose-leaf format, and was available for 50 cents.

Other Programs

The School of the Air, by the late 1930s, had fairly extensive offerings available to elementary and high schools throughout the state. There were programs offered every day of the week, ranging from a history program for upper grade students, to a rhythm and games program for kindergarten through grade three, a French Program for high school students to a geography program, "This Land of Ours," for grades five through seven. A popular program in the late 1940s was called "Book Trails" and introduced young people to good books. Here are excerpts from a 1946 script for a program on the book, *The Black Stallion.*

"HORSE GALLOPING UNDER

The Wisconsin School of the Air invites you to come along on Book Trails.

UP

(EXAGGERATED) Down the road he comes with the sound of thundering hoofs and the cry of 'Hi-O! Black Stallion!!. . . .The Trailalong rides again!

OUT

Are you sure you're on the right program? Well, this is a program for boys and girls who want to hear a good story, isn't it?

Yes.

And for boys and girls who want to read more stories like that?

Yes.

That's the program, all right. . . to tell you a story, and to tell you where to find more stories to read for yourself.

Yes, I know all that.

Book Trails is a series planned to help boys and girls in the intermediate grades find fun and enjoyment in their leisure-time reading. Lots of our listeners know that too because they're trailalongs from way back. And those boys and girls who are tuning in for the first time today won't be long in finding out what fun it is to be a trailalong on the reading road of Book Trails.

What I want to know is . . . this. . . (IMITATION) "Down the road he comes with the sound of thundering hoofs and a cry of 'Hi-O! Black Stallion!'

What was that for?

Jerry, I'm surprised. I'll bet the boys and girls know. It's the name of our story for today: "The Black Stallion" . . . ready to take us for a wild ride to adventure down our first Book Trail of the year. It's an exciting story, all about the Black Stallion who was born wild and Alec who first found him aboard ship."

Jerry Bartell goes on to read the book.

The Wisconsin Idea

In the early 1900s the phrase, "The Wisconsin Idea" was coined. It had several meanings, but one important dimension of The Wisconsin Idea was in the slogan, "The boundaries of the campus are the boundaries of the state." The University of Wisconsin was to make itself available to the people of Wisconsin, no matter where they lived, or what their occupations or economic circumstance. Farmers were the early beneficiaries of The Wisconsin Idea as agriculture professors traveled to the far corners of the state with their message of scientific agriculture.

The School of the Air, directed primarily toward country school children, was another important dimension. At a time when country school children were essentially isolated in their local communities—few of them traveled more than thirty miles from their homes by the time they were twelve years old—the School of the Air expanded their horizons. With the radio programs, offered over battery powered radios in the early years, farm kids from throughout the state had a link to the university and its resources. There was also a kind of camaraderie that developed among the school children who participated in the radio programs. They knew that they were listening with thousands of other young people each week, and now, at least for a few minutes, they were not a little cross-roads school, but part of a huge congregation of students all gathered by their radios at the same time. If some of them had difficulty believing there were so many students listening, they had only to attend one of Pop Gordon's spring meetings in Madison where up to 4,000 young people gathered to sing the songs they had learned during the year.

The country schools emphasized the basics—reading, writing, and arithmetic. Areas such as nature study, drawing, music, and literature were in second place. Teachers were generally prepared to teach the basics; they were often less well prepared to teach topics that broadened students' visions, and helped them experience the joy of music, the creativity of art, and the deeper messages of the out-of-doors.

Elementary students sometimes developed a "one answer, stay with-in the lines" approach to learning. The School of the Air helped to challenge the "one right answer" approach. Bonnie Trudell, a former country school student, and now a university education specialist, said, "Our views were very much—there is a right answer. The radio programs taught us that we could 'go outside the lines.' This was particularly so in 'Let's Draw' where we were encouraged to develop our creativity. We worked with pencils, crayons. We did some stuff with watercolors and the picture I remember the most was wet paper and the watercolors were running and that was OK. We picked the best drawings from our school and sent them into Madison. I got an honorable mention for a painting of a forest fire—it really was outside the lines."

The School of the Air not only supplemented the country school's curriculum, and provided a break with a new form of teaching, it clearly provided pupils with alternatives, new ways of thinking, new ways of doing, and alternative ways of looking at the world.

Today, educational institutions at every level are using what is called "Distance Education." Now of course the technology includes TV, computers, satellite communication and more. The Wisconsin School of the Air was one of the early applications of distance education, at a time when technology was scarce and electricity was viewed as a novelty for many.

The School of the Air made a phenomenal contribution to the education of Wisconsin's rural young people, beyond anything those who worked with it ever imagined. The School of the Air connected Wisconsin's rural communities to the world, via the radio.[1]

Chapter Notes

1. Material from University of Wisconsin-Madison Archives, from *Wisconsin Public Broadcasting 75th Anniversary*. Madison, WI: University of Wisconsin Extension and Educational Communications Board, 1992, and from interviews with former students and teachers.

Here Comes Santa Claus

At most country schools, Thanksgiving time meant colder temperatures, first snow fall, turkey cutouts, stories about Pilgrims, and first mention of the upcoming Christmas program. Most country school teachers had been planning for this yearly community event since the last one. They had been selecting plays, recitations, and musical numbers for months. In most rural school communities, where everyone was Christian or said they were even if they never attended church, no one questioned the appropriateness of a Christmas program in the local school. It was the accepted, and the expected, thing to do. Hildegarde Engle, a former teacher said, "It was a known fact that a new teacher's contract for the next year was contingent upon the success of the Christmas program."

James Otis School, Fond du Lac County, 1945. Children practicing for the nativity scene for the annual Christmas program.

From Mary Hanley.

Elmer Marth, a retired University of Wisconsin professor, attended the Polk Dairy School in Washington County where Christmas programs were annual highlights. "Currently, a program of the sort described would probably cause problems in many communities because of the obvious reference in a public school to a religious event. This was never considered a problem in the Polk Dairy School of the 1930s. In fact, a program of the sort that I described was expected by residents of the district and anything less would have been found objectionable. To better understand this, consider the ethnic and religious makeup of the students. The ancestors of nearly all the students had come to the United States from Germany in the middle or late 1800s. Besides the German families, one family was Swiss but originated in the German speaking part of Switzerland, and one name, DeCaluwe, suggested French, but Mrs. DeCaluwe was German and Mr. DeCaluwe spoke German. Three families were Lutheran, four were Catholic, and the rest were members of the Evangelical-Reformed Church (now United Church of Christ). All students shared a common background in Christianity."

But not everyone, in every school district was Christian, as many assumed. Myrtle Natzke, Merrill, a former teacher, recalled the family of children whose parents were agnostics. They did not want their children joining in the celebration of Christmas. She said, "I finally found poems about winter and New Year that the children were allowed to recite, but during the program the sixth-grade girl boldly joined the other girls and sang 'Silent Night.' When the family got home the parents took the disobedient child to the barn and whipped her with a harness strap."

Christmas Program Memories

Former teachers and students alike have fond, and sometimes not so fond, memories of country school Christmas programs. Mary Klug began teaching in Shawano County in 1929. She had sixty students in eight grades with thirteen first graders. She remembered her first Christmas program as the night of Santa's misfortune. The program went well, except for Santa who missed his cue. Finally, after a long delay he appeared at the door, a bit disheveled. It seems some older neighborhood boys had held up Santa and stolen his gifts. Someone had overheard their plans, retrieved the gifts, and sent Santa on his way, a little embarrassed and a lot late.

Santas caused other kinds of problems. Myrtle Natzke, a former teacher, told about Santas she had known:

James Otis School children in a Christmas program. Fond du Lac County, 1946.

From Mary Hanley.

"One came in his barn boots—they were so strong they could have walked by themselves. One Santa was so stricken with stage fright that he forgot his own kids' names. One fortified himself with a bottle of scotch under his belt. He fell off the stage, sprained his ankle, and as some men escorted him out to his car he swore so loudly that he fairly shook the building. Another Santa came on stage, jingling the bells and shouting, 'Ho, Ho, Ho' before the program was completed. The rest of the program was in shambles, much to the disappointment and anger of the children who had not yet performed and the loud-voiced anger of their parents."

"I, the teacher, was numb for days," said Myrtle Natzke.

Larry Meiller, host of the noon show on Wisconsin Public Radio, attended the Hope School in Dane County, in the early 1950s. He recalled one of the memorable roles he played in a Christmas program skit. He played the part of a tire in a one-act play about an automobile. Two children sat in the cardboard auto, and two more played the parts of the tires on the side of the auto toward the audience. Meiller, as a tire, had to explode at one point in the skit. At the appropriate time, he yelled, "Boom!" and then spread out his arms and legs and lay flat on the floor. He was clearly a flat tire. The crowd loved it, and Meiller has never forgotten this rather unique theatrical experience.

Lola Olsen, of Pine River, attended the River View School, Town of

White Rapids School, Marinette County, 1942.

From Shirley Bennett Madden.

Leon, Waushara County. She told about the beauty of the school room prepared for the Christmas program. "Christmas colors and decorations were everywhere. How different and wonderful it was to see the kerosene chandelier spreading its soft light over everything; it was used only on dark and stormy days, and for evening programs. The Christmas tree sparkled and shone with our handmade ornaments, enhanced by the chandelier's bright glow. Hanging in the northeastern corner of the schoolhouse, the lamp could be, and was used, for the Christmas star."

Christmas programs also evoked many memories of what went wrong. Rosemary Boxrucker, Rhinelander, attended a country school in the 1940s. About Christmas programs, she said, "I was always a nervous child who never did anything right. I would get my lines mixed up, and during one program I even lost my skirt right in the middle of the folk dance."

Doris Lund, Rhinelander area, told about the little first grade boy who "bravely started reciting the Christmas poem he'd tried memorizing, but after three lines couldn't remember it. He stopped reciting and called out, 'What comes next, Ma?'"

Doris also shared the exchange a teacher had with her students about the Christmas holiday. "The teacher asked, 'What do you know about Christmas?' Up shot a small hand and from the little mouth came this worldly wisdom, 'If Jesus hadn't eaten the apple Mary gave Him, we wouldn't have to work so hard.'"

One more from Doris Lund's recollections. "A little boy learned the poem, 'Why Do Bells For Christmas Ring?' and did it very well during practice, performing perfectly. The night of the Christmas program he got on stage, stood straight and tall, and said in a clear voice, 'Vy do bells for Christmas ring?' There was silence for a moment and then he continued, 'Dat's the reason vy,' bowed and left the stage. He knew how to shorten a poem!"[1]

Phyllis Uminski taught in various country schools, several in Grant County. She remembered when she taught at Boice Creek School during World War II. All the preparations had been made for the Christmas program. It was Friday afternoon with the program scheduled for that evening. Like many one-room schools, this one was heated with an aging pot-belly stove. The last thing she did before leaving that afternoon was to shake down the old rusty stove before taking out the ashes and laying a new fire for the evening program. As she shook down the ashes, the grates came loose and fell to the bottom of the stove. Of course the fire wouldn't burn without the grates in place. She dashed back to her rooming house in Lancaster, changed clothes for the program, enlisted her friend to help, and rushed back to school. In their best clothing, they wrestled the grates back into place, started the fire, and had everything cozy warm by 8:00 p.m. when the program started.

Christmas Seals

At the same time that everyone was preparing for the Christmas program, all the students were encouraged to sell Christmas seals. They sold for one penny each, and pupils could take as many as they thought they could sell. Selling one hundred, a dollar's worth, was considered a major achievement in a community where money had always been scarce.

I recall making the rounds of our neighbors, trying to not visit those farms closer to my schoolmates. I would walk to Allen Davies farm, and could expect to sell five cents worth, then on to Joe Hudziak's place for another five cents, and then to Bill Miller's for maybe a dime. It took a long time to sell one hundred Christmas seals so I could return to school with a dollar. Usually my parents would buy what I couldn't sell, often around fifty or so.

A Memorable Christmas Program

The Monday following Thanksgiving break, Miss Thompson who taught that year at Chain O' Lake, my school, announced the one-act plays, and who might be good for which parts in our Christmas program. Everyone participated. No exceptions. The tiniest, most shy first grader to the most program experienced eighth grade student had a part in a play. Everyone also had a recitation, we called them pieces, to deliver in front of parents and the entire community who crowded into the school room on this most important school night of the year.

For this particular year, Miss Thompson tried an experiment, something that was totally her idea. Johnny French, basically a good kid, came from a family where profanity was so common that little third grade Johnny could scarcely speak a sentence without at least including one damn, hell or worse. What Miss Thompson planned was risky, and she knew it, but country school teaching was filled with risk taking.

An important part of each year's Christmas program was the nativity scene. A straw-filled manger was erected on the stage, and in it was placed a naked baby doll wrapped in a clean white dish towel. Were swaddling clothes really dish towels, some of us wondered. An upper grade girl was dressed as Mary. She wore a white sheet and a towel around her head, held in place with a shank of clothesline rope.

Johnny French was selected to read the Christmas story: "Jesus Christ was born this day . . ." Miss Thompson's experiment was this—

James Otis School children in a 1946 Christmas program. Fond du Lac County.

From Mary Hanley.

given the responsibility for narrating the Christmas story, Johnny might develop a new sense of meaning for some of the words that slipped easily into his everyday language, but for purposes far afield from the Christian religion.

Planning and practicing began slowly that first week after Thanksgiving, only an hour or so each day, and the last period in the afternoon. By the second week practice time doubled. By the third and final week, every afternoon was devoted to fine tuning this elaborate, finely honed event.

The Saturday before the program (it was always held on the Friday night before Christmas break) the school board slid the oak planks down from their storage place in the woodshed, and dragged out the wooden sawhorses from the corner of the pump house. Within a couple of hours, a stage appeared in the front of the school.

When the students arrived the following Monday, there was a new sense of excitement for now they could practice on stage, and begin to experience a little more of what the real program would be like. By Wednesday Miss Thompson and the older students had strung a wire across the front of the school, above the stage, to which they fastened the brown stage curtains. Bed sheet side curtains were fastened to wires along each end of the stage, making two small dressing places on either end of the stage.

Along with planning for the program itself, a host of other activities was taking place. Children in the lower grades made paper chains for the Christmas tree which the school board had put up after they'd constructed the stage. Children exchanged names and purchased Christmas presents to be placed under the tree for Santa to distribute at the program. Fifty cents was the limit for a gift to assure some fairness, particularly for large families where finances were always stretched extremely thin, especially at Christmas. Gifts were often highly practical—pencils, writing tablets, a handkerchief (a most disappointing gift when I received one), or maybe a comb.

One of the school board members, Arlin Miller, had been a regular as Santa Claus and Miss Thompson asked him if he could do it again this year.

"Wouldn't miss it," he said, pleased that he was asked once more to perform this honored task.

Thursday, before the day of the program, nothing was going right. Lines hadn't been memorized. The brown stage curtain stuck and an eighth grade boy had to unkink the wire with pliers. A side curtain fell

Light

The night has a
*   thousand eyes*
And the day but one;
Yet the light of the
*   bright world dies*
With the setting sun.
The mind has a
*   thousand eyes,*
And the heart but one.
Yet the light of a
*   whole life dies*
When love is done.

—1911
School Souvenir

James Otis School children practicing for a 1947 Christmas program. Note curtains to the right that were closed between the various pieces and skits.

From Mary Hanley.

when its wire broke, and both Joseph and Mary were home sick.

Johnny French was taking his role as narrator seriously enough, but he was speaking just above a whisper and Miss Thompson knew that no one beyond the first row would hear him. She left school that Thursday night confident that the program was doomed and the chances for another year's teaching contract were slim.

Friday afternoon Mary and Joseph were back practicing, the children knew most of their lines, and the curtains worked, most of the time. Unfortunately, Johnny French continued to whisper his lines, and everyone was so giggly and nervous that Miss Thompson closed school at three and sent everyone home with the instruction to return no later than 7:30 that evening.

Miss Thompson sat quietly after the last student had left, wondering why she did this every year. It was always the same. Hours spent planning, hints of impending disaster, and then a wonderful program. Would this year hold true she wondered.

By eight the building was packed with standing room only. The men gathered around the stove in the back of the room. The women and preschool children slid into the school desks, sometimes with considerable difficulty.

The brown curtain parted; older students took turns pulling the curtains when they weren't involved in something on stage. A first grader, Ned Olson, stood in center stage, wearing new bib overalls, a bright red shirt and freshly combed hair. He thrust his hands into his pockets and looked out across the sea of faces, or so it seemed to a six-year-old participating in his first Christmas program. For what seemed like an eternity to his parents, and to Miss Thompson, he said nothing. Then, in a small but clear voice he said, "I wish to welcome one and all to our Christmas program. We are all happy you came." A broad smile spread across his freckled face before he turned and proudly walked off stage to the loud applause of everyone in the room. The Christmas program had begun.

It is the supreme art of the teacher to awaken joy in creative expression and knowledge.

—Albert Einstein

One after the other recitations, one-act plays, songs ("Jolly Old St. Nicholas," "Up On The Housetop") and skits were presented. A few times a child had to be prompted on a forgotten line. Once the curtain stalled, briefly, leaving four youngsters who had just completed "Emil's Holiday Surprise" not knowing what to do. They remained on stage, giggling, before the reluctant curtain was finally yanked closed.

The time for the nativity scene, and Miss Thompson's experiment, had arrived. She wondered if Johnny would, or could, speak the words loudly enough for all to hear.

A reverent hush fell over the too warm school room as the curtains parted revealing Joseph, Mary, and the baby Jesus in his sawbuck crib with fresh yellow straw hanging to the stage. It was a religious scene, played better by the girl who was Mary, and the boy who was Joseph than any in recent years. Even the manger with its baby doll Jesus looked more authentic, more real.

At the appropriate time, Johnny French walked onto the stage, pushed a strand of unruly hair out of his eyes, and looked straight at the damper of the stove pipe in the back of the room. This was a trick the teacher had taught him so he could avoid looking at the audience, yet appearing to do so.

A quiet whisper slipped off his lips, "Jesus. . . Jesus. .."

Johnny stopped, cleared his throat, stood up as tall as his four foot eight inches would allow, and spoke in a voice that could be heard in the entry way beyond where the men were standing, and that was with the entry doors closed. This fact was made known later by Arlin Miller who had slipped out to the entry way to put on his Santa gear and reported hearing Johnny without difficulty.

With everyone straining to hear, and not needing to do so, Johnny boomed, "Jeesus Kee-rist was born on Christmas Day."

It was like a bolt of lightning had shot through the crowd. Johnny forgot what he was supposed to say next. There was stunned silence. Miss Thompson buried her head in her hands, hoping no one was looking at her.

Then a giggle sneaked out from back stage, then more giggles. Then everyone was laughing, the entire audience, and finally, even Miss Thompson began laughing. Johnny was smiling, proud of himself, pleased that for the first time he could stand on stage and speak loudly enough to be heard. It didn't matter to him that he had spoken the words as he had learned them at home rather than as Miss Thompson had tried to teach him.

All of the children assembled on stage to sing Jingle Bells, the cue for Santa to run around the schoolhouse a couple of times, shaking the sleigh bells he kept each year for this purpose. Santa burst into the school room yelling, "Ho, Ho, Ho and a Merry Christmas." He carried a white pillow case filled with bags of candy with one hand while trying to adjust his Santa mask with the other.

"You kids all been good?"

"Yes," the children cried in unison.

Santa then began distributing the presents that were under the tree, assisted by several of the older students. A few surprise gifts always managed to find their way under the tree. This year was no exception.

Fred Everson, a school board member, ripped open his package and found a pig's tail with a red ribbon tied to it. Ed French, Johnny's father, opened his beautifully wrapped present to find a small wooden cheese box. He slid back the cover which allowed an angry sparrow to fly free, circling the school room before perching on the wire holding the curtain. It chirped loudly as the children pointed in amazement at what they had just witnessed.

A bachelor, who had recently moved into the community, provided a bushel of red delicious apples, enough so everyone in the room got one. No one could afford to buy delicious apples for themselves, so this was a special treat. Children tore open their presents and the teacher began opening hers. Parents came by to thank the teacher and praise the children. Fred Everson was showing everyone his pig's tail, Santa disappeared to the woodshed to shed his Santa uniform, and the sparrow continued to chirp from its perch above the stage. Another Christmas program to remember.

To avoid using the word "ain't":

*A fat little boy
    said ain't.
Fell in a can of
    red paint.
When he got out,
    he said with a shout,
I'll say isn't and aren't
but not ain't.*

—Rural Schools Research Committee. Good Old Golden Rule Days: A History of Sauk County Wisconsin Country Schools. *Baraboo, WI: Sauk County Historical Society, 1994, p.9.*

Values From Christmas Programs

There was always a certain amount of controversy associated with Christmas programs, including the fact that not everyone in a community was Christian. Some of the county superintendents questioned whether the program was worth spending so much time in preparation, particularly when it meant taking time away from academic studies. Hildegarde Engle from Merrill remembered it this way: "The County Supervisor would send a notice saying: 'What are you doing about the so-called Christmas Program? Can you afford to waste three to four weeks of valuable school time to put on a slap-stick type program for cheap entertainment at Christmas when we celebrate the birth of Christ?'" On the other side of the issue was a community expecting a Christmas program and a good one.

As someone who participated in eight such Christmas programs, and with benefit of hindsight, I believe there were many values associated with the Christmas programs that went well beyond the celebration of Christmas. The benefits to the children were many. I remember my first program, when I was five years old and in first grade. Always a shy kid, not unusual for farm children who were often alone more than with others, I had to stand on the stage, in front of the entire community, and say my piece, as the recitations were called in those days. Miss Piechowski, our teacher then, made sure that all of us "spoke up" loudly enough so people in the back of the school could hear. This was no small task for a shorter than average first grader who was more comfortable by far doing farm chores than standing on a stage. Each year it got a little easier, until I was in the upper grades and then had the opportunity to work with the first and second graders as the older students had worked with me when I was just starting out. Gaining skills in public speaking was a great benefit, and frankly, put me ahead of the "town kids" when I attended high school and participated in public speaking (forensic) contests that were popular in those days.

We also learned the rudiments of play acting, how to memorize lines, how to leave behind who you really are for a few minutes and act a part. And we learned how to cooperate with each other. It took the entire school, all the students and the teacher, to put on a Christmas program. Everyone was involved. At one moment we were in a play, the next we were pulling the curtains, and a few minutes later, helping a first grader get ready to say his piece.

Beyond benefiting the students, the Christmas program brought the entire community together. In a farm community, most people never spent a night away from home, had little entertainment in their lives, and limited opportunities to see and talk with each other. The Christmas program was a special night, a night away from the worries of drifting snow and ever demanding dairy cows, a night to relax, talk with neighbors, and see their children and their neighbor's children perform. The Christmas program helped to make the community a community, and it was the country school, its children and teacher that made it happen.

Chapter Notes

1. Doris J. Lund in *A History of the School District of Rhinelander*, Rhinelander Area Retired Teachers Association, 1982, pp. 179-180.

Recess

Riverview School, Dunn County, 1937. Marshmallow roast.

From Janet Creaser.

Ask any kid what was best about attending a country school and you'd likely hear, recess! Ask kids today you'll probably get the same answer. Country schools had little playground equipment. At best, there was a teeter-totter and a couple swings. So recess was a time for playing games, exploring friendships and getting acquainted with the out-of-doors. Recess was also a time for, what some today might call, unusual activities.

In many parts of the Midwest, gophers were common in the school yards. Gophers are little brown and tan ground digging animals with stripes down their backs, and an uncanny ability to avoid capture. They usually made their appearance in spring, and were often spotted by spring-sick pupils who took every chance to glance out the schoolhouse windows. Upon spotting a gopher standing upright by its hole, the word was quietly passed among the boys, "It's time to drown a gopher."

Coher School children standing on a storm shelter. Crawford County, c.1950.

From Ada McKnight, teacher.

What this meant was that one kid poured water down the gopher hole, while another waited by a second gopher hole, hoping the wet gopher would emerge. Here is how Bill Stokes, once a student at the LaFollette School in Barron County, described the process. "We divided the kids into groups. One group did the pumping. These were bigger kids who could move the pump handle up and down quickly, providing a necessary supply of water. We called this group 'pumpers.' A second group of kids was designated 'haulers.' They ran from the pump to the gopher hole and dumped in the water. The third group, one person per gopher hole, was called the 'bat boys.' These were big boys who had the job of trying to hit a wet gopher when it dashed out of its hole." Stokes went on to explain that he didn't remember that they ever killed a gopher. "The wet gophers usually ran between the bat boy's legs, or they missed the gopher when they tried to hit it. Of course, we then always had gophers to drown another day."

Wilfred Humburg, who attended a country school in Faribault County, Minnesota, also recalled their attempts at gopher drowning. He explained it this way. "Well, gophers usually had two separate holes.

They had an escape hatch and an entrance hole. You simply pump buckets full of water and poured the water in the hole until a gopher came out. If you'd put a gunny sack over the hole, you'd catch a gopher. We'd then release the gopher in the old coal shed. Sometimes we'd have as many as four or five gophers running around in the coal shed. Eventually they'd get out."

There were other things to catch during recess, such as grasshoppers. Everett Refior of Whitewater learned how to catch grasshoppers for his pet Buff Orpington chicken who particularly relished this delicacy. One day, while he was playing softball, he noticed a giant tan grasshopper. "Neglecting my outfielding duties for a moment," he said, "I deftly snatched it and stowed it in my overall pocket." His plan was to take it home for his pet chicken.

Back at his desk, he wondered if the grasshopper was still in his pocket. His teacher, they called her Goldie, and he discovered the grasshopper at the same time. Goldie ordered Everett to toss the grasshopper into the furnace. She even held open the furnace door. Refior tells the rest of the story this way. "Slowly I rose, grasshopper in hand, but half way there, I eased my grip and it bounded away. To make it look good, I crawled under the seats and desks in pursuit, much to the amusement of the other kids. The grasshopper kept a jump ahead, as I clumsily grabbed at the spot where it had been. All school work came to a halt. Nobody dared to speak, but the girls tittered, the boys guffawed, and Goldie glowered. Finally, the grasshopper leaped in her direction. She snatched it and gave it to me to throw in. I fumbled the grasshopper and went crawling after it.

"Goldie's face twitched with suppressed anger. All eyes were fixed on me as I continued the farce of grabbing tardily at the grasshopper. At last it repeated the fatal mistake of bounding toward Goldie. Taking no chances this time, she deftly nabbed it and threw it in the furnace herself. I watched in horror as the little form, legs outstretched, disappeared into the swirling flames." [1]

In most country schools, there was a fifteen minute recess in the morning, and another of similar length in the afternoon. Noon included an entire hour, enough time to quickly wolf down a sandwich, and then rush out into the school yard. In warmer weather, we ate lunch outside as well, under the large old white oak trees that were scattered around the school yard. Recess included doing many things, some of them best forgotten. For example, I remember so clearly the recess day when we frightened Mac Jenks' horses.

Chain O' Lake School, Waushara County. Built in 1902, closed in 1955 and not used for several years. Now a home.

McKinley Jenks, whose farm is closest to the Chain O' Lake School, had the contract with the Town of Rose to grade the roads with his team and the township's rusty old road grader. All the recess games stopped as the team and the grader began climbing the little knoll in front of the school. The small gray horses strained in their harnesses as the grader rolled up a heavy thread of gravel in front of the shiny blade. Mac, as everyone knew him, took one of his hands off the controls of the machine to wave at us as we lined up along the fence to watch the team and the grader move by.

We could smell the sweaty horses, and the freshly turned gravel, not at all unpleasant smells for farm kids accustomed to smells of the land. When the horses and grader were closest to the schoolhouse gate, one of the older boys began jumping up and down and waving his handkerchief. The rest of us soon joined this mischief, having no idea of the consequences.

Mac Jenks' horses, mustangs everyone called them, were good workers but always on the skittish side. When they saw our animated group with handkerchiefs flailing, they reared on their hind legs, their front legs pawing the air. Mac struggled to control them, alternatively yelling "whoa" to the horses, and "Stop it" to us.

Mac was never known for polite language, even when women and children were around. Soon a stream of invectives gushed out of his mouth, words that many of us had never heard before, even those of us who prided ourselves in knowing the current cuss words in the community.

Never expecting to happen what happened, we stood wide-eyed as the horses continued to rear with their driver trying to control them, now alternately cussing us and his out-of-control team. One of the horses slipped, and fell on the road grader's tongue, the wooden pole that separates the team from each other while they are hitched to the machine. Like a rifle shot the tongue snapped, and with the noise the team stopped its thrashing. For a moment there was silence.

When Mac Jenks discovered the damage that had been done, and realized that this was the end of road grading until he could make a new tongue for the machine, the stream of cuss words increased in intensity. Many of the smaller children had already run toward the schoolhouse, hoping that the building would shield them from this man who seemed to have lost control even more than his team of gray mustangs. We older ones knew that Mac couldn't physically harm us because he could not leave the team. The school bell rang twice, recess was over, and we all filed back into the schoolhouse to leave Mac Jenks, his team of mustangs, and the broken road grader behind. I overheard Jimmy Steinke say to Norman Hudziak, "Geeze, that Mac Jenks sure can swear, can't he?"

"He sure can," replied Norman with admiration in his voice.

Recess, no matter what the season of the year, was the time for games, many passed on from generation to generation of country school children. (See Appendix A for instructions on how to play several recess games.) Popular games included "Anti-I-Over," "Pom-Pom-Pull-Away," "Drop the Handkerchief," "Ring Around the Rosy," "Kick the Can,"

A little black cricket
Lives down in a thicket,
O, a jolly young
Cricket so gay!
For he hops with delight
And chirps all night,
And he keeps very
still in the day.

—Stella H. Seed
1900 Reader

"Run Sheep Run," and "London Bridge."

At the South Natwick School in Vernon County, the children attending there played a rather unusual and complicated game with sticks. Burton Olson, a former student at the school, describes the game in great detail. He said, "One of the first signs of spring in our school was when we started to play a game we called 'Flipstick.' This started as soon as a reasonably sized patch of bare ground appeared. To play Flipstick, you needed two sticks about three-quarter inch to one inch in diameter. The short stick was about five to six inches long, and the long stick was about 24 inches long, pointed at one end. Sides were chosen, one was up and the other side in the field. A side could be as small as one person up and one person in the field. See Appendix A for a complete description of how to play the game.

In commenting on the game, Olson said, "I don't know how many generations played Flipstick, but I know my dad played it. My dad told the story about how he, his brothers, and some neighbor boys couldn't get enough Flipstick during recess, so they decided to skip school one nice spring day and play Flipstick all day. They met in an isolated clearing in a woods, and commenced to play the game. They didn't have watches so when they thought it was noon, they ate their lunches and got back to the game. In those days, the first and second graders were let out of school at 3:00 p.m. while the older children stayed until 4:00 p.m. When they thought it was about 3:00, they sent my Uncle Lee, who was in second grade, home. They were not very good at estimating time, because when Uncle Lee got home, it was just after noon. The cat was out of the bag. In those days, violation of school rules resulted in *two punishments*—one by the teacher, and another when you got home. Needless to say, this was their first and last experience skipping school for Flipstick or for any other reason."

Various forms of softball, beyond the traditional with teams, were also played during recess. Because my school usually didn't have enough students to play with two sides, we played a game called "work up," which I say more about in the chapter on softball.

Inez Thompson Hawley taught at the Progressive School in Waushara County from 1937 to 1942. They played a game called "Norwegian Ball." She described the game this way. "That was when you just had one base. You would bat and if you hit the ball you'd run to the one base instead of going around three of them. While you were running, the person who got the ball threw it at you. If the ball hit you, you were out."

"Cops and robbers" was another game sometimes played. Jan Otten Mawhinney recalls an experience when she taught at Blooming Prairie School (Walworth County) in the early 1940s. "It was noon hour and I was outside playing cops and robbers with the children. The robbers were locked in the woodshed when they were captured. I was caught and locked in the woodshed with one boy. I glanced at my watch and realized it was 12:55 and time to ring the bell to resume studies. Suddenly it dawned on me that if the children wanted to, they could keep me in the woodshed all afternoon. I had a vision of the school board firing me, and my reputation as teacher going down the drain. I called out, 'Time for the bell!' Immediately one of the children unlocked the door and we all trooped into the schoolroom to get a drink. I silently breathed a prayer for my deliverance."[2]

On rainy days, when students were forced to stay inside during recess, various kinds of indoor games were played. Some of these included "Button, Button, Who's Got the Button," and "Musical Chairs." Some children, on bad weather days, preferred to read, or to chat with their

White School, Dane County.

Photo by Steve Apps.

Daisy Chapin School, Rock County, c.1873. Moved to Beloit where it is now a museum.

friends. There were choices. But when the weather was nice, no one stayed inside the school building. The teacher moved everyone outside, even those who preferred staying inside.

John Palmer, who later became Dean of the University of Wisconsin-Madison School of Education, attended the Wilson School near Aurora, Illinois. He started in 1932, but even then the number of students was small, with never more than five students. One of them was Palmer's brother. Palmer and his brother were the only students one year. During recess they read books or fought with each other. "I remember," Palmer said, "the one teacher who lived in the city and who would bring three to four boxes of books every month. We just read and read."

Twyla Hart Kieffer, a student at Shadow Lawn School in Walworth County, recalled the day when everyone wanted to go outside for recess, but they couldn't. The problem wasn't the weather either. Shadow Lawn School was next to a farm and a bull got loose and ran around and around the schoolhouse. As she said, "We were prisoners in the building. Having no telephone to call for help, the teacher decided on a plan.

She stood at one side of the building and got the bull's attention while a student in the upper grades slipped out to the neighbor's. The neighbor corralled the bull and took it away." [3]

Winter, even with its inconveniences, provided wonderful recess opportunities. A large open field, with two long, gentle slopes, provided unending opportunities for sledding and skiing at my school. Nearly everyone owned a sled of some kind, and most of us had skis as well. For some of us, skis were a fairly common means of transportation in the winter, over snow covered roads, and even, sometimes through the fields, when the roads were blown shut and impassable to car travel.

When we weren't sledding or skiing, we were playing fox and geese, a form of tag where a wheel-like track with four spokes and a center hub was laid out in the snow. See Appendix A for a detailed description of how to play the game.

We can't forget those days when the temperature crawled above freezing. We built snow forts, snowmen, and of course organized elaborate snowball fights. I don't recall how we chose sides for the snowball fights, except they were serious business. Sometimes we would spend an entire morning recess constructing our snow forts and making snowballs for the noon hour confrontation. The morning recess was a kind of preparation truce.

One year, when we had several days of thaw and lots of packing snow, we constructed an elaborate snow house, trying to mimic the igloos we saw pictured in one of our books about the northland. We never quite caught on to building the roof. So the next best thing we did was to stack up an enormous pile of snow, let it freeze overnight, and then, the next day excavate the inside into a large and cozy room, large enough so some of the first graders could stand up inside.

Recess was more than fun time. During recess we developed friendships that lasted a lifetime. We learned how to play, how to relate, how to get along with both boys and with girls, with those older, and those younger. We learned how to put up with older kids who sometimes wanted to pull tricks on us and make sure that we knew they were older, and more important. We learned how to cooperate and how to follow rules for all of the games we played had elaborate rules. We learned about disagreement and how to deal with it. Sometimes it meant rolling in the dirt, wrastling we called it, to show someone his place. Invariably, when this happened, the teacher used the moment to teach both of us something about getting along, for getting along and cooperating with each other was a prerequisite of attending a country school.

When the distant sun is sinking
And your mind from school is free,
When of others you are thinking,
Won't you sometimes think of me?

1880 autograph book

Lucile Bisegger, Marjean Bondele, and Harriet Halloran. Wiota: William S. Hamilton's Diggings—1828-1993. *Gratiot, WI: Privately published, 1993.*

Chapter Notes

1. *Wisconsin Writes Home Stories to Remember.* Madison, WI: Yarns of Yesteryear Project, July/August, 1991, p. 27.

2. Walworth County Historical Society, *Good Old Golden Rule Days.* Elkhorn, WI: Walworth County Historical Society, 1994, p. 63.

3. *Ibid.*

Softball

Softball season began early in most country schools. As the winter sun climbed higher in March, the snow began to melt a little, the icicles grew longer from the schoolhouse roof, and even the most serious scholars had thoughts of softball in their heads. The badly scarred bat and the dirty, scuffed softball rested on the shelf in the entry way, just above the pile of oak wood that had to be fed regularly into the ever hungry wood stove in the back of the school. The older boys, who took turns carrying in wood and feeding the stove, eyed the ball and bat and stood for just a moment in the chilly entry way, thinking about the softball season now many months passed, and the upcoming season a few days away, surely not more than a few weeks.

When the snow had mostly exposed the ball diamond (loosely called a diamond because no one had ever thought to measure the distances between the bases, or even wanted to) children began their favorite recess and noon-hour pastime—softball. Country school kids didn't play baseball, at least I never heard of a school that did. The balls

Union Valley School, Iowa County, c.1905-1910.

From Marilyn Knutson.

were too hard, and too small, and flew too fast and could injure someone far more readily than the slow moving, often clumsy softball. Besides, if you played baseball, we called it hardball, then you had to own a baseball glove, and none of us had enough money to buy such a fancy piece of equipment. We farm kids even scoffed at those who owned baseball gloves—mostly our city cousins. We told them it made no sense to own a glove for only one hand.

Randy Jablonic, now University of Wisconsin men's Crew Coach and formerly a student of the South Bright School in Clark County, told me how much he and his fellow students enjoyed softball. "We all played softball at our school," Randy said. "From the eighth graders right on down to the little first graders. And we played because it was fun not because we wanted to win." He explained how each day someone different got to "choose up sides" so each day's team was a different one, and everyone got to play with everyone else, and against everyone else. "And everyone played, too, everyone who wanted to, boys and girls, older kids and younger kids. Even the little first graders who could scarcely hold the bat. The older kids helped them, showed them how to do it."

At my home school we usually didn't have enough pupils to make two full teams. Several years we had only fifteen or sixteen kids total. So we played a softball game we called "work-up." You could play work-up with only seven or eight kids, but it was better if you had ten or more playing. The game went like this. Someone chose to play a position at each base, and three more kids played in the outfield—that makes six kids accounted for. We didn't use the shortstop position, or maybe we didn't know about shortstops—I don't recall. Another student pitched, and one caught. Batters got to keep batting as long as they didn't make an out. As soon as the batter made an out, it was off to left field and everyone moved up a notch, with the catcher becoming the next batter, the pitcher becoming the catcher, the first baseman becomes the pitcher and so on. It was great fun and besides, we learned how to play every position on the field. The downside was that some of the better players spent a lot of time batting, but eventually they hit a ball for someone to catch, or they dribbled a little grounder and were called out at first. It all worked out.

Often the game was modified somewhat for the younger students. The smaller children were allowed to swing until they hit the ball, no matter how many times they missed before connecting. Also, a temporary first base was established, about half the distance of the normal run to first base. Because there were no sides involved, there was no real competition in the game.

At the South Natwick School in Vernon County, located in the hills not far from Westby, Wisconsin, softball teams were chosen when school started, and stayed together throughout the fall. Usually new teams were created in the spring. Burton Olson, a student at this school in the 1940s, describes the process of choosing the teams this way. "Two of the older kids served as team captains. This was considered a prestigious position and usually reserved for an eighth grader. One would throw a bat to the other, and after catching it, the two would go hand over hand until reaching the tip of the handle of the bat. The one who had the next turn when only the tip was left to grab had to grasp the tip of the bat and circle the bat three times around his head without dropping it. If successful, he got the first pick of the players. It was somewhat disturbing to be the last picked. This was usually the littlest child, and usually a girl. This was long before the days of gender equity and equal opportunity. Some of the girls, however, were just as good as the boys at hitting and catching, even though most boys wouldn't admit it.

"Like most of the land in the Westby area, our school ball diamond had a slope to it. It was up hill to first base, down hill to second, on the contour to third, and up hill again to home. We pretty much took hills for granted, not knowing there was such a thing as flat ground, except for a little in the valleys."

A Game to Remember

I suspect the highlight of softball was when we played teams from other schools, which we usually did in the spring, but sometimes in the fall as well. I remember one of the more interesting games my home school played. I was in eighth grade that year, 1946-47, and the only student in my class at the Chain O' Lake School.

There are certain advantages associated with eighth grade, especially if you are the only one in it. One definite advantage was I could decide where I wanted to play on the softball team. In the lower grades someone else was always telling me where they wanted me to play, now I could decide for myself.

During that school year there were about eleven boys and girls interested in playing on the school softball team. We needed nine on the field at any one time, and with two in reserve we were in good shape. And it was a pretty good team. This might be the year when we could win a game or two against the other one-room schools in the vicinity, I thought. Because of my eighth grade position, I declared myself captain. Both Jim Kolka and Mildred Swendryznski were excellent ball players, but they were in seventh grade. Neither of them contested my self-proclaimed designation as captain as we began organizing the team during recess one chilly day in late March. I had enough sense not to stand up and proclaim, "I'm captain of the team this year." I just called the bigger kids together back of the woodshed for an organizational meeting.

Organizing the team didn't amount to much. We had all been together the previous year, in fact most of us had been together since we could remember. It was rare when someone new moved into this rural community, but it did happen on occasion and this sometimes caused a problem in organizing a softball team. If a city kid moved into the community, who knew how well he or she could play softball? But there were no new kids this year. It was the same old bunch. Jim Kolka, Dave Kolka, Jim's younger brother, Mildred Swen (we always dropped off the rest of her Polish name in the interest of efficiency), my twin brothers, Donald and Darrell who were in fourth grade, Joyce and Nita Dudley (we called Nita, Tink for reasons unknown), Jerry and Norbert Zubeck, who had a few years earlier moved into the neighborhood when their mother married a local farmer, and Lyle York.

I said that I wanted to play first base and pitch on occasion. Jim Kolka would be our regular pitcher. That's how it worked out. No arguments. No fights. No rolling in the dirt to work out a disagreement. Not this year anyway. Maybe some reluctance to put up a fuss was because of our new teacher, Faith Jenks. Although she was my cousin, she was obviously much older than I and a person who I had only seen at family gatherings and knew hardly at all. She was tough. She didn't put up with any foolishness either in the school room or outside.

We began practicing every morning and afternoon recess, and during the lunch hour. Soon three or four of us could sail the ball over the school yard fence which was an automatic home run, even if the distance wasn't as far as what was common for softball diamonds.

As softball diamonds go, ours was unusual. The backstop for home plate was the privacy wall for the boy's toilet. First base was a scraggly box elder tree that was scarcely ten feet tall. Its leaves had a rather sickly yellow appearance from the time they first emerged in May until they fell off in October. Each year we expected the tree to die, but it never did. Somehow it seemed to know that it held a place of considerable importance for the Chain O' Lake softball team. There were few arguments at first base. Either you got hold of the box elder tree or you didn't. But visiting teams always wanted to argue, particularly those with those fancy movable bases (they used sawdust filled gunny bags). But we always held our ground. When you played Chain O' Lake, you played on our diamond, with all its rather unique features.

Second base was an oak tree, a black oak and a huge one, maybe three feet across at the base. The first branches were probably fifteen feet or more in the air, allowing ample room for a well-hit line drive to make its way well into the outfield, if not over the school yard fence for a home run. If by chance a ball hit the tree, we always played it where it landed. This, too, added some interesting features and often unexpected events to the game. Outfielders had to be especially alert because they never had a hint where the ball was going to light once the batter hit it past the pitcher and in the air. Of course you never slid over second base, you only slid into it and once you made contact you stopped rather abruptly. There is absolutely no give in a full-grown oak tree.

Third base was another oak tree, not quite as large as the one that was second base, but a good size tree. It nuzzled the side of the woodshed, and had a kind of bow in its trunk. It was possible to hit a ball through the bow in the tree, and over the roof of the woodshed and still have it fair and probably earn an "in the park" home run. But I don't recall anyone doing it during my eight years of observing and playing the game on this diamond.

The distances between bases, in case that might be a question, were not equal. The squirrels, who planted the acorns from which the oak trees grew, obviously didn't have softball in mind when they did the planting. The distance from home plate, which was a bare spot on the ground, to the box elder first base was a fair hike. Enough so most of the shorter-legged kids didn't really have much of a chance, particularly if the first baseman was halfway proficient at catching balls.

From first base to second base was about as far as from home plate to first. But it was only about half that distance from second base to the oak tree which was third. That's likely as it should have been. If you're good enough to get to second base, you ought have an easier time moving onto third. And the distance to home plate from third was even shorter, following the same logic. Make it tough in the beginning, and then easier the further you move around the diamond. I don't recall we ever referred to the ball field as a diamond either, because it was scarcely a diamond with its odd-shaped sides.

Anyway, by mid-April we had a well honed softball team looking forward to our first game. The Dopp School was our first competitor

The following are penmanship exercises:

The biggest trees do not always bear the most fruit.

He is to be pitied who cannot distinguish his friends from his enemies.

A little nonsense now and then is relished by the wisest men.

that spring. Dopp School sat on a little knoll east of Wild Rose a few miles. They played ball in the neighbor's cow pasture. Their field was wide open, no trees to contend with, nothing but wide-open spaces. There was, however, the occasionally "land mine" left when an inconsiderate cow wandered across the ball field from time to time. But usually, the teacher or sometimes the farmer was careful to remove such inconveniences from the ball field before the games.

Well this open space ball team was beside itself when they arrived at our school. Dopp had never played us before and they howled when they saw the ball diamond with its trees and uneven distances. And one thing more. From home plate to the outfield was somewhat of a hill. So as you ran from home to first, you ran uphill, more uphill from first to second, and then downhill to third and on home. That, too, was at it ought be, I thought. Uphill at first, and then down hill when you're close to your goal.

The teachers at Chain O'Lake and Dopp had been friends; that's how the game had been put together. But our teacher had been a little less than up front with the Dopp teacher about the condition of our ball field. They stood off to the side arguing and shaking their fingers at each other, and saying words I suspected they didn't want their students to hear.

Finally, I overhead the Dopp teacher say, "Well, we came all this way to play ball, I suppose we should go ahead and play."

Another argument they had to settle was the question of gloves. The Dopp team came with both the catcher and the first baseman wearing gloves, huge leather things as large as watermelons. None of us had ever seen anything quite as big before. So we protested and said the game would be totally unfair if they wore gloves and we didn't. I could see the compromise coming. If they were going to play on our rather unusual ball field, then their first baseman and catcher got to wear gloves.

We were finally ready to play. A cheer went up from the Chain O' Lake pupils and our team jogged to our places. As visitors they had first at bat. Jim Kolka was pitching. The Dopp teacher was the umpire. (Our teacher called balls and strikes when we were up to bat.) Jim had perfected a pitching style that made batters hit the ball into the air, which allowed our outfielders time to trot underneath the ball and catch it easily with their bare hands.

Dopp's first batter was a huge kid, maybe six feet tall with enormous shoulders and muscles in his arms that resembled those I'd seen in the Charles Atlas advertisements.

All that you do.
Do with your might;
Things done by halves
Are never done right.

—Handwriting
exercise

"Ball one," yelled the Dopp teacher. Jim was a little nervous this first game of the season.

"Ball two," yelled the umpire.

"Go gettum, Kolkie," I yelled. "Throw 'em your screw ball."

Chain O' Lake's lower grade kids had lined up just off to the side of home plate and cheered each time Jim tossed a pitch.

The warm early May sun beamed down on home plate, and on the pitcher's mound, really not a mound at all but a scuffed up place where the grass wouldn't grow. The rest of us were mostly in the shade, depending on where we stood in reference to our respective bases. I could see perspiration beading on Jim's face as he moved the ball in his hands and stared down on this hulk of a kid waving his bat as if it were a piece of kindling wood.

"Strike one," the umpire called. I heard the swish of the bat as it missed the ball. The little kids cheered more loudly.

Jim brushed his sleeve across his forehead and looked over at me with a "What do I do now?" look.

"Strike em' out, Kolkie," I yelled.

Jim wound up and let go. It was a perfect pitch. I knew it the moment it left Jim's hand.

"Crack!" Wood against softball.

Jim turned and covered his head with his arms, a natural reaction under the circumstances.

The pitch had worked. High, high, higher the ball flew, directly over second base and well above the majestic old oak tree. Our second baseman, Dave Kolka, got himself into position under the old oak about where he figured the ball would come down. All eyes were in the air. The little kids were cheering. They hadn't yet figured out that you don't cheer when the opposition hits the ball.

Soon I could hear the sound of the falling ball as it began its descent through the limbs and leaves of the old oak. Then nothing. Silence. The ball had become stuck in a crotch high up in the tree.

This was not something new. During practice it occurred rather often. Dave stationed himself directly under the crotch and waited, along with everyone else. I could see the ball from my station at first. The batter had already cleared all the bases and was standing at home plate, ready to celebrate his home run. But all eyes were on the tree.

Then the sound of the ball crashing through the leaves began again. Dave was ready. The ball gently fell into his hands, and a great grin spread across his face as a cheer went up from the Chain O' Lake team.

"You're out," yelled our teacher.

"You're not the umpire this inning," yelled the Dopp teacher.

"It's the rule of the tree," said our teacher.

"Well it's a dumb rule," retorted the other teacher.

We all watched as the two teachers squared off behind home plate, shaking their fingers at each other and raising their voices. Finally, the game got underway again. When it was over, we had won by the lopsided score of 10 to 5.

Up Hill Both Ways

11

When I begin telling my children about my country school days, they often interrupt and ask, "Were those the years, Dad, when every-day was winter, you walked five miles to school, and it was up hill both ways?" The truth of it is I walked a mile each way, and one way was indeed up hill, at least part of the trip. Winter also seemed to go on for-ever. Walking to school each day, you got to know winter well, from its early hints in November, its full blown fury in January, and its last reminders in April.

The walk itself was part of country school education, for some chil-dren an important part. Mary Bray, a student at Finch School, Walworth County, in the early 1940s, said, "One of the most delightful parts of those long ago days was the walk to school. To go by the road would be two plus miles, but it was shortened by going cross lots—tres-passing by today's rules."

Eagle Valley School, Buffalo County, c.1922. Note dirt road and woodpile.

From Hulda Stettler.

"We would go down the long lane-like driveway to Anderson's Resort and along the shore of Turtle Lake, checking to see what washed up dead or alive along the shoreline. Sometimes all we'd see would be maybe a turtle or snake resting itself. Then we crawled through a fence to pass the only other dwelling on that side of the lake. Here there was a plank to cross a narrow stream of water flowing from the spring where we might get a drink of cool, clear spring water. Then on along the willows to the next fence to crawl under, later a stile was made at this point. Now we were in a woods which was a cow pasture, too. If it was a very cool morning, it was a precious delight to step on the warm earth where a cow had slept all night, and there warm your toes, for of course, in those days we were barefoot until there was no way to postpone putting on those sturdy shoes necessary for fall and winter. Many plants to check in the woods from spring time to fall: a lone gnarled apple tree in fall and a patch of dainty, fragile hepatica in spring and nest of birds in the trees. Then to the last fence and under it to the road to the two places on the north side of the lake, and the school. The teacher and other students would be there."[1]

Esther Luke Niedzwiecki, a student at the South Bright School in Clark County, recalled, "I lived about a half mile from the school. My mom had a very hard time getting me to go to school when I was six. I was always busy with 'things,' and being shy I just didn't want to go. I did make a couple of friends early on, but Mom still had to watch me. In those days our road wasn't paved. So quite often the big old road grader came along. I was deathly afraid of it, so when I even heard it coming way over the next hill, I would scoot under the fence on our hill, and wait until it passed, and was clear out of sight way down the road over the next hill.

"When the frost came out of the ground in the spring, the road softened and got like Jello. Then, too, Mom had to watch me. I was always intrigued with how things happened, and how they got here—sticks, bugs, trickles of water, birds. I did well once I got to school, but it was before and after that took so much time. I guess I'm still that way, always curious."

Winter

Winter always provided a challenge for the trip to school. Marcia Staton attended the Sentinal Ash School, nestled next to the foot of the Blue Hills and near Bruce, in Rusk County, from 1937 to 1943. "My sister and I walked two miles to school. Usually we could catch a ride with the milk hauler, but sometimes we had to walk. We had a huge snowstorm one night. The next day Mary and I walked the unplowed road. I had an easier time of it since the snow was heavily packed and I could usually walk on top of the crust. She was enough heavier that she kept breaking through. We struggled the mile to the corner and turned, only to see a snow drift that went from the roof of the cheese factory on one side of the road to the top of a tall pine tree on the other. The snow had drifted to twenty feet deep. We looked at each other and without a word, we turned and walked home. There wouldn't be any school for us that day."

Some of my most vivid and sometimes terrifying memories were walking home during winter blizzards. I recall the time when I must have been in third or fourth grade at Chain O' Lake School in Waushara County. The winter had been a fierce one, with many days of below zero weather, and a stretch of ten days when the warmest it got was ten below zero with night time temperatures slipping well below minus thirty.

Ed Davidson bringing his children home from the Nelson Dewey School, Barron County, 1909. Horses and sleighs were a common mode of transportation, after walking.

The snow plows had managed to keep our road open to travel—the most important vehicle on the road was the milk truck that made the daily rounds to pick up the milk from the neighborhood farmers. If the milk truck couldn't get through, and this particular winter it had happened two or three times, we had to find a place for the gallons of milk that the cows kept producing.

Even though the roads were open, the snow plows had piled up huge banks on each side of the road, sometimes fifteen feet high. Walking along the road was ever so much like walking along an open topped white tunnel. Sometimes we walked along the tops of the frozen banks on our way to school, making believe we were mountain climbers; other times it just seemed more fun to walk the banks because we could see so far.

On this particular day, the temperature had risen into the plus twenties. The walk to school, along the narrow, snow packed road was pleasant, even though all you could see were snow banks until you got

Union No. 1 School, Pierce County, 1937. Lloyd Fox, teacher.

From Edna Runquist.

to Miller's place where they had shoveled out their driveway so you could see their house and barn.

The sky was cloudy and a brisk wind was blowing out of the southwest. "Think we're in for another snowstorm," Dad had said when I left for school that morning.

At recess I noticed the first fine flakes of snow beginning to sift downward, but we mostly ignored the possibility of yet another storm. The sledding on the hill back of the school was perfect, after each snowfall and spell of cold weather it got better.

Before noon, working at our desks, we heard the wind thumping against the side of the school, and howling around the corners of the building. Glancing toward the window, I could see the snow continuing to fall and swirling on the wind. From time to time the teacher walked over to a window and looked out, but she didn't say anything. An older boy, whose job it was, periodically shoved sticks of oak wood into the always hungry school stove that stood in the back of the room.

At noon, when we went outside to play, it was snowing so hard that we couldn't see the hill back of the school, beyond the school yard fence.

"Stay inside the school yard," our teacher said. "It's too dangerous to slide on the big hill. You might not find your way back."

No one argued with her, and no one went out on the hill that noon.

By 2:00 p.m. we were in the midst of a full blown blizzard. The wind blew unmercifully; the snow fell ever harder. Looking out the school window, the school yard fence was invisible as were the outhouses. No one should go out to an outhouse unless it was absolutely necessary, the teacher warned.

By 2:30 the first of the fathers arrived to take his children home. He, of course, walked. "Wicked storm," he said, stomping the snow off his feet and rubbing his hands together in front of the stove.

One after another fathers came for their children. Dad came about mid-afternoon. After he had a chance to warm up by the stove, he made sure I was bundled up for the trip home. My grandmother Witt had knitted a huge shawl for me that usually served as a scarf, but when the weather was bad could be wrapped around my head so only my eyes weren't covered. Some of the kids said I looked like a mummy when I was all wrapped up, but it was warm.

We started the mile hike toward our farm, Dad walking ahead. I tried to step in his tracks but my short legs made this difficult. The new snow was already more than a foot deep, but with the strong wind it was difficult to know how deep it was.

In the snow tunnel which was the road, the snow swirled around, from time to time it nearly took away my breath and I had to stop and rest.

"We can't stop," Dad yelled over the the storm. "Got to keep moving."

Snow sifting off the tops of the snow banks made visibility along the road impossible. Dad walked only a few steps in front of me, yet at times I couldn't see him as he disappeared in a wall of white.

"We should be to Miller's place soon," Dad yelled during one of the few times when we stopped to rest. The fury of the wind blew away his words as soon as they left his mouth. He looked like a walking snowman, every inch of him was covered with snow from his six buckle rubber overshoes to the top of his red and black plaid cap with the cat fur ear flaps.

Finally we came to Miller's farm, their driveway a dim break in the roadside snow banks. I was sure that I couldn't walk another step, at least for the last half mile of the trip, but Dad kept encouraging, kept coming back to where I staggered along to tell me we had only a little further to go. And then, what seemed like forever, we arrived home. Mother had a huge kettle of vegetable soup cooking on our kitchen wood stove. The smells of soup and wood smoke engulfed me as I stumbled into the house, exhausted but thankful to have made it home.

*Thirty days
   have September,
April, June,
   and November;
All the rest
   have thirty-one
Save February,
   which alone
Has twenty-eight,
   but one day more
We add to it
   one year in four.*

Dad warmed up a little and then went out to the barn to start the evening chores.

Most of the time the trips to school were more pleasant than this one was. But winter blizzards are a part of the upper Midwest, and we all had great respect for them. On the other hand, although the schools often let out early during bad snow storms, they almost never closed because of the weather. I don't remember our school closing, no matter how snowy or how cold the weather.

Extreme cold was more hazardous than snow storms. Alva Mott, who attended a country school near Wascott in Douglas County, recalled walking to school when it was fifty-four below zero. "When it gets down in the thirties, or forties, or fifty below, you are always cold when you get to school. Kids would come with frozen toes, they would be white, and their noses were white with frost bite as well. If you came to school and your hands were white, we got a dish pan of snow and you'd rub the snow on your hands. You cried a little. You'd take your shoes off and put them up. While you were getting warm, you'd work on your lessons. We stayed around the stove until we thawed out, and then we would go to our seats and the day would go right ahead."

Union Valley School, Iowa County, c. 1900. Caroline Slamer, teacher.

From Marilyn Knutson.

Many Ways to School

Carol Mattson-Port attended the Chapp Creek School in Chippewa County starting in 1936. She remembered, "We had to walk or take a bike or ski two and half miles each way to school. It was pretty flat country. There was a boy who was a month older than I and lived a half mile away. We would walk to school together. Often times we were an hour late because we kind of took short cuts, and we would explore squirrel nests and wild animals and birds and such. The road went through open farm country. There were trees along the road, and a wooded area that we'd sometimes cut through, a swampy area. I can remember watching the muskrats as we went to school, and falling into the water in the spring. I also remember taking animals with us to school, and leaving them in the cloakroom. I remember taking a squirrel to school one time. We found it in the woods."

Children traveled to school in a variety of ways. Most walked. Some rode bikes. Skiing was popular transportation in winter. In the northern counties, it was not unusual for children to ride the train, the Chicago Northwestern and the Soo Line Railroad. In the early days, some students rode horses to school, or were transported with horse drawn vehicles of various kinds, from pony carts to sleighs, to horse drawn wagons with covered boxes—the forerunner of today's school bus.

Alva Mott attended a country school in Douglas County, in the far northern part of Wisconsin from 1926 to 1935. "One of the ways we got to school," she said, "was with a high covered wagon pulled by a team of horses. In the winter, my father made us a sled with a covered canvas over it. We piled in there with blankets over the top of us. Dad built a little barn by the school. We unhitched the horse and he stayed in the barn until we were ready to leave at the end of the day.

"One year we didn't have a horse because Pa needed it. He told us, 'In the old country they make the oxen do things,' so we had to train an ox to take us to school. But the ox wanted to eat all the way to school. It was morning and that was eating time. One of us tried to lead the ox while the other switched it with a stick. We got to school an hour late; it took two hours to make the trip. Of course on the way home the ox hustled right along because he knew he was headed home. We'd rather it had been the other way around because we had chores to do when we got home."

Hazel Udelhoven taught in various Grant County one-room schools for more than sixteen years, in the 1930s and 1940s. Some of her children rode to school on horses. She recalled one little second grade boy,

Dale was his name. "One morning he came walking into the building crying, carrying his dinner bucket. 'What's the matter, Dale?' I asked. Between sobs he answered. 'Queenie shied and I didn't shy. I fell off and Queenie ran home.' It seems that Queenie shied every time she got as far as the cement culvert. The other children would sometimes give notice beforehand. 'Dale must have forgotten to shy this morning and had to walk.' As I remember, he finally learned how to get Queenie past the cement culvert."

Beyond the Trip

The trip to and from school each day was much more than overcoming the challenges of muddy roads, blizzards, unruly horses, and slow moving oxen. Settling personal disagreements often took place along the way.

Bill Stokes, a student in the LaFollette School in Barron County, and long-time newspaper columnist recalled this incident:

"A couple of boys didn't get along all that well, and often got into fights on the way home from school. Willard and Roger went at it often. One day Roger hit Willard over the head with his lunch bucket, a syrup pail. Willard went down in a heap and just lay there in the snow. Several of us were walking by and asked about Willard's condition. 'Don't worry about Willard,' Roger said. 'He's just faking it. Nothing wrong with him.' So we all walked on, wondering if he was really OK or whether he had been knocked out. He must have been OK because he wasn't there when we came along the next morning."

Vieno Keskimaki, commenting on the event of school closings in Clark County said, "Some shiver as they recall the pre-bus days when children were bundled in scarves, mittens, long stockings and overshoes to face the wintry weather on the long hike to school on drifted, unplowed roads. But these long hikes, alone or with your school mates, had a therapy value missing today.

"It was a time to forget or a time to reflect on the pleasures or frustrations of the day as you hurried or dawdled along the road under the open sky. Biology, science and art were silent teachers on these walks. None knew better than a rural teacher when the first mayflowers, cowslips or violets bloomed. Pussywillows, cocoons and frog eggs hatched and grew in quart jars on the window sills as reminders of life's ever changing nature. The first robin in spring, the first southward flight of geese in the fall were topics of interest."

Be kind to all as far as you can; you know not how soon you may want their help; and he that has the good will of all that know him; shall not want a friend in time of need.

—Webster's American Spelling Book 1831

*Sunnyview School,
Green Lake County,
1939.*

From Ruth Plautz.

Bill Stokes said it this way, "As much education occurred on the way to school as occurred in school. It was an opportunity to get in touch with the weather and with the natural world.

"When I was in the upper grades, I cared for a trapline on my way to school. The Peterson Swamp was a good place to find muskrats and mink. That year I trapped thirty or forty muskrats and a few mink. I stored the pelts in a box in the cellar, and mother accidently burned the box of pelts. She felt terrible, but I felt worse because I had been counting on the income.

"One time I set a trap with a dead chicken. I had hoped to snag a crow but caught a fox instead. Unfortunately a huge blizzard swept over the area about that time and I couldn't get out to my traps. I found the fox frozen to death in my trap. I still feel bad about that; I really wanted to catch a crow and then this poor fox happened along at the wrong time."

Along with the memories of the county schools are the recollections of the trips to and from school, day after day, in all kinds of weather, during each of the seasons of the year. The out-of-doors is a great educator. It is one thing to learn about nature in the classroom, in books, or even in modern science laboratories. It is quite another to learn about nature each day, as part of the trip to school. Traveling to and from school was also more than nature study and learning first hand about weather. It was a reflective time, an opportunity to think through a problem, to get over a hurt, to spend some time contemplating, whether intended or not. Contemplation is in short supply these days. People don't believe they have time for it, there is just too much to do. The walks to and from school gave children at least two times a day to reflect. They were natural times, built into the rhythm of their lives. As they interacted with each other, as they were challenged by their teachers and their school books, and as they faced the demands of ever changing weather, they had time to think, to make sense of what was happening in their lives.

Chapter Notes

1. Walworth County Historical Society. *Good Old Golden Rule Days.* Elkhorn, WI: Walworth County Historical Society, 1994, p. 13.

12

Beyond The School Room

Lynxville School, Crawford County, c.1950s. Eighth graders practicing for musical number, "Walking My Baby Back Home." Presented at a school program.

Country schools were much more than buildings where farm kids learned to read, write, and work with numbers. They were the center of their community, defining the geographic boundaries for the people who lived in the school district. In my home community, people knew they were part of the Chain O' Lake School District, just as those who lived south of us knew they were in Willow Grove, those to the west in the Oasis district and so on.

Community Center

Many wedding receptions, birthday celebrations and anniversaries were held at the school. When soldiers returned from duty, a welcome home party was held there. When I completed Army basic training and was on leave, the community turned out to see my pictures and learn about my adventures at Fort Eustis, Virginia, a far distant place to most of the people in our central Wisconsin school district.

The school was the social center for the entire community. I recall the receptions and parties held at my school when I was growing up. Three farmers played musical instruments. Frank Kolka played the concertina, Pinky (I never new his real first name) Eserhut strummed a banjo, and Harry Banks sawed on a fiddle. What wonderful music they made.

It was an amazing feat that Harry Banks could play at all because he'd severed a finger on his left hand in a haying accident. He learned how to use his remaining fingers in creative ways. No one listening to his fiddling would ever guess that he had a missing finger.

Country schools sponsored many community activities during the year. Some were open only to parents, others were available for everyone. Parents were invited to the annual Halloween party. Because Halloween always fell in the midst of fall harvesting, only a handful of mothers showed up. Those who did enjoyed watching children bob for apples in a galvanized wash tub where the only way to retrieve an apple was to force it to the bottom of the tub, completely immersing one's head in the process. Children, blindfolded, were asked to feel grapes (a ghost's eyeballs), smell vinegar (a witch's brew) and experience other scary sensations. A couple of mothers helped plan the party and arrange the various activities.

Thanksgiving meant another party, with parents invited. After a few Thanksgiving readings, and a song or two, the highlight was diving into the fresh pumpkin pie furnished by one of the mothers. Valentine's day was one more time for parents, again usually mothers, to watch children retrieve their homemade valentines from the huge valentine box that sat on the teacher's desk for a couple of weeks before February 14. Bad weather often kept the numbers of mothers attending low.

Lelah Bruso, Rhinelander, recalled a mother's club that met at the school she attended. Mothers came to school one Friday afternoon a month. "We kids had to learn poems or write something and be able to read it, or some would sing. We had to put on a little performance for our mothers. It was good training." Doris Soderland, also of Rhinelander, remembered that they had a literary society in her school. "A man came in and taught us how to conduct a meeting, showed us how to follow Robert's Rules of Order, and even how to conduct an election. We took turns at being officers so that everybody through the years would have a chance to conduct a meeting."

End of Year Picnic

Along with the Christmas program, the picnic held on the last day of school was open to the entire community, and almost everyone attended. Even though many farmers were in the midst of planting corn or other spring work, it was customary in nearly all school districts for everyone to attend the school picnic.

Different from the Christmas program, nothing was really planned. It all just happened. The featured event was the noon potluck. Everyone was asked to bring their own sandwiches, silverware, and a dish to pass. The teacher brought the ice cream. In the Chain O' Lake district, the teacher always brought two, two and one half gallon tubs of vanilla ice cream that was packed in a huge padded container to slow the melting (the school board covered the cost).

After the meal, it was tradition for the fathers to form a softball team and play against the students. Bonnie Trudell, a former student at Squaw Lake School in St. Croix County, described the softball game this way. "The mothers would visit, up in the yard, but the softball game was the school kids against the fathers and older brothers and sisters. I don't know if this was true for other children, but this was one of the few times I saw my father play. He would come to the school picnic and play softball and all these other farmers with their big leathery farmer hands would get up to bat, and that was really fun." Farming was known for its hard work, but the school picnic was one of those rare times when it was OK to play. And play they did, all afternoon, while the women cleaned up after the noon meal and then sat under the oak trees and visited.

Rogers School, Waupaca County, c.1897.

From Lillie Ann Rasmussen.

The teacher usually organized sack races, three-legged races and such for the children who didn't want to play in the softball game. By three p.m. people began drifting off for home; there were chores to do and spring work that never seemed finished. Children bid goodbye to their teacher for the summer, and often forever, as the teacher moved to another school, got married, or for some reason quit teaching. Many tears were shed because for many pupils, the teacher was clearly their second mother. Children often gave their teacher a little end-of-school-year present, and the teacher, in turn, gave each student a gift.

In many schools it was common for the teacher to give each student an attractive folder that included a photo of the teacher, a list of all the students, plus the names of the school board members. Students prized these mementos and often kept them with the family Bible, as a remembrance of their school years. One such 1928 souvenir folder included these words:

> "This souvenir of the school year now closing is presented to you with the best wishes of your teacher. May it serve in the years to come as a pleasant reminder of your school day associations."

On the cover of the folder, along with a painting of a pond and a schoolhouse, were these words:

> "Your teacher's wish on closing day
> Is that, in years to come, you may
> Recall the joy the hours here spent,
> And all that each dear friendship
> Meant."

Box Socials

Country schools were always short of money. There were never enough library books, maps, reference books, and the like. Not different from today, school boards were always stingy with money because they knew that it was their neighbors, through taxes, who were footing the bill.

Teachers constantly searched for ways to raise additional money. The box social was one way and besides, it was a splendid way to bring the community together for an evening of fun and good dining.

The idea of a box social was for the older school girls, and the women in the community to prepare a box lunch that was packed in a shoe box, oatmeal box, or other container about that size. The box was then wrapped as attractively as possible, and brought to the school where an auctioneer sold them to the boy or man prepared to bid the highest amount. The person who fixed the box lunch then ate with the person who bought it. All sales cash, all money to the school.

Of course many asides occurred. A young lady who wanted to make sure a favorite boy friend would buy her box lunch would describe it to the young man ahead of time. Unfortunately, when the other young men saw one of their friends bidding on only one box, they began bidding on this box too, making sure the young man paid dearly for the right to sit with his girl friend and taste her cooking.

Phoebe Bakken attended a one-room school, starting in 1927. Later she taught at the Hope School in Dane County. She remembered a particular box social she attended. "I remember one guy who was auctioning and made a big mistake. He held up a nicely decorated box and said it must be a good one because it was nice and heavy. Every woman there knew that if you had a cake in it, it shouldn't be heavy. Cakes should be light and fluffy. He pulled a boner there."

Doris Lund, Rhinelander, remembered a box social when she was a country school student. "When we kids were in the country schools of Sugar Camp, we had get togethers of all schools for certain events. At about ten years of age, I had my first school 'crush' on a young man who attended the Kathan Lake School. The school sponsored a box social. Dad and Mom decided to go and I excitedly planned to take a box, too, hoping the 'right' person would buy it.

"After decorating a cardboard box (usually a round large-size oatmeal box), Mom would bake some of her big sweet buns for the box. Sometimes she would fry chicken. But other times she would buy minced ham at Mangerson's store in Rhinelander. To me that was a real treat and cold cuts today can not match it for flavor. With fresh produce from the garden tucked in and topped off with a home baked pie or cake, any man was well rewarded for his purchase price.

"I don't remember what I put in my box, but I expect Mom helped me with it. I do recall it was prettily trimmed with crepe paper flowers and 'he' did buy it. But after all that preparation and anticipation, can you imagine I was too bashful to eat with him? That young man got his money's worth, since each box contained enough food for two." [1]

Hazel Udelhoven taught more than sixteen years in Grant County country schools. She remembers a box social where somehow the young men found out which decorated box belonged to the teacher. The competitive bidding began with one thought in mind, buy the teacher's box and see what goodies are inside for lunch, at whatever cost. This was during the Depression years, but even so the box brought more than

Happiness in this world, when it comes, comes incidentally. Make it the object of pursuit, and it leads us on a wild goose chase, and is never attained.

—Nathaniel Hawthorne

twenty-five dollars, a lot of money in those days, particularly when the final bid on most boxes was between five and seven dollars.

Arbor Day

Not all teaching took place in the school room. Most schools, in the spring of the year, observed Arbor Day. Judy Lee Tarbox attended a country school near Gays Mills. "On Arbor Day we planted a tree on the school property, nearly every year. We also raked the school yard."

Larry Meiller attended the Hope School in Dane County. He fondly remembers Arbor Day activities at his school that consisted of about 30 children in all eight grades. Eleanor Dahl, Hope School teacher, began focusing on Arbor Day well before the day arrived. "Throughout the school year, as a part of each day's opening, she read a chapter from a book to the entire school. As Arbor Day approached, she read from books associated with the environment and understanding the out-of-doors. She was well ahead of her time in her concern for the environment."

When Arbor Day arrived, the Hope School children spent the entire day outside the school. A wooded area surrounded the school grounds, and one of the tasks was to spend time in the woods, cleaning up debris. They also planted a tree each year. Additionally, they raked the school yard, and then culminated the day's activities with a bonfire and wiener roast.

I affirm that the good is the beautiful.

—Plato

"I've never forgotten Eleanor Dahl," Meiller said. "She helped us become more aware of the woods and the plants, and she made a point that I've never forgotten. She helped us understand that many of these plants will be here long after we've gone. I'll never forget that lesson."

Bill Stokes attended the LaFollette School in Barron County. He said, "On Arbor Day we got to walk down to the Yellow River which was about a mile and a half from the school. A highlight of the year. One time we found a dead beaver, next to a tree it had cut off. The tree had slipped off the stump and landed on the beaver's tail, preventing it from moving. We found it when the snow melted in the spring, on our annual Arbor Day trip. Something I've never forgotten."

At the Chain O' Lake School, we celebrated Arbor Day by walking around a lake, about a half mile from the school. It was clearly a highlight of the year as we gathered frogs, turtles, and other creatures to bring back to the school. Upon returning, we raked the yard, and built a huge bonfire with the dead grass and leaves. To top the day, we roasted wieners and marshmallows.

World Wars

During World War I, everyone was asked to make sacrifices. Patriotic meetings were held in the rural schools. In Sauk County, every school district was encouraged to hold patriotic meetings. President Wilson had also asked the nation's schools to organize Junior Red Cross societies to make a variety of items for the war effort such as quilts and knitted items.[2]

During World War II, schools contributed to the war effort in a variety of ways. In some schools, students were asked to bring ten cents a week for defense stamps. These were pasted in a book and redeemed for war bonds. In Sauk County, and perhaps in other counties as well, in 1942, 4-H fair prizes were awarded in defense stamps.

Many school children collected milkweed pods for life vests. Kapok from the Dutch East Indies had been used until the Japanese overran these islands, making it necessary to find an alternative. Milkweed floss became the choice. It took two bushels of milkweed pods to stuff one life vest, and 1.2 million life vests were needed. A milkweed stuffed life vest was called a Mae West. The government paid twenty cents for a well dried mesh onion bag of pods.[3]

4-H Clubs

In 1946, with World War II slowly fading into history, my father inquired about starting a 4-H Club in the Chain O' Lake community. Henry Haferbecker, County Agricultural Agent for Waushara County, was invited to a meeting at the school to explain 4-H work, and how to organize a club.

At school I announced an upcoming Friday night meeting, inviting pupils older than ten and their parents to come and discuss forming a 4-H club. Every student over ten was there, promptly at 8:00, to hear what Mr. Haferbecker had to say. He passed around 4-H record books, and pamphlets on raising dairy calves, growing field crops, 4-H Victory gardens (left over from the war emphasis), woodworking projects, sewing, cooking, canning—enough information to whet the interest of every youngster in the room. Before the evening was over, we had organized a 4-H club, elected officers, and had a discussion on what to call it. Mr. Haferbecker said we could name our club whatever we wanted— it was our club. One kid suggested naming the club the Royal Dizzy Daisies. The name had a nice ring to it, and I voted for it. In fact all of the kids voted for it.

Our parents and Mr. Haferbecker were listening to our delibera-
tions. It was during this meeting that I learned for the first time of the
importance of a higher power, and how sometimes what seemed evident
isn't so evident. It soon became clear that most of our parents didn't care
much for the name, Royal Dizzy Daisies. I believe it was my father who
gently suggested we might want to reconsider our club's name. "After
all," he said, "Do you want to read in the *Waushara Argus* about what
the Royal Dizzy Daisies has done?" Some of us began to have second
thoughts about our earlier decision, and we voted a second time. Chain
O' Lake 4-H became the new name, a logical, but not very creative,
alternative to Royal Dizzy Daisies. That club met often at the school, as
well as at the homes of the club members. It continued to meet many
years after the school closed in the 1960s.

The Wiota Handy Helpers 4-H Club (LaFayette County) organized
in 1931 with the Wiota School teacher, Magdalen Holland (Flanagan)
of Darlington, as its leader. It later changed its name to the Wiota
Happy Hour 4-H Club. Forty-six members enrolled in various 4-H projects. The club met at the Wiota schoolhouse. The Chain O' Lake and
Wiota schools were not unique. 4-H Clubs were associated with country schools throughout the state, often serving as meeting sites.

When the country schools closed, rural residents experienced a vacuum beyond no longer seeing their children hike off to school each
morning. The school served purposes that went well beyond the formal
education of the community's children. Unfortunately, not many of the
decision-makers responsible for closing the schools fully appreciated the
role of the school beyond what happened in the classroom. For many
residents, the school was the hub for community activities. It served as
a central meeting place, but more importantly the school gave the community around it an identity.

Chapter Notes

1. Doris J. Lund. "Basket Socials" in *The History of the School District of Rhinelander*. Rhinelander, WI: Rhinelander Area Retired Teachers Association, 1982, p. 180.

2. Rural Schools Research Committee. *Good Old Golden Rule Days: A History of Sauk County Wis*. Baraboo, WI: Sauk County Historical Society, 1994, p. 35.

3. *Ibid.*, p. 36.

It is impossible to say something about every one-room school that ever operated in Wisconsin; there were just too many of them, over 6,000 at one time. Each one had an interesting history and a fascinating story. In the following selection of schools, I've tried to pick some from throughout Wisconsin.

I've tried to give some flavor for the history and particular circumstances of each school I've selected, as a kind of representative sample of all of them, knowing full well that each school was unique and different from all the rest.

Pleasant Ridge School. Grant County. 1890s. Likely the first integrated school in Wisconsin. The school was built by black and white settlers on land donated by Isaac Shepard, a former slave who came to Wisconsin in 1848.

State Historical Society of Wisconsin. Whi(x3)28262.

Chain O' Lake School
Located on the corner of Cty A and 15th Rd., Town of Rose, Waushara County

The original school was built c. 1870s and replaced with a new building in 1902. The school closed in 1955.

From the Treasurer's Record, 1902.

Paid to Radley Brothers	
for building school	$705.19
Black board and freight	16.75
Putting up black board	1.75
School seats (purchased from District No. 5)	71.50
Stove	20.00
Oil Paint and brush	6.00
Lock	3.25
Dictionary and holder	12.70
Globe	16.00
Step Ladder and chalk	.90
Broom	.30
Clock	5.00
Desk and chair (teacher)	17.50
Firewood	2.00
School insurance	3.00
Teacher's salary 4 months @ 36.00 per month	144.00

Income: 1902-1903

From State for school bldg.	800.00
District taxes	200.00
State taxes	121.75
County taxes	113.83
Sale of old school	18.00
Balance on hand	$180.59

From the records for 1954-1955, the last year the school operated.

Balance on hand, 1954	$1,327.39
Teacher salary 9 months @ 210.90	$1,898.10
Withholding	343.80
Retirement	143.10
School supplies	367.34
Repairs	81.55

Board services	55.73
Electric bill	32.33
Coal	25.71
Two cords firewood	10.00
Fire insurance	4.00
Cleaning school	15.00
New radio	13.79

Summary: 1954-1955

Expenses	3,127.81
Income	3,756.00
Balance on hand, June 30, 1955	$628.19

The income for 1954-1955 included the sale of the school for $1.00, to the Chain O' Lake Community Club. The building was used several years as a community meeting place, then became a home which is its current use.

County Line School
On the boundary between Green Lake and Dodge Counties [1]

The school building was bought and moved to Gilmore's corner, where County Line Road, and County Hwy A meet. It was leased to the County Line Lutheran Church for three years. In the fall of 1901, the building was moved again, this time across County Hwy A to the east.

Zona Schwandt Justiss and her brother attended the school and she recalled details of the building and what they studied. "The schoolhouse had two front doors. Girls entered at the right. Just inside was the coat room where each child was assigned a hook for a coat. Overshoes were placed just underneath along with their lunch boxes. All of us, teacher and children, brought our lunches of sandwiches, fruit and dessert with an occasional variation such as a hard-boiled egg. Sheldon and I had the latest in lunch pails, gray granite buckets with tin lids. It was easy to tell which was Sheldon's by the many dents in the lid.

"Art appreciation was a study I didn't comprehend in those young years, but I liked being able to give the correct name of the picture and its artist on review days. I remember very well sitting on the little chair for recitation at the front of the room. I can still see 'Feeding Her Birds' as it was held up for us to identify. The pictures were on five by seven sheets supplied for each pupil. The story about it and its artist were on the back side. As the years pass, I appreciate this early introduction to

Raphael, Bonheur, Millet and others. My parents and I may not have heard of these great artists but some curriculum planner must have had dreams of adding to our culture.

"Each spring we had a contest. Each pupil's name was listed on a chart posted in the school room. When I saw my first robin, song sparrow, flicker or others the date was marked on the chart. My interest in birds began with this contest. As we walked to and from school we had time to notice the birds. Our quiet steps did not frighten the song sparrow as he sounded his lovely notes from a fence post. Nor were the larks, bobolinks and red-winged blackbirds in the tall grass disturbed. In those years each box of Arm and Hammer Soda had a bird card enclosed. I still have a stack of them within easy reach."

Zona Schwandt Justiss went on to become a teacher at the County Line School, beginning in the fall of 1943 when she was nineteen years old. The County Line School, also known as the Kelly School, was closed in 1956.

Fauver Hill School
Town of Medary, LaCrosse County [2]

The first school in the district was log and built in the Hartley pasture in 1867. In 1878, the voters decided to build a new school in the district, on a different site. Joseph French bought the old building for $10.00. A tax levy of $400, in two installments, was approved to build the new school which was completed in 1879. It was then called Campbell School. The site for the new school was donated by David Fauver, with the provision that the land would go back to the Fauver family if the school was abandoned. In 1919 the school's name was changed to Fauver Hill, in honor of the man who donated the land.

In 1924 a new brick school building was constructed on the site at a cost of $8,900. Works Project Administration (WPA) workers modernized the school with sanitary facilities and running water in 1936. A $90,000 addition was completed in 1957, and in 1960 the school joined the Onalaska School District.

Francis Creek School
Manitowoc County [3]

The Francis Creek District was organized in the early 1850s. The first wood frame school building was constructed about 1852 and was

18 x 24 feet with four shuttered windows on each long side and one in the entrance side. A small entry was attached to the front of the building, and a lean-to addition for fuel was added to the rear.

The school's equipment consisted of homemade desks and seats, accommodating six to eight pupils each. This first building was sold for $43.45 on February 27, 1892 and moved a mile west. It was remodeled into a cheese factory. A new school with brick veneer was constructed in 1891 at a cost of $708 for material and $747.41 for labor. The building was 28 x 38 feet with a smaller brick fuel shed attached to the rear.

New blackboards, double desks and a bell were purchased, and two years later, the district bought a new large Webster dictionary. The school was heated by a wood stove. Summer and winter sessions were held to about 1875 with older boys and girls attending during the winter. In 1870, sixty-nine students attended. By 1875 and 1880, the average attendance numbers had jumped to ninety. Even as late as 1915 the enrollment was near sixty. Since then, the enrollment declined rapidly until 1948 when the daily attendance was only eight. The school closed in the early 1960s and was sold to the Francis Creek Sportsman's Club for $1.00 on September 30, 1964.

Be a good child; mind your book; love your school, and strive to learn.

—Webster's American Spelling Book, 1831

Hochungra Indian Mission School
Town of Komenski, Jackson County[4]

Part of the Black River Falls School District, it was the only school with only Winnebago students attending. In 1934, the government allowed the Indian children to remain at home and attend public schools rather than the Government Indian School in Tomah, which was a boarding school. The sixty-eight children that attended the school first met in the mission church.

The Indian Mission School was an experiment, to see if parents would send their children to school. The answer was a resounding, yes. A school building was erected in 1936 to serve eight grades.

Mrs. Lawrence Olson, a white woman, taught at the school until it closed. She came to the school as a five-day substitute teacher and stayed for twenty-nine years. In the early years the children were so shy they refused to walk onto the stage to receive their diplomas. Mrs. Olson helped the children to excel in music, creative arts, sports, and of course academics. She also instilled in them the pride of their heritage. The children, whenever they performed in a school activity, were encouraged to wear their bracelets and beadwork. The school was closed in 1963 when the

Hochungra Indian School. Jackson County, operated 1932-1963. All Winnebago students. Emma Olson, teacher.

From Betty Epstein.

Indian Agency, The Department of Interior, and the State Department of Public Instruction integrated the children into the white community.

Hugunin School
LaPrairie & Rock Townships, Rock County[5]

Most country schools have more than one life—after serving as schools they become homes, farm buildings, museums or the like. The Hugunin School building had two lives as a school. It first opened before 1864. It was then a one-room building with a dirt floor. J.V. Hugunin offered a more centrally located site for the school, as many people wanted, at no charge, about 160 rods to the south. The only restriction was that at anytime the site was not used for school purposes it would revert back to his farm.

Everyone agreed it was a good idea. They moved the school to the new location in 1900 by placing poles under the building to act as rollers, and then hitching four horses to the building. A wooden floor and several other improvements were added at this time. In those days, the older boys attended school in the winter months because they were needed on the farms in the spring, summer, and fall. If possible, a man teacher was hired for the winter terms as the big boys "got a little rough and rowdy at times."

In 1917 the school closed for lack of attendance, and children were sent to Janesville to attend classes. The school district paid tuition of $10 per student but by the late 1930s the tuition had risen to $60 per student, and taxes became a great burden for the farmers in the district. So they reopened the Hugunin School which had been closed for twenty-four years. Now the problem was too large an enrollment, with fifty children in one small building with one teacher.

After many heated debates, part of the district was annexed to Janesville, and the rest consolidated with LaPrairie District in 1956. The school was closed and returned to the Hugunin farm, as earlier stipulated. The school was converted into a home in 1957.

Louisville School
Town of Dunn, Dunn County[6]

The first Louisville School was a log building constructed in 1858, 16 x 24 feet. A seat was built around the walls, and two rows of combination plank desks and seats were in the center. The first teacher was

Richfield School, Washington County, c.1893.

From Marlene Reinders.

Nettie Barnum.

Back of the school, a high board fence stretched from the school building to the rear fence. Its purpose was to separate the boys' side of the playground from the girls.

A stove was located in a hole under the schoolhouse. The teacher carried a lantern to the dark dungeon under the school to build the fire each morning. She used a draw shave to make pine slivers that served as kindling for starting the fire.

In the early years there were no grades, and no report cards. There was first level of reading, and so on. At the completion of eight years, pupils were given a rigorous test in the subjects they had been taught.

The teacher lived with various families in the community. The custom was for the teacher to have the spare bedroom, usually off the parlor where no fire was kept. The winter nights were long and chilling.

Remembering her first year of teaching there, Myrtle Cotts commented, "The building was old and it creaked. The lamps were oil; their odor was stronger than their candlepower. No one had better ones."

In 1921, just before a Christmas program, the school burned. Over the holidays a tar paper shack was built and it was used for the remainder of the year. In 1922 a new brick school was constructed with a basement, including a well and a furnace. The Louisville School merged with the Downsville District in 1960. Since then, each year on the Saturday after the Fourth of July, former students, neighbors and teachers gather at Wakanda Park to recall memories of former school days.

Lower Wilson Creek School
Troy Township, Sauk County [7]

Built in 1856, the first school, 15 x 18 feet, was constructed of logs. The site for the building was purchased from a Mrs. Wheeler for one cent. Miss Crandall was the first teacher and received the handsome sum of $8.00 per month. She boarded with her students' families.

The next school on the site, also of logs, was larger, 20 x 22 feet. Logs for the building were purchased from local residents for fifty cents each. The wife of a school district officer, Mrs. Robinson, claimed, in 1908, that the school "is as warm and comfortable and as good as a $2,000 house. It is not on the main road which prevents teams from being bothered with the scholars as so often occurs." W.H. Lonsdale taught in the new school receiving $26 a month for a five month term.

This school became the last log schoolhouse in Sauk County. The *Baraboo News*, 1909, reported, "The age of the old log home, the old

Lower Wilson Creek School, Sauk County, 1911.

From Sauk County Rural Schools History Project, William C. Schuette.

barn and old log schoolhouse is forever gone. Probably never again will there be built in Sauk County a building of logs to be used as a place of learning. Amongst the older inhabitants, who does not recall the spelling schools, the literaries, and other evening gatherings in these formidable structures built on the outer rim of civilization."

The old log school was condemned in 1918 and moved to a site about four miles northeast of Spring Green. A new stucco-covered wood frame schoolhouse was constructed in 1918 and served until 1935 when it burned. It was replaced with a brick structure that included a basement—a vast improvement over the humble log building of 1856. Lower Wilson Creek School joined the River Valley District in 1960, operated one more year, and closed. The building became a home.

North Bend School
Jackson County[8]

The original school building, shared by students of North Bend and Wilson Creek, was built in 1861. The site was near the creek, west of the North Bend Cemetery.

Bert Gipple, a former resident of North Bend and later publisher of the *Galesville Republican* newspaper, at an April 15, 1938 anniversary celebration said, "The little building which stood below the North Bend cemetery, and which district was named Hard-Scrabble, a shabby little structure it was, unpainted with some of the siding gone from the entrance, its rough plastered walls and pine benches nailed to the floor, yet to me it was a school in every sense of the word. It was there I received my education. And let me say right here, that although the school was not even graded, and examinations unheard of, there was something about the education I and other boys [and girls] received, that is not in the courses today, with all the fads and frills. That was to learn to get back on your feet if you were knocked down, and not whimper about it. Also, if the teacher 'tanned' you, not to go home and complain to Ma and Pa."

In the early days, boys, some as old as eighteen or twenty, attended. Generally men teachers were hired for the winter term, and women for the summer. Younger children attended during the summer sessions.

A new, larger and more modern school was built in 1904, and the old school was torn down. Because it was located in a village, and two rooms were in operation at the time, the school was classified as a state graded school in 1948-49.

Hillside School, Sauk County, 1907.

From Sauk County Rural Schools History Project, William C. Schuette.

Burritt School, Dane County, c.1950.

From Mrs. Gerhard R. Schedel who graduated in 1927. Her parents attended 1889-1893, and her children graduated 1959-1962.

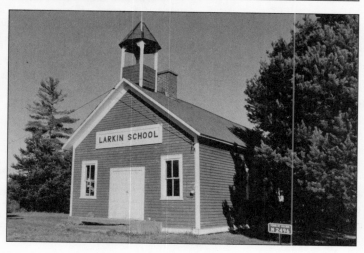

Larkin School, Price County.

Photo by Steve Apps.

Teacher salaries in 1881-82 were $28 per month for the school term; in 1902 teachers received $30.00, by 1918 the teacher's salary had climbed to $69.30, in 1938 it was $85 per month, and in 1948, $245 per month.

The school closed in 1966 and the equipment and building were sold at auction. The building sold for $2,200. Florence Heineck Spors, who contributed this information, attended the North Bend School from 1934 to 1942, when she graduated.

Pleasant Ridge School
Beetown Township, Grant County [9]

True worth is in being, not seeming; In doing each day that goes by Some little good, not in dreaming Of great things to do by and by.

—Alice Carey

Pleasant Ridge School opened in 1870. In this community, about five miles southwest of Lancaster, approximately one hundred African-American freed or escaped slaves settled. The community included, in addition to the school, a church and many small farms scattered over the rolling hills. Many believe that this was the first integrated school in Wisconsin, with both white and black children attending. The *Flora Fountain School*, also located in Beetown township, had black children attending as late as 1942, when Hazel Udelhoven taught there. She also recalled the one non-landowner African man who lived "in very meager circumstances not far from the school." Hazel said, "He worked as a farm hand when various farmers in the district needed him for cropping, plowing, hay making, threshing, etc. at a time when the going wage was about one dollar a day, your dinner at noon, and supper at night.

"One fall day, as he often did, he came at noon to the school when I and the pupils were eating lunch out on the schoolhouse step. Being a frequent visitor the children looked forward to his coming. Often he received a handout. Visiting with him was interesting and all the children called him by name, Charlie. He enjoyed the various games with the children and teacher such as anti-over, squat tag, free tag, and prisoner's base.

"Being a new teacher in the district one of those first days after Charlie had gone, one child said, 'You know, Mrs. Udelhoven, Charlie has "taking ways," but my dad doesn't care because Charlie is a good worker.' People around here knew about his 'taking ways' but didn't care because he was always willing to work and help out. It seems he often raided chicken houses."

Quarry School
Waukesha County [10]

The first school, located southeast of the present site, was log and began operating in 1849. The first recorded minutes, September 24, 1849, stated, "There are no outdoor conveniences for the different sexes, no blackboard, no entry or closet, no ground belonging to the district." The building itself was said to be in very poor condition with an estimated value of five dollars.

Salary for the teacher was $15 per month, with yearly total expenditures amounting to $50. The minutes also stated, "Resolved that each family furnish one-half cord good hardwood per scholar, cut two feet long, well fitted for stove, also to pile the same. If anyone fails to furnish his proportion of wood as stipulated, the District Board shall furnish it and the delinquent will pay .75 per cord."

A blackboard and outline maps were available in the school by 1851. In 1853, the Board began planning for a new school but shelved its plans until after the Civil War. The Board recommended raising $1,600 to build a new stone building. It was completed in 1868. This was the same year that stone quarries in the area opened and began flourishing. In 1878 an addition was added to the school, providing a second room.

In 1924 the school was officially listed as Quarry School. Quarries had always influenced the school, including the ethnic make-up of its students. Polish people came first to work in the quarries, then Italians, all mixing with the various ethnic groups that had settled to farm in the area. At one time the school had as many as ninety children under one teacher. The school closed in 1959.

Richmond Island School
Walworth County [11]

Because of a fire in 1918, this school was left without a building. Gail Olson Folkers tells the story: "On this particular day in February, 1918, the education of youngsters was put aside for their safety. The schoolhouse was on fire! It was the fault, no doubt, of an overheated stove and chimney.

"My grandfather, Dewey Olson, looked up from his farm work and started running down County Trunk P to the smoking scene. His neighbor, Morris Johnson, joined him. Both of these gentlemen were con-

Wakefield School, 1893. Now part of Folklore Village, Dodgeville.
A "life in a one-room school" program offers children a taste of earlier school days.

Photo by Steve Apps.

Dodd School, Fond du Lac County, 1949.

From Aileen Straseski.

Wiota School, Lafayette County, 1911. Closed in 1975. Today, school is part of Wiota Recreation Park.

Photo by Steve Apps.

cerned for the safety of the children, and the teacher, Mildred Knoll. It was apparent that the school would be a total loss. How would they finish the school year?

"My grandmother, Lizzie Holloway Olson, had been a teacher before her marriage and realized the importance of an education, so she offered her parlor as the substitute school room until the end of the term. It was an ideal location. There was an outside door leading to the parlor. The pump organ that her parents had bought her when she was ten years old would supply the music.

"Twenty desks replaced the horsehair sofa, chair, the what-not, and other antique pieces of furniture. A bucket for drinking water and dipper were added. The fire in the wood burning stove was started early each morning before school by my grandmother. After the students arrived, the mahogany doors were slid shut so that the remainder of the house was free from daily recitation.

"The students ice skated during recess on a frozen pond in the cow pasture. My grandfather put on his skates and joined them. In the spring the scent of lilacs and new farm soil being tilled would flow through the open windows."

The teacher received $50.05 per month. She was excused from building fires during the time they met at the Olson house. The Olson's received $43.10 for the use of their parlor as a school room.

Rogers School

District No. 2, Town of Dayton, Waupaca County [12]

Lillie Ann Rasmussen attended this school, graduating in 1939. So did her parents, her older brother and younger sister (to third grade when the school closed). The school records go back to 1869.

"When I attended," Mrs. Rasmussen said, "There was only one room, the heat was a large jacketed stove in the back of the room. There were blackboards across the front and a small one on each side. Water was carried from an outside pump into a stoneware bubbler. Coats were hung on hooks in the opposite rear corner from the stove. There were two front entrance doors, but usually only one was used.

"A woodshed was next to the school and wood was deposited in a woodbox inside the school. Two outside toilets were on the back of the property, one for the boys and one for the girls. These were in use all the years and never improved upon. There was a merry-go-round, and a swing from a tree for student recreation. In the winter time we skied on a hill back of Wilde's property. During our hour noon, we would eat fast and then head the quarter mile to the hill."

"The school had an outside bell that the teacher rang ten minutes before school started so we could make it back in time. We also played Fox and Geese on trails we made in the school yard snow. In the summer there was Hide and Go Seek, Anti-I-Over the woodshed with a ball, and Prisoner's Goal, with the school building and the woodshed serving as goals."

"We also played softball, not enough kids for two teams, so we played work-up; when you finally got up to bat, if you struck out you then went back out as a fielder to the outfield to gradually work your way up again."

The school closed in 1940 when it was consolidated with Pleasant Valley School. Written in the school deed was the provision that if the building was no longer used as a school the land would revert back to the farmer who donated it. In 1948 an auction was held and the school building sold.

Round Lake School
Town of Trade Lake, Burnett County [13]

Records for the Round Lake School go back to 1878, but there was an older school located southeast of the present schoolhouse. In the early years, the school term was five months. The winter term began the first Monday of January and went on for three months. The summer term was two months, beginning in May. Generally, men taught the winter term, and women the summer term. In 1882 teachers' salaries were not to exceed $30 per month and district school taxes were $15 annually. At the annual meeting, the voters contracted for someone to cut and haul five cords of wood to heat the school for $3.50.

In 1890 there was concern about ventilation in the school. A trap door was cut in the roof to remedy the situation. In 1879, when someone inquired about water for the school, the reply was "get water at the most convenient place."

In 1901 a new school building was approved at a cost not to exceed $650 and to be ready before February 1, 1903. The building was to be on one acre of land, and 28 x 40 feet.

The new school opened in February, 1903 with 110 school age children in the district, sixty-three boys and forty-seven girls. The district bought and installed a bell in 1904, for $45, and in 1906 bought eight reflector wall lamps, and dug a new well. The district also voted at the annual meeting to place six new hitching posts on the school ground. They were to be eight feet apart and not less than six inches in diameter. A furnace was added to the school in 1908.

A full basement was built in 1934 and the building was wired for electricity in 1939. In 1951, Round Lake was integrated with the Frederic Common School District. At this time the school was remodeled with a new well, new sewer system, a fire proof furnace room, new playground equipment and a modern kitchen for school lunches. The school closed in 1953.

The school had always been the center of community activities. Organizations meeting there included the Farmers Union, 4-H, and the Parent Teachers Association that was organized to support the hot lunch program that had begun in 1949. After closing, the school continued to house sixth grade classes from the Frederic School for a few years. But then it closed for good and is now a home and antique shop.

Woodprairie School
Western Taylor County [14]

Woodprairie School opened on September 13, 1913 with Dorthea Heagle as teacher. She had seven pupils that first year, three boys and four girls. One was in grade six, three in grade four, one grade two and one in grade one. By April, two students withdrew, leaving five. Attendance was always a problem, but two students managed not to miss one day. Of those who continued all year, one missed forty-five days.

Miss Heagle received a salary of $45 per month, which amounted to $2.50 per day. In addition to teaching, she was expected to do all janitorial work. She noted in her year end report that the school library included forty-two books; the general condition of the school building was good, but needed plastering; and the condition of the out buildings was good. She also noted one visit from the county superintendent and five visits from district school board officers.

Wiota School
Lafayette County [15]

The first school in Wiota began operation in 1833 and was taught by George Cubbage. It likely operated with private funds. The first public school in Wiota, built sometime after 1848, was located northwest of the present building, which was constructed in 1911 at a cost of $2,000. The school closed several years later, after becoming a part of the Darlington and Black Hawk Districts in 1967. Today the school is part of the Wiota Recreation Park.

In an 1891 school report, the following statistics were noted:

> Number of days taught 79
> Number of scholars enrolled 60
> Average daily attendance 43
> Scholar not absent during term: Roy Pinney.
> R.J. Gilmore, teacher.

Chapter Notes

1. From Leona Weber, Markesan.

2. From Florence Spors, Onalaska.

3. From *The Midweek Lakeshore Chronicle*, September 11, 1991.

4. From Betty Epstein, Millston.

5. From Gwen Daluge, Janesville. *In LaPrairie Country Schools*, 1982.

6. From Janet Creaser, Menomonie.

7. Rural School Research Committee. *Good Old Golden Rule Days: A History of Sauk County Wisconsin Country Schools*. Baraboo, WI: Sauk County Historical Society, 1994, pp. 214-215.

8. From Florence Spors, Onalaska.

9. From Hazel Udelhoven, Lancaster.

10. From Joy Buslaff, Big Bend and prepared by Charlotte Boyd McCombe and Mabel Chapman.

11. In Jane Rahn, *Good Old Golden Rule Days*. Elkhorn, WI: Walworth County Historical Society, 1994, p. 10.

12. From Lillie Ann Rasmussen, Scandinavia.

13. From Shirley Ganter, Amery and Carolyn Wedin, Whitewater.

14. Material from Paul Nagel, Eau Claire.

15. From Lucile Bisegger, Marjean Bondele, and Harriet Halloran. *Wiota: William S. Hamilton's Diggings—1828-1993*. Gratiot, WI: Self published, 1993.

Modern Day One-Room Schools

The one-room schools in the upper Midwest are nearly all closed, except for here and there a privately operated one. The privately operated ones generally are sponsored by various religious groups. For instance, the Amish communities scattered throughout the region often operate one-room schools, some of them nearly identical to the one-room schools that operated throughout many of the northern and eastern states until the middle 1900s. They have no electricity, no indoor plumbing, and depend on wood burning stoves for their heat. Some of them are even constructed of logs.

One-room public schools are extremely rare, however there is an interesting one operating on an island in Lake Superior.

Pledge of Allegiance, La Pointe School, Madeline Island, 1994. An operating one-room school.

Photo by Steve Apps.

The School on Madeline Island

La Pointe School is found on Madeline Island, in the Apostle Island chain and about two miles across the unpredictable waters of Lake Superior from Bayfield. It is a kindergarten through seventh grade school, with all of the children working together in one room. At this writing, the school included four kindergarten students, two first graders, three second graders, two third graders, three fourth graders, one fifth grader and one sixth grader, for a total of sixteen students. Eighth grade and high school students ride the ferry to Bayfield each morning where they attend school, returning to the island again in the afternoon.

Early Schools on Madeline Island [1]

La Pointe School, Madeline Island, 1994. An operating one-room school with grades kindergarten through seven.

Photo by Steve Apps.

Ojibways were Madeline Island's early inhabitants. The first white people on the island were French traders who began arriving in the middle 1600s to trade for furs with the Indians. In 1693, Pierre LeSueur arrived and built a fort on the southern tip of the island which was abandoned in 1698 when the market for furs declined. A new fort was built in 1718 on the western shore of the island.

The first schools on the island were mission schools. Trader families, Lyman and Truman Warren, convinced a lay teacher from the Protestant mission school on Mackinac Island to come to Madeline Island which he did in 1830. Curriculum at the mission school included lessons in Chippewa and in English, simple arithmetic and religious exercises.

A Catholic mission school began in 1835 under the leadership of Reverend Frederick Baraga. With the treaty of 1854, many of the Ojibway left Madeline Island for Red Cliff and Odanah.

Bay View School was the first public school on the island. It was built in late 1872 or early 1873 on the west side of the island, in La Pointe. Cost of the land for the school was $525. The 1880 census revealed that thirty-three children had attended school during the previous year. The school district included most of the other twenty Apostle Islands as well as Madeline Island.

Meanwhile, people on other parts of the island were complaining that their children had to travel too far to school, and that an additional school ought be built. In 1897, the original school district was divided into two, and The Christensen School was built on the south side of the island. Ten students attended this school in its first year.

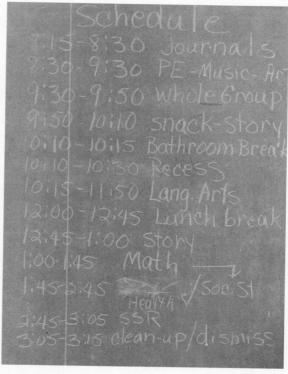

Daily schedule, LaPointe School, Madeline Island, 1994.

Photo by Steve Apps.

In 1904, the town of La Pointe was once more petitioned concerning school districts, this time to divide the town into three school districts instead of two. A third school, Lake View School, was constructed on the east end of the island, on what is now known as School House Road. This rather small school enabled students on the north and east end of the island to attend school regularly because it was within easy walking distance for most of them. The school soon became the center of community activities as well, with dances, and even church services held there during the summer months.

The old Bay View School closed in 1927 and was renamed Memorial Hall. It was used as a community center for many years and in 1960 became a public library. Meanwhile, a new Bay View School was built in La Pointe and was ready for students by the 1927-1928 school year. This school is the present center section of La Pointe School.

Both Lake View and Christensen Schools closed in 1938, with all of the students now attending Bay View School. In that year, an additional room was added to Bay View School to accommodate the extra students, and two teachers were hired. One taught grades one through five, the other six through ten. Ninth and tenth grade instruction was offered on alternative years; ninth one year, tenth the next.

With declining enrollments, Bay View School once more became a one-room, one-teacher school in 1947-48. In 1950, La Pointe School District Number Four was dissolved and attached to Joint School District Number One, which included the city of Ashland and six other towns. (Madeline Island is in Ashland County, although Bayfield is but two miles away by water.) The school was renamed La Pointe. With increases and decreases in students over the years, the school varied from a two-room, two-teacher school to a one-room, one-teacher school. A gymnasium was added to the school building in 1981.

Present Day La Pointe School

Upon visiting the brightly decorated school room at the beginning of the school day, children were quietly working at their desks. "The children are writing in their journals, and doing silent reading," Kathy Klein, La Pointe's teacher told me. "It helps to settle the children down, and gets them going into their day's work."

Soon, all the students were standing, and one of them led the class in reciting the Pledge of Allegiance to the flag. As in country schools of the past, big and little students worked together, helped each other with lessons, and played together during recess. A physical education teacher from Bayfield was in charge of the recess, leading the children in a variety of active games.

Different from one-room country schools of an earlier era, Klein had considerable help from the school district—a part of the Bayfield school district since 1987. A teacher's aid (one of the mothers) worked with several students, an intern worked with several others. One day a week an art teacher from Bayfield worked with the students, as did a music teacher for a half-day a week. The physical education teacher spent three mornings a week with the La Pointe students. There was also a part-time cook, and a part-time custodian, plus several parent volunteers. Yet, the school was essentially a one-room school operating

All words are pegs to hang ideas on.

—Beecher

like the hundreds of other country schools now closed.

"Teaching all seven grades is quite a challenge," Klein said. "I have to do a lot of integrating so I'm not spreading myself too thin. If I went back to teaching a one-grade classroom, it would be a piece of cake."

Before coming to La Pointe, Klein taught three years in Rhinelander and one and a half years in Bayfield. 1994-1995 was her eighth year at La Pointe.

"I select a theme each year," she said. "Something that can cut across all the grades. For example, last year we did a flight unit. We studied bird flight with the younger kids, and moved up to rockets with the older ones. Everything in our reading and writing had to do with flight. At the end of the unit, the older kids put together rockets and we had a rocket blast-off day."

We talked about advantages and disadvantages of attending a one-room school. The most obvious advantage for the children who live year-round on the island is the easy access to the school. The trip across two miles of Lake Superior waters, particularly in the late fall and winter months, can be at best a challenge, and at worst dangerous and life-threatening. But there are many other advantages as well, related Klein.

Children working at La Pointe School, Madeline Island, 1994.

Photo by Steve Apps.

Kathy Klein, teacher at La Pointe School, Madeline Island, 1994.

Photo by Steve Apps.

"We have a real strong parental support group. The parents are really into their child's education. The children learn how to work together; it's almost like a family unit. I can highly individualize my teaching. I can shift children around based on their ability not on the grade they are in. The children also become independent learners. I haven't got enough time to spend with the older students, so they learn to do much of the work by themselves. They help out the younger kids who need help, particularly with subjects like reading."

There were disadvantages in attending this fairly isolated one-room school on an island. "The kids are a little shy, a little less socially inclined when they go over to Bayfield for activities with the children there. When they're out here they seem real comfortable in their social atmosphere, but when they go to Bayfield, they're a little more reserved. They are real comfortable with a small group, but in a larger setting, they become a little intimidated."

Living in Bayfield, Kathy Klein traveled across the two miles of Lake Superior twice a day. In warm weather, the trip was by ferry and usually uneventful unless there was a storm. As a "frequent floater" she was entitled to special ferry boat rates. The school district paid for her trip to and from school.

In late fall, winter, and in early spring, the trip across was more of a challenge. "Clear, cold days in winter are the best," Klein related. The ice is then thick enough to drive to and from the island. Crews keep an ice road plowed and open to the island. But even in winter there are surprises.

"One year when I was driving," she said, "they had plowed two roads. One had cracked up and they plowed a new one. So I came down to the ice and it was blizzard conditions, a white-out on the ice. I drove out there, and I didn't know which road I was on. I kept going, hitting potholes until I finally arrived on the other side. I found out the next day that I was driving between the two roads. That night I followed the van back (vans make the trip regularly in winter between the mainland and the island) because it was still snowing and blowing hard."

When the ice was not frozen deep enough to support a car, the trip across was made with a wind sled, a canvas-topped boat on wheels powered by a propeller. The machine hauls from twelve to fifteen people sitting on benches. "It's a cold and windy ride," Klein said. "But there seldom is more than a day a year when I can't make it to school."

I asked her what she liked about one-room school teaching, on an island, with sometimes hair-raising trips across Lake Superior to arrive at work (compare her commute with the typical complaints of bumper-to-bumper traffic on auto clogged highways).

"It's the challenge," she said. "I'm afraid if I went back to a regular classroom, I'd get bored. Because I've got the same kids every year, I have to change the curriculum, and that's what I do every year. I also have the freedom to organize the curriculum the way we want it."

The children were doing well with their academics. A recent class of third graders traveled over to Bayfield for the state third grade reading test. Almost all of them got one hundred percent on the test. One of the slowest readers got only four wrong.

Until a bridge is built from the island to the mainland (no one is talking about doing it), or the population on the island declines, the La Pointe one-room school will continue to operate. Everyone, especially the teacher, will collect new stories about winter and the trip across the ice. And the children will learn as children before them did, in one-room with all of the children in the community present.

What you are to be you are now becoming.

—Anonymous

Home Schooling [2]

Several thousand students are taught each year by their parents, who, for an assortment of reasons, choose to keep them out of the organized school systems in the state. One home school family has gone a step further. Vern and Jean Elefson of Prescott provided home schooling for their two boys in the Trimbelle Town Hall, which was set up like a traditional one-room schoolhouse. Jean Elefson was the teacher, and her two boys were the only students. Jean Elefson, a former UW-River Falls Agricultural Journalism professor, attended a one-room country school when she was a child.

The 1924 town hall had the basic necessities for schooling. It had two rows of old-fashioned school desks, an American flag, a wood burning stove, and a stack of wood piled in the corner.

The curriculum Elefson followed included speaking, listening, arithmetic, science and social studies. When the boys were at home they worked on computer basics. She tailored the curriculum to fit the agricultural community in which they live, and related it to things they were doing as a family.

"Aside from giving them a sense of history, by using the one-room schoolhouse setting, we're also trying to instill a respect for the environment, for family, and for the importance of agricultural communities in our country," said Elefson.

"These days kids from farm families are going to school in town where they are often looked down on as socially 'un-cool.' I think its partly because examples from agriculture are rarely used any more in reading, writing, social studies, math and science classes. I start right at the beginning with the alphabet, using words like 'ax', 'beets', and 'carrots', for their A, B, C's. It's not that we don't want our children to learn about the world of business and industry or about advances in technology or medicine. We just think they also need to know about the major roles that agriculture, environment, and family play in all our lives."

Jean Elefson and sons, Prescott. Jean conducts home schooling in the Trimbelle Town Hall which is set up as a one-room school.

Photo by Jeff Milfred.

The Elefson's also did many things as a family, including taking nature hikes, and involving the boys in the operations of their forty-acre farm where they learned practical ideas about farming.

Some worry that home-schooled children, such as the Elefsons, will grow up with inadequate social skills. Each Monday the Elefson boys attended a story-hour at the Prescott Library where they have developed friendships with other children. They also met and played with other children through their church and through social activities that the Elefsons set up. The Elefsons believed there was something special about the one-room country schools, and they wanted to capture a little of it for their children.

Chapter Notes

1. From *Madeline Island Schools and Highlights of Island History.* LaPointe, WI: Madeline Island Historical Preservation Association, Inc., 1992.

2. In part from Jeffrey Milfred, "Home Schooling: Unique Settings, Creative Choices," *Prescott Journal.* September 29, 1994.

Consolidation

Imagine the following meeting. It is a crisp fall evening in 1953. Voters in the Chain O' Lake School District in Waushara County are gathered for a special informational meeting to discuss why their country school should close and consolidate with the Wild Rose District. An outside speaker, a specialist in educational reform, has come to explain the advantages of busing the Chain O' Lake pupils three to five miles to the more modern grade school in the village. School bus service had begun in 1947, to transport the high school students in the district, so district voters already knew something about busing, both its advantages and considerable disadvantages.

Maple Grove School, Rusk County. Closed 1955 and torn down in early 1960s.

From Nora Walnoha.

Nearly as many people pack into the school building that evening as do for the annual Christmas program. All want to hear about the fate of their school, and a majority want to know how they can stop the landslide of country school closings that are already taking place throughout the state.

Arlin Handrich, a member of the local school board, calls the meeting to order and then introduces the speaker. The young educational researcher from Madison begins by talking about the number of school districts in the state that have already consolidated, and the almost uniformly positive feedback he and other researchers are receiving from children and especially from their parents when children attend newer, more up-to-date consolidated schools.

The speaker points out that children attending the larger schools do better academically, proven repeatedly by tests scores. He goes on to say that the larger schools provide more opportunities in music—children can learn to play an instrument. More opportunities in art—there are classes in drawing. Up-to-date ideas about science—modern equipment is available.

Quite a number of heads are shaking in agreement as the speaker continues. "Additionally," he says, "your children will participate in an organized physical education program."

"What's that?" one of the fathers asks.

"It's exercises and games like basketball and volleyball—it's an opportunity for children to get into physical shape."

A quiet comes over the school room as people allow the words from the educational reform expert to come down from the ceiling and settle in among the seats. Then there are looks of utter disbelief.

A deeply tanned farmer stands up, thrusts his huge calloused hands in his bib overall pockets, clears his throat and says, "You mean to tell us that our kids are supposed to ride a school bus for a couple hours so they can run around a gym? Right now they help with the morning chores,

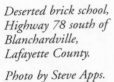

Deserted brick school, Highway 78 south of Blanchardville, Lafayette County.

Photo by Steve Apps.

walk to school, then walk home in the afternoon, and help with the evening chores. I don't think there's much of a problem with them being in physical shape." After this exchange, everything the young researcher said was suspect.

This meeting was typical of hundreds of meetings held during the years of rural school closings and district consolidation. To understand something of the vastness of the consolidation task, we need to look at some numbers. According to the United States Office of Education, in 1935-1936, 121,311 one-teacher schools operated in the United States. Approximately 91,000 of these were in the Middle West. Illinois and Iowa each had more than 9,000 school districts.[1]

In 1939-1940, the year I was a first grader in a country school, Wisconsin had 7,325 school districts, including 258 in Dane County, 194 in Dodge, 228 in Grant, 158 in Vernon, 109 in Waushara, and 12 in Florence County.[2] Just two years before that, 1937-1938, Wisconsin reached its peak of 7,777 school districts with 6,181 one-room schools.[3]

In 1993, there were 418 school districts in Wisconsin, 6,907 less than in 1939, and there were essentially no one-room schools.[4]

The fate of empires depends upon the education of youth.

—Aristotle

Rural-Urban Differences

Through the early and mid-1900s, it became clear that the differences between one-room country schools and the village and city schools were growing larger, and that change was necessary. Until the beginning of World War II many farmers still farmed with horses, milked cows by hand, and essentially followed the farming practices of their fathers and grandfathers. The Great Depression of the 1930s put much of the country on hold, with millions of people in the big cities unemployed. Rural people had work, food, and their country schools.

However, just as farming practices had changed little over the years, few changes occurred in the country schools. More dramatic changes had occurred in the village and city schools. These schools usually had central heating, running water, and electricity as well as better paid teachers, larger libraries, and a broader curriculum.

Because of their isolation, one-room schools had a less visible problem that former students later identified. Bill Stokes attended LaFollette School in Barron County. He said, "We were isolated from the rest of the world. To the kids living in town, even in Barron which had a population of only a thousand or so, we were not worldly. We weren't as good as the city kids in many respects. This is something I have been trying to overcome all my life. It is built into who I am. Maybe it explains why I always wanted to move to yet another large city [After graduating from college, Stokes was a journalist for newspapers in Stevens Point, Madison, Milwaukee and Chicago]. I wanted to prove that I could live and work in a big city, that a country kid could make it in an urban area. I'm still trying to do that I think."

Stokes continued, "We seldom met people outside our community. This led to poor social skills. I still feel uncomfortable in social settings, particularly with larger groups."

John Palmer, a long-time Dean of the School of Education at the University of Wisconsin-Madison, attended a one-room school in Illinois and related a similar concern. He said that a serious shortcoming of the country school was the social dimension. "I don't think I ever got over it, I still don't enjoy crowds," he said.

Country schools did not develop tolerance for different kinds of people and their many varying viewpoints, unless the community was more diverse than the typical rural community. Bill Stokes said he didn't learn to appreciate people different from him without always trying to decide whether they were better or worse off than he was. This was particularly true of his relationship with city people. "On the one hand you compared yourself to them in a negative way; they were so much better than you were. On the other hand, you were better than they were, particularly when it came to understanding the ways of the outdoors. You knew many skills from butchering a pig, and helping birth a calf to shocking grain and splicing a broken hay fork rope. You held these skills in high esteem, and you wanted to share them with city kids that you ran across in church, at the free movies, or perhaps in your 4-H club that included both country and city kids."

With the many societal changes swirling around, it became clear that changes were necessary in the one-room country schools. But for some national leaders, rural school had no redeeming qualities, and could not be improved.

Ellwood Cubberley, Professor of Education at Stanford University, writing in 1912, said, "The country school lacks interest and ideas; it suffers from isolation and from lack of that enthusiasm which comes only from numbers; and it realizes but a small percentage of its possible efficiency. Its site is usually unattractive; its building is too often a miserable, unsanitary box; it too often lacks the necessary equipment for proper instruction; its instruction is usually limited to the barest elements of an education, and lacks vocational purpose; its teacher is often

Beautiful lips are those whose words
Leap from the heart like songs of birds.
Beautiful hands are those that do
Work that is earnest, brave, and true.

—1904 text book

poorly trained or entirely untrained, and is poorly paid; the supervision provided is utterly inadequate, and usually exists only in name; and the management of the school is often of a very inferior type.... The children coming from the same little area, and often from related families, bring no interests to the school...the country school is poor, often miserably poor, and the numerous classes, overburdened programme, absence of equipment, and lack of ideas and impulses to action offer odds against which the best of teachers can make but little headway." [5]

A few educational leaders defended the country school, and pointed out its advantages. Homer Seerley, President of Iowa State Teachers College in 1913, wrote, "There is no cause for any apology for the necessary peculiarities of the country school. It is what it is, and it can be what it can be, because of these very individual characteristics that are sometimes unnecessarily deplored by those who do not recognize the efficiency and strength of its position as a factor in civilization. The distinctive mark of a country school is its normal and natural environment. It has thus far escaped the devitalizing influences that the artificial and the conventional can produce. It is strictly original in its characteristics and decidedly individual in its work and its development. Its strength lies in its closeness to nature, in its practical relation to the every-day occupations of everyone, and its possibilities for simplicity, sincerity, and sanity." [6]

In the eyes of many national educators, the one-room country school was beyond reform. There was only one solution. Small school districts should be consolidated, and the little cross-roads country schools should be closed.

Not A New Idea

The idea of consolidating school districts had been around a long time. In the 1848 and 1849 school laws, power was given to the township school superintendent to consolidate township school districts. In 1897, a law passed authorizing school district boards to work with adjoining districts so that children in those districts could attend the same school. There were several joint district schools in the state.

In 1899 a report on consolidation and free transportation to consolidated schools was prepared by the state superintendent of schools. He reported that "consolidation and free transportation of pupils wherever it was tried conserved the health of children, greatly increased the regularity of attendance, reduced the cost of maintaining schools, and systematized and improved instruction." [7]

Audubon School, Wood County. Now used as a hunting lodge.

From Jim Everts.

There was no evidence, however, of a groundswell of interest in school consolidation following the report. Transportation of pupils had always been a sticking point when school consolidation was discussed. Most parents did not feel good about having their children transported out of their neighborhoods, particularly when they could walk to a nearby one-room school. Imagine the transportation difficulties before automobiles and all-season roads.

Organizing Efforts [8]

Starting in 1904, a succession of state superintendents led the fight for school consolidation in Wisconsin. The Wisconsin legislature passed laws in 1907 and 1911 providing $75 and later $150 to a school district which would close its school and consolidate with another. Earlier laws, in 1860 and 1900 encouraged consolidation. All these laws proved futile because they were voluntary and most schools simply ignored them.

The disparities between rural and town schools continued growing larger, and the number of rural children attending high school remained at an extremely low level. In 1940, only fifty-two percent of Wisconsin's sixteen and seventeen-year-old farm children attended high school.

At the national level, the Committee on Rural Education, affiliated with the American Country Life Association, took up the problem of rural education in 1939. Roscoe Pulliam, chairman of that committee, said, "A real democracy must provide a good educational program for all children in all communities. Although the United States has provided reasonably good schools for most of its communities, there are many rural areas in this country where the schools have not been able to give the amount or kind of education needed by American citizens."[9] This report offered six recommendations to correct what the participants considered the major problems with rural education:

"1. The financial support of rural education is inadequate and unequal.

2. There are too many school districts.

3. Professional personnel for rural education is inadequate.

4. Teaching materials related to experiences of rural children are limited.

5. The rural school program is not coordinated with the other educational activities of the community.

6. War emergency problems in rural education are not receiving adequate attention."[10]

The report went to great lengths to explain how society and rural life were changing, and that rural education must keep up with the times. Point 2 in the report, by implication, recommended consolidating school districts in order to improve rural education.

Rural District System

The rural district school system frustrated educational reformers. Iman Schatzmann, in 1942, said, "Since the Constitution of the United States did not specifically provide for public education, the pioneer had to create such educational opportunities for his children as time and finances permitted. The American public school system has never been dominated by the federal government or by the church. Therefore education simply grew, district by district, like wild crops in untilled soil, according to local school arrangement made by groups of farm families. These rural school districts represented the smallest units of local government."[11]

Those who lived in rural areas took great pride in their schools, and were deeply involved in local school district affairs. For its time, it was a form of government that worked and worked well. But for those seeking educational change, the district was often seen as a major block. One team of writers said, "It is possible that the independent district was a mistake in the first place." [12]

New Laws

In 1939, the Wisconsin legislature finally accepted that local areas, on their own, were not going to change their schools. The legislature, in that year, began cutting school aids to schools with ten or fewer students, and no district could be created with an assessed valuation of less than $150,000. Also, under the provisions of this new law, the state superintendent of schools was authorized to attach to a neighboring district any district with less than $100,000 valuation.

The 1939 national Committee on Rural Education was followed by the first White House Conference on Rural Education held in October, 1944. A "Charter of Education for Rural Children" emerged from the conference. Some of its provisions included:

> "*Every rural child has the right to a satisfactory, modern elementary education.*
>
> *Every rural child has the right, through his school, to health services, educational and vocational guidance, library facilities, recreational activities and, where needed, school lunches and pupil transportation facilities at public expense.* Such special services, because they require the employment of specially qualified personnel, can be supplied most easily through enlarged units of school administration and the cooperation of several small schools.
>
> *Every rural child has a right to attend school in a satisfactory, modern building.* The building should be attractive, clean, sanitary, safe, conducive to good health, equipped with materials and apparatus essential to the best teaching, planned as a community center, and surrounded by ample space for playgrounds, landscaping and beautification." [13]

Without saying so directly, the conference was advocating school consolidation. Many of their recommendations were simply impossible for the current, small one-room country schools to adapt.

By 1944-45, only 884 small school districts had been abolished or attached to contiguous districts. Many people were angry about the 1939 law because they thought it gave too much power to the state and the state superintendent's office. No matter that the local districts, themselves, did not want to take the initiative to upgrade their schools. Whatever was happening with their schools, the local districts and their voters wanted a major say. In 1945, opponents of the superintendent attachment authority, as it was called, were successful in repealing the law.

By the end of World War II, an ever increasing number of people pointed out the disparities between the living standards of rural and urban people, including the ever widening variations between country, and village and city schools. The pressures were mounting to improve rural education. To do this, many people concluded that the small rural districts and the one-room school were standing in the way of progress and must be replaced. No one said this to rural people directly. Most knew better, because when rural people discovered they were going to lose their local school, they protested loudly. Closing the one-room schools was not going to be easy. Rural people knew that if they lost their school, they would lose the core of their community. The one-room school was an integral part of who everyone was. It defined not only the geographical location of a community, but it gave the community its identity. The country school was the link to a community's history, and through the community's children, it pointed to the future. To have a community without a school was like having a body without a soul. Rural people, who had attended the school just down the road, as did their parents and grandparents, could not envision their community without a school, no matter how powerful the arguments to close it.

Outside educational reformers didn't, wouldn't, or couldn't grasp this deeper level of love and concern for the one-room school. When they heard local people talking about their school in such personal terms, they dismissed the argument as old-fashioned, nostalgic, or blindly conservative and out of step with the times. Stanford's Professor Cubberly represented those who didn't understand these deeper values. About local school board members, he wrote, "One of the most serious obstacles to educational progress in the rural schools is presented by these hundreds of school trustees, who as a rule, know little about educational needs or progress. As a body they are exceedingly conservative, and hard to educate; they usually possess important powers; and, because they control the purse-strings, they frequently assume an authority unwarranted by their knowledge of school work."[14]

Those leading the charge for school consolidation soon discovered they had taken on a formidable task. A rational, logical, scientific approach where the test scores comparisons between those who attend-

*One thing at a time
And that done well,
Is a very good rule,
As many can tell.*

—1904 textbook

ed country schools and those who attended the village and city schools was not enough. Tampering with the soul of a community required more than logic and statistics.

Emeritus Professor Burton Kreitlow of the University of Wisconsin-Madison researched differences between rural and urban children. He said, "In the research reports that were beginning to come out, the academic achievement of students from one-room school weren't coming up. There was no question at all that academic achievement for students from larger schools was greater, particularly in the early years."

Beyond providing for enhanced academic opportunities, proponents of consolidation argued that children would be exposed to young people with a wider range of life experiences, and they would have more competition in their academic work. The school buildings would be better lighted, more adequately ventilated, include indoor plumbing, central heating, and a school lunch program. Supplies and equipment for learning would be more up-to-date, teachers would be better trained, and opportunities in such areas as art, music and physical education would be available for all students. With fewer grades to handle, teachers would have more time to give individual help.

When many of the country schools closed, the property returned to the original owners and the buildings were sold. The Rogers School in Waupaca County was sold at auction in 1948.

AUCTION SALE
School House and Supplies
Roger School Dist. No. 2, Town of Dayton

Located 11 miles Southwest of Waupaca on Highway 22 to Town Road, then ¾ miles West, or first Town Road West of Stratton Lake.

SATURDAY, NOV. 6   *1948*

What the advocates didn't say was some students would spend a hour or more each morning and evening bouncing around the country on rough dirt roads in a noisy school bus. No parent wanted to hear that their six-year-old must climb on a school bus in the dark and return in the evening in the dark. The thought of a school bus filled with children stuck in a snow drift on some remote Wisconsin road with the temperature dropping below zero was too much for many parents to even consider.

Advocates of consolidation also avoided talking about how decisions would be made in the larger, consolidated districts. Parents would surely not have as much say about the education of their children as they had under the old system. The chances that a member of the school board would be their neighbor were not great, and being able to pop in and talk to the teacher at anytime was simply not as easy. Besides, attending various parent functions became more difficult when the school was several miles away rather than at the crossroads across the cow pasture.

Some parents simply didn't want their kids going to a town school, where rural values were likely not understood or appreciated. In the 1940s, 50s and 60s, country kids were often looked down at by city kids. "Now we've got to put up with these country 'hicks,'" was often heard whispered around the village schools when they heard the country kids were coming to their school. Rural people had opposite perspectives. City kids were lazy and didn't know how to work; they had too many "things" and didn't appreciate working together as a family. Country kids would surely pick up some of these negative values from their urban school mates.

Many country people had another fear. It was expressed this way, "Once our children get to town, even if only for school, we'll lose them when they grow up. They won't want to work on the farm." Of course the reality of the times was that many of the farm boys and girls simply had to leave the farm; there was no room for them as smaller farms became larger, and fewer and fewer people lived on and made a living from the land.

Some of the advocates of consolidation said that combining school districts would lead to greater efficiencies, and that school taxes would go down. Farm people were very skeptical of this, and their skepticism was well placed. In most instances, school taxes went up after consolidation, not down.

The decision to consolidate the rural districts, and in many instances, integrate the rural children with nearby village children, thus became a far more complicated proposition than most people imagined it would. The issue quickly became more than increased academic opportunities and indoor toilets.

School Committees

To move the process of consolidation along, the Wisconsin state legislature, in 1947, directed each county board in the state to form a committee and develop a plan for the consolidation of the county's school districts. After holding hearings in the districts to be reorganized, the committees had the power to dissolve, alter, combine, or create school districts by majority vote of the committee membership. The committees were made up of six members elected by the county board. Half the members were to be from rural townships in the county. The county superintendent of schools, an elected position, was to serve as secretary of the committee, but did not have a vote.

The committee, in addition to its organization powers, also had financial incentive and penalties it could evoke. These included additional state aids for transportation.

The county school committee's task was tremendous. In 1948 Wisconsin still had more than 6,000 school districts, down only about 1700 from its peak number reached some ten years earlier. Further, the severely compromised 1947 law was to expire in 1949; some people considered it "emergency" legislation. Nevertheless, by 1949 several counties had moved well into school consolidation. Some of these counties to close schools included Forest, Jackson, Oneida, Vilas, La Crosse, Marinette, Trempealeau, Waushara, Bayfield, and Dane. Forest and Jackson counties had consolidated ninety percent of their districts by 1949.

A modified school consolidation law was passed in 1949, with the basic idea of the earlier law intact. One addition was the requirement that each school committee had to submit to the state superintendent of schools a reorganization master plan for its county by 1951. If the committee didn't comply, it could be dissolved and a new one formed. Thus a slow and always painful process of school closings and district reorganization began, going on for twenty years, with sour memories lingering to this day.

Wilmer Gorske, Superintendent of Schools in Green Lake County at that time, recalled the process used. He said, "School committees were created by Wisconsin Statute in the late 1940s to formulate a renewed system of education that would take us from 150 years of rural education to an urbanized industrial type of education that would develop after World War II. This new type of district would be called an 'Integrated District.'"

Today when we talk about integration we mean bringing together children of various ethnic backgrounds such as African-American, Native American, and so on. Then it meant bringing rural school districts together.

As in other Wisconsin counties, the Green Lake County Board elected the members of the school committee, attempting to represent a cross section of both city and country interests in Green Lake County. Each committee member had one vote, except for the county superintendent who was ex-officio. Philip Lehner, Princeton, was appointed chairman.

The committee was charged with developing a master plan for the

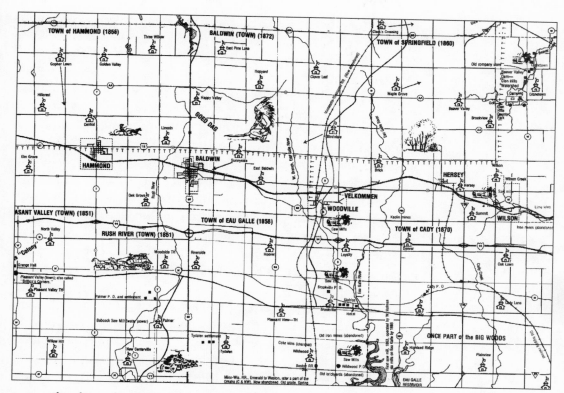

Partial map of St. Croix county showing locations of early country schools.

county by the early 1950s. The master plan should include: integrated K-12 districts for all areas of Green Lake County, school bus routes, approval of tuition and transportation costs, and approaches for meeting other educational goals.

As integration plans moved forward, every high school district in Green Lake County was looking for students and adding territory in order to increase their valuation and tax base. High school districts often competed with each other for certain areas. Gorske said, "Every high school was trying to attract students and this was no different in the township of Green Lake. Markesan and Green Lake High Schools were covering every road with school buses. Some roads were traveled with no student pick-ups just to say, 'This territory belongs to us.'"

An example of contested area was property in the township of Green Lake where property valuations were high because some of the land was on the shores of Big Green Lake. Any property that could be brought into a school district added to the increased valuation of the school district as well as adding students.

Gorske said, "One specific piece of land caught the attention of both Hal Hornby, Superintendent of Schools in Green Lake, and

Norman Larson, Superintendent of Schools in Markesan. This was 200 acres of land on the shoreline of Green Lake that had not yet been developed. It belonged to the Wabiszewski family associated with Maynard Electric Steel of Milwaukee. The Guderski family lived and worked on the land. Their children attended Markesan High School on a tuition basis—the money paid by the township of Green Lake for nonresidents of a high school. Each school district, at different times, had petitioned to add this property to their school districts. The Green Lake County School Committee held public hearings, but they couldn't decide to which district the land should be attached.

Mr. Gorske suggested, as a solution to the problem, that the owner of the property should help make the decision. Mr. Gorske proposed the Green Lake and the Markesan superintendents meet with members of the Wabiszewski family, explain their school programs, discuss property taxes, educational costs, each school's curriculum, and the prospects for future development."

"I traveled to Milwaukee," Mr. Gorske said, "and went down to South Milwaukee on 27th Street to the home office of Maynard Electric Steel. I met with a very elderly gentleman who I believe was Andrew Wabiszewski. I arranged to have Mr. Larson of Markesan and Mr. Hornby of Green Lake meet with Mr. Wabiszewski and have each one explain the advantages of joining their school district. Times and dates were arranged."

"The meetings were held with Mr. Wabiszewski in early November, at State Teacher's Convention time so no extra time was taken from daily work. The meetings were in private."

A few weeks later, Mr. Gorske and the committee received a one sentence reply to the meetings. Mr. Wabiszewski wanted his land in the Markesan School District, and that is where it was placed.

Once this decision was made, most of the township of Green Lake agreed to join the Markesan District, except for the south shore of Green Lake which joined the Green Lake District.

This is an example of thousands of such decisions that were made by county school committees throughout Wisconsin between 1947 and 1962. Not different from other county school committees, the Green Lake County Committee met for fourteen years and held more than 100 official meetings in every area of the county. In 1949 there were fifty-six school districts in the county. Upon completion of the committee's work in 1962, Green Lake County had four districts. The first district to reorganize was Princeton, but with several legal challenges, it was delayed

*So nigh is grandeur to our dust
So near is God to man,
When duty whispers low, "Thou must,"
The youth replies, "I can."*

*—Emerson
1888 Reader*

two years before it was recognized. Mr. Gorske became Elementary Supervisor for the Markesan School District in 1960. All County Superintendents of School lost their jobs after consolidation.

In 1942 Sauk County had 164 districts and 153 rural schools. By 1945 there were 115 rural schools, in 1959, sixty-four were open. In 1962 there were none. And so it went, county by county throughout the state.

Lingering Results

People in many Wisconsin rural communities remember vividly the days of school consolidation, and the many heated arguments that took place. Many rebelled then, and continue to despise the county school committees and the "arbitrary way" in which they made decisions. Estella Krohn Bryhn of West Salem recalled the 1950s this way. "Meetings were held far into the night. At one, a veteran township officer, with tears in his eyes, pleaded for the continuance of the rural school. He said the annual meeting in the rural school is 'the only true democracy left in America.' Another opponent of consolidation feared schools would become so large, so centralized, that people would have no voice in running them, and no control over the curriculum...." [15]

The County School Committees had a near impossible task. In some ways it was similar to meeting a grizzly bear in its den, and trying to convince the bear that life would be better in another den. Is it any wonder that the bear might growl and show its teeth. No one, especially not grizzly bears, wanted to be told that what they had was inferior, and they should change and all would be improved. Better to live with the devil you know than climb in bed with an angel who speaks nice words but hasn't walked in your shoes was the feeling of many rural people when the school consolidation people showed up at their doors.

Some communities never reached consensus on school consolidation. Some would have returned to the country school they once knew and so dearly loved in a minute, if they had been offered the opportunity. Others, as they looked around their communities and beyond, knew that their children needed an education that was more than the country school could provide. They fondly remembered their school days, the ringing of the school bell, the caring, motherly teacher, the long, but interesting walks to school, but they knew all of this was history. Something to remember fondly, and perhaps learn from, but not something that could be reconstructed. There were those who lamented the passing of the draft horse, my father was one of them, but he and I both knew that we must own a tractor to be a part of an ever-changing rural life. We kept horses for many years after we owned a tractor. There were tasks the horse could do that no tractor could. There were tasks the country school could perform that no large consolidated school could. Unfortunately, not until recently have people gone back to examine what took place in these country schools that has application today.

Chapter Notes

1. Iman Elsie Schatzmann. *The Country School: At Home and Abroad.* Chicago: The University of Chicago Press, 1942, p. 141.

2. *Wisconsin Official School Directory, 1939-1940.* Madison: State Department of Public Instruction.

3. William Thompson. *The History of Wisconsin: Volume VI, Continuity and Change, 1940-1965.* Madison, WI: State Historical Society of Wisconsin, 1988, p. 495.

4. *Wisconsin School Directory, 1992-1993.* Madison: State Department of Public Instruction.

5. Ellwood P. Cubberley. *The Improvement of Rural Schools.* Boston: Houghton Mifflin Company, 1912, pp. 13-14.

6. Homer Seerley. *The Country School.* New York: Charles Scribners Sons, 1913, p. 10.

7. Conrad E. Patzer. *Public Education in Wisconsin.* Madison, WI: State Department of Public Instruction, 1924, p. 192.

8. See William Thompson, pp. 495-506 for a useful discussion of legislation and related school consolidation issues.

9. Roscoe Pulliam. *Still Sits the Schoolhouse by the Road.* Chicago: The Committee on Rural Education, 1943, pp. v, 3-4.

10. *Ibid.*

11. Schatzmann, p. 139.

12. Horace M. Culter and Julia M. Stone. *The Rural School: Its Methods and Management.* Boston: Silver, Burdett and Company, 1913, p. 223.

13. Mildred Welch Cranston. *What Can We Expect of Rural Schools?* New York: The Woman's Press, 1948, pp. 24-25.

14. Cubberley, p. 7.

15. Estella Krohn Bryhn. *Early Schools of LaCrosse County.* West Salem, WI: Privately printed, 1985, p.182.

Learning From The Past

Round Lake School children, Burnett County, 1906.

From Carolyn Wedin.

With consolidation of rural districts, nearly all one-room country schools had closed by the 1960s. Educational reformers, policy makers, and many others had great expectations for an improved educational system. Some reformers gleefully proclaimed that the primitive and out-of-date country school had finally become a part of history. They saw one-room schools replaced by modern educational buildings with the most technologically advanced teaching aids. The great disparities between city and country schools would no longer exist. The weaknesses of one-room schools such as lack of plumbing, drafty, poorly heated buildings, inadequate libraries, and isolation from a broader world would be finally overcome.

Unfortunately, many of the strengths of one-room schools were left behind as well. Ben Logan said it well when he wrote about his country school experience, "We didn't know it at the time, but we just may have been participants in the best educational system ever devised. In that richly varied one-room community there was no artificial separation of children into good and bad, smart and dumb, young and old. We were all in it together. Subjects and years weren't tied into neat bundles. They were overlapped, so that there was only one subject: education."[1]

Strengths of One-Room Country Schools

One-room country school strengths that reformers overlooked or didn't understand included a focus on community, dedicated teachers, special classroom activities, low number of pupils in the school, development of a love for learning, learning how to deal with unexpected events, and a positive attitude about the importance of education.

Focus on Community

The one-room country school and the area around it were one. The community defined the school, and the school defined the community. During school district consolidation, many advocates of consolidation did not appreciate or understand the close relationship between the school and its community. Yet, this close relationship was viewed by rural people as the cornerstone for the country school's success.

The American Association of School Administrators, although they supported consolidation, did seem to understand the community's important role. In a 1939 document, they said:

> "Keep the schools and the government of the schools close to the people, so that the citizens generally, including the parents and taxpayers, may know what their schools are doing, and may have an effective voice in the school program....The relationship of the schools to the natural community and the closeness of the school to the people are of first-rate educational significance and are not to be sacrificed in the interest of 'efficiency.' If such a sacrifice is made to establish economical districts, we will find in a generation that something of deep significance which money cannot buy has been destroyed." [2]

School reformers demonstrated that village and city school children did better than rural one-room school children on academic tests, and that this was a sufficient reason to close the little country schools. Burton Kreitlow, a Professor of Education at the University of Wisconsin-Madison, researched this topic and affirmed academic test score differences. But he also discovered that rural children always

Stone School, Winnebago County, 1949. Jennie Frees, teacher.

From Marcie Kirk Apps.

scored higher than city children on surveys measuring personal security. Country kids were comfortable with their school and with their community. They knew that they were wanted, and that they mattered. Each of them knew that somebody cared about them, and that they belonged. They were all part of their rural community. They knew everyone, and everyone knew them. This may not have translated into higher academic test scores, but it did demonstrate that a good education was more than doing well on academic tests.

A community existed among the pupils as well. Children learned how to work and play together. After all, they were together with each other for eight years. Bigger kids looked out for littler kids. School yard bullies attended some schools, boys picked on girls, girls picked on boys, and big kids sometimes picked on little kids. But underneath, everyone cared about each other and they shared what they had with their fellow pupils.

Concern for community had other dimensions as well. What happened in the neighborhood, the work of the people who lived there, and the natural world of which the neighborhood was a part were integral to the school's curriculum. The walk to and from school, in all seasons of the year and in all kinds of weather, was a profound course in nature study. It was especially so when children were encouraged to record observations of new birds seen in the spring, of wildflowers when they first opened, and of the effects of weather changes.

Although the textbooks usually had an urban slant with few pictures or references to country life, the teacher, often born on a farm, used examples that fit a rural setting. In arithmetic, students talked about numbers of cows and loads of hay, and children were encouraged to share stories about happenings on their home farms.

Community also meant an unwritten partnership between the teacher and the pupils' parents. Parents were involved deeply in the education of their children. If the teacher had a problem with a youngster, she visited the parents and it was immediately straightened out. The teacher was in partnership with the school board, too. She knew them well, and expected and usually got their full support. For instance, in my country school the school board saw to it that the woodshed was filled with split oak wood each fall, that the schoolhouse floor was cleaned and oiled before school started each term, and that the stage for the Christmas program was put in place when the teacher wanted it.

Teachers

Teachers have always been central in schools. It was especially true in one-room country schools. Ask people what they recall about their schooling, and almost to a person they will remember one or more teachers that made a difference in their lives.

In today's educational context, computers and on-line services, videotape machines and individual audio stations, modern science labs, and shiny buildings all enhance learning. But never will a machine or a fine building replace a human being as a teacher. No computer or video tape machine has ever given a hug to a six-year-old with tears streaming down his face, or took the time to listen to the excitement of a ten-year-old who has just received a new puppy for her birthday.

To teach is to touch a life forever.

—Anonymous

The teacher was the soul of the one-room country school. Teachers knew their students and their students' families well. They knew their home circumstances, the joys and sorrows the families were experiencing. In some instances teachers had taught the parents of the children they were now teaching. Many teachers cared for their students as if they were their own.

With modern teacher training, teachers are well prepared in subject matter, in understanding child development, and in employing a variety of teaching strategies. But as many have long known, teachers who make a difference know more than subject matter and teaching strategies. They are concerned about what they do, and they care deeply for their students. Good teachers teach from the soul of who they are as they attempt to touch the soul of their students.

Most country school teachers fit the model of excellent teacher. A few, to be sure, were mean, incompetent and ought to have chosen other work. But these were clearly the few. The many were human beings trying to touch other human beings, and make a difference in their lives, often in near unbearable physical surroundings.

Classroom Activities

An unspoken set of rules existed in country schools that influenced all that went on there. Some of these rules included:

- Everyone can learn.

- We are here to help each other learn.

- Parents and teachers are partners.

- There are no divisions into bright and dumb, or winners and losers.

- Everyone respects everyone else, no matter what their religion, ethnic background or economic condition.

- Everyone respects the teacher.

- The material studied is mastered, from learning how to read to doing long division, from knowing the capitals of the states, to spelling.

- No one advances to another grade who is not ready to do so.

- No one graduates from eighth grade without meeting all the standards.

- Everyone is expected to work alone as well as with others.

- Everything is done on time, from the start of school in the morning, to the end of school in the afternoon.

Within these rules, country school pupils and their teacher were a family. They depended on each other. Older children helped younger children with assignments they found difficult. Also, by overhearing what the older students were studying, younger students knew what to expect. By listening to lower grades, upper grade students could review points they may have missed, or not fully understood when they studied it. Some said country school children learned to listen with both ears—one ear tuned to what they would learn next, the other listening to what they had previously studied.

All of the children helped with the necessary chores to keep the school operating: carrying in wood and water, pounding the erasers, cleaning the blackboards, sweeping out the outhouses and so on. Just as a family worked together, so did the school family work together.

Because of the small numbers, everyone had an opportunity to perform in such events as the annual Christmas program. In the eight years that I attended a country school, not one student ever missed standing on the stage, in front of parents and neighbors, and speaking a piece or performing in a play. Farm kids often were considered shy, and many were. But they knew how to speak in front of an audience. They had eight years of practice doing it by the time they completed their elementary education. This early training in public speaking was invaluable. Ask any of the former country school children who are now mayors, farm or business leaders, college deans and professors, pastors, research scientists, elementary teachers, or county board members.

The development of values was an important part of what happened in the day-to-day activities of the country school. Learning values occurred naturally, as students worked together. Values that were a critical part of the operation of the country schools included hard work, cooperation, honesty, integrity, "There is nothing more important than your name," fairness, friendship (many developed lifelong friends in the country school), patience, being on time, self-discipline, and the importance of doing quality work.

Number of Students

One reason for school consolidation was to increase the size of schools, to make them more "efficient and effective" educational units. It was a time when nearly everyone was proclaiming "bigger is better." Larger farms, bigger dairy herds, bigger business—everything large, and growing larger.

Today, educators, and parents, too, have second thoughts about bigger education with larger schools. Researchers are discovering that big education is not better education. Educational researcher Bruce Barker compared small schools, those with less than 300 students, with those larger. He reported his findings in 1987 and said: "There exists in the small school a sense of pride, and an attitude and sense of personal possession and involvement on the part of students, parents, teachers, administrators, and community residents. To a great degree, the school is the community center...." He then pointed out the strengths of smaller schools. These included: An attitude that all children can learn, and that each child is challenged to learn up to his or her capacity. A place where teachers are more likely to know their students as individuals. Less red tape and fewer regulations. More opportunities for every student to participate in sports, drama, and serve as leaders in clubs. And an emphasis on basic subjects such as reading, math, and writing. Because of low pupil/teacher ratios, the small school was more likely to be learner-centered with strong emphasis placed on individualized and small group instruction. [3]

To things observe with care:

Of whom you speak, To whom you speak, And how, and when, and where.

—Anonymous

Currently, small rural schools in the Midwest and West register the highest Scholastic Assessment Test scores in the United States each year. Why? Researchers have found that school size is a key to student performance. Students do better in schools where the principal knows the name of each student, and this translates into schools that are 300 students or smaller. In these research studies, some schools had larger than average classroom size, but students still did better than those in larger urban schools with smaller class sizes.

After an analysis of twenty years of data on school spending and student performance, the researchers discovered three key qualities for a successful school:

1. A belief all children can learn, and a strong emphasis on core academic classes (reading, writing, and arithmetic).

2. Less administrative overhead.

3. High level of parental involvement.

States whose students ranked highest lived in Iowa, Kansas, Minnesota, Montana, Nebraska, South Dakota, Utah, Wisconsin and Wyoming. And, incidently, none of these states ranked in the top ten in spending on education. Most of them spent less than the national average.[4]

Development of a Love for Learning

Most country school children developed a great love for learning, and they learned how to learn independently. For many rural children, the one-room school was their first exposure to an interesting, exciting world that they knew little about because their farms were quite isolated and most of them had traveled less than twenty or thirty miles from home when they started school.

For many country school pupils, learning became one of the most exciting things they ever did. That attitude continued to serve them well as they went out into the world. Today, everyone must keep on learning. Much of this learning is self-directed. Country schools taught students how to take charge of their own learning, and how to seek help from fellow students when they were stuck. Learning was thus at the same time an individual effort and a cooperative endeavor.

Dealing With Unexpected Events

Today is a world of constant change. Very few students will follow the occupations of their fathers or mothers. Around every turn, there is something different, something that wasn't expected to happen. Some people today adjust to these changes quite easily, others have considerable difficulty.

Those who attended a one-room country school learned how to deal with unexpected events, and take them in stride, and have fun doing it. Winter in the one-room country school often included unexpected events. Blizzards and below-zero temperatures disrupted school activities. I recall so vividly below zero days when we all gathered around the wood stove in the back of the school and conducted our lessons. It was different from sitting in our regular seats, and brought us all closer together. We learned to do the best we could with what we had.

Importance of Education

The old saw "Too much book larnin' spoils a farm kid" was a myth. True, some parents believed schooling prevented their children from spending more time on the home farm. In the 1800s and early 1900s there was sometimes poor school attendance in rural areas—or attendance only during the winter months, when farm work was at a low ebb.

Mostly though, rural people gave tremendous importance to education. Immigrant families knew the schools helped their children adjust to a society that was unfamiliar to them. Many immigrant children started country school knowing essentially no English. They knew the language of their parents: German, Polish, Czech, Swedish, Norwegian, and a host of other languages. For these children of immigrant parents, the school's first task was to teach them English. Their parents also wanted them to become "good Americans" and they saw the school as essential for doing it.

By the time of the Depression, and then World War II, most farm families already sensed that not all, indeed perhaps none, of their children would return to the land. As farmers retired, they sold their land to their neighbors, and farms became ever larger, and the numbers of farmers became fewer. For these farm families, an education was essential for children who had to seek employment off the farm, as thousands of them did starting in the 1930s and continuing to this day. For many farm parents, the most important thing for their children was the country school. In some cases, even more important than the church.

The importance of education and the one-room country school permeated rural communities at every level, from parents to teacher, from school boards, to the entire neighborhood. What would happen to a child who did not know how to read, or write, or work with numbers? Nobody wanted to even talk about it. Some of us knew what it meant. On our

Y OUR TEACHER'S WISH
on Closing Day
Is that, in years to come, you may
Recall with joy the hours here spent,
And all that each dear friendship
meant.

From 1928 "End of School" souvenir. Russell Flats School, Marquette County.

home farm, our hired man could neither read nor write. He signed his name with an X. He was a young man, seventeen when he lived and worked with us. When he received a letter, which he did on occasion, I read it to him. He sat and listened, carefully, but I knew how much he wished that he could read it by himself. This young man, a handsome, strong fellow, was destined to a life of farm labor, which was what he knew. He had few options and extremely limited opportunities.

Consider the Best, Leave Behind the Rest

Educational researchers and policy makers are scrambling to find solutions to the failings of many of today's public schools. Revisiting the country school can provide ideas about teaching approaches, curriculum, and organizational strategies that likely have application today. But caution is necessary. Today's society is not the society we knew when the one-room country schools operated.

A place to begin is to examine the strengths of one-room country schools, and see which might have merit in today's educational context.

Some ideas from the country school are returning, often under the guise of "new and innovative" educational ideas: smaller class size, more than one grade in a school room, older children helping younger children, parents heavily involved in the education of their children, and a focus on neighborhood schools. These ideas were extremely important to the operation of the country school. But there were other, more fundamental, ideas as well. Values such as everyone can learn and is expected to, children learn at different rates and in different ways, and high expectations for achievement permeated the one-room country school. Perhaps it is time to examine our past, and consider the one-room country school as more than merely an interesting page in the history of public education.

Chapter Notes

1. Ben Logan. *The Land Remembers.* New York: Viking Press, 1975, p. 197

2. Quoted in Andrew Gulliford. *America's Country Schools.* Washington, D.C.: The Preservation Press, p. 45.

3. Bruce O. Barker. *The Advantages of Small Schools.* ERIC Clearinghouse on Rural Education and Small Schools, 1987.

4. Jane Fyksen. "Small, Rural Schools get A Plus," *Agri-View.* September, 1994.

Appendix A

Recess Games[1]

Country schools included children ranging in ages from five to fourteen or sometimes even older. Many of the games played during recess were fun for children of all ages. In the winter months, sledding and skiing were favorite recess activities, especially if the school had a nearby hill. Snowball fights were also popular on those days when it thawed enough for the snow to pack. With several days of warmer weather, the children sometimes built elaborate snow forts for conducting their snow ball fights. During the snow-free times of the year, children played on the teeter-totters, and the swings—about the only playground equipment most schools had available. Softball was a universally accepted recess game at country schools. But beyond the teeter-totters, swings, and softball, many other recess games were popular with country school children. Here are a few of those games, with instructions on how to play them.

Louisville School, Dunn County. School burned in 1921. Note syrup pail lunch buckets on the steps.

From Janet Creaser.

Anti-I-Over (Also called Annie-Over, Andy-Over, Aunti-Over)

The game requires a rubber ball, at least eight players, four for each side, and a low roofed building. For most country schools, the pumphouse or the woodshed served the purpose well. Team members gather on opposite sides of the building. A player from the "tossing team" throws the ball over the building, yelling "Anti-I-Over." The ball must be tossed in such a way that it bounces at least once on the opposite side of the building's roof. A player on the opposite side "catching team" tries to catch the ball. If the player is successful, the entire catching team runs around to the tossing team's side of the building. The person who caught the ball tries to tag members of the tossing team, either by touching them with the ball, or throwing the ball at them. If the ball touches a member of the tossing team, this person joins the catching team. The game continues with the catching team now becoming the tossing team. The purpose of the game is for one side to capture all the players from the other.

Bear in the Pit

This game tends to be a bit rough and is best left to the older children. All the players form a circle and hold hands, except the one selected as bear. The bear attempts to escape from the circle by going over or under the players clasped hands. If the bear escapes from the circle, everyone chases the bear and the person who catches him becomes the bear for the next game.

Button, Button, Who's Got The Button.

Players stand in a circle holding hands, with one person in the center. The players pass a button from one to another, as inconspicuously as possible. The player in the center tries to guess who has the button. If the right person is guessed, this person then becomes "It" and the former "It" joins the circle.

Dodge Ball

Players form two groups. One group forms a circle and the second group stands inside. Those players in the circle, using a basketball, or a rubber ball, throw the ball at players inside the circle. Those inside dodge as best they can. When players are hit, they join those in the outside circle. The last remaining player inside the circle is the winner.

Drop the Handkerchief

A popular game with younger children. Needed for the game is a handkerchief or a chalkboard eraser. At least eight players are needed to form a large circle. The person who is "It" runs around the outside of the circle and quietly drops the handkerchief behind one of the players—say player A. Player A chases after "It" and tries to catch "It" before "It" reaches A's place in the circle. If Player A does not catch "It," Player A becomes "It" for the next round of play.

Farmer in the Dell

One child is selected as farmer and the others form a circle around the "farmer." The children walk in a circle, singing:

"The farmer in the dell,
The farmer in the dell,
Heigh-O, the dairy-O,
The farmer in the dell."
Then,
"The farmer takes a wife,
(With these words, the farmer selects one of the children as a wife.)
The farmer takes a wife,
Heigh-O, the dairy-O,
The farmer takes a wife."

The game continues with the words, "The wife takes a child." (The player designated wife selects another player as child.) Then, as the song goes on, players are selected as follows: The child takes a nurse, the nurse takes a dog, the dog takes a cat, the cat takes a rat, the rat takes the cheese, the cheese stands alone. The cheese then becomes the farmer and the game starts over.

Fetch the Bacon

Someone is selected as game leader, often times it is the teacher. Two teams are formed and they face each other about twenty feet apart. An object such as a cap, or a chalkboard eraser is placed halfway between the two teams on the ground. Players on each team are numbered, starting with one (each team will have players numbered one to ?? depending on the number of team members). The game leader calls out a number, let's say number three. The player who is number three on each team races to the center to grab the object and return to his or her team before the other player can tag him or her. The team with the most steals wins the game.

Flipstick [2]

Equipment for flipstick includes two sticks about three-quarter inch in diameter. The short stick is five to six inches long, the long stick is about 24 inches and pointed at one end. Box elder or willow make ideal sticks, but other wood will work, too. Sometimes a broom handle was used, but this was considered too "commercial," particularly by those who didn't have one.

A slit or hole is dug in the ground, and two teams are formed. A team could have as few as one person, with no maximum number. Everyone in the school could play at one time. If the group got too large, it could be divided and two games of flipstick could go on at the same time.

One side is "up," and the other side is "in the field." The field's boundaries are previously marked to avoid later arguments. The side that is up assembles to the rear of the hole in the ground. Each player, in turn, follows three differ-ent steps until he is out. Points earned for each step are variable and adjustable, and agreed on before the game begins.

Step 1. This move is called "flip." The first player on the side that is up places the short stick across the hole at a right angle. This player then places the long stick in the hole, under the short stick, and flips the short stick out into the field, trying to make it difficult for some-one in the field to catch it. If a player in the field catches the flipped stick, the field team earns 100 points and the player who flipped the stick is out.

Step 2. If no one catches the flipped short stick, the "up" player now moves to the second step called "Hit." He proceeds to hit the short stick with the long stick toward the field. Those in the field, if they have the courage, try to catch it. If someone does, the field team earns 200 points and the player is out. Most of the time, if the stick is well hit, the players cover their heads and get out of the way since the short stick is traveling end over end and making a sound like a swarm of angry bees.

Also, if during step 2, the player should happen to miss the short stick, he is out and suffers hearing the hoots and appropriate comments from the oppos-ing team, and often from his own side as well.

If no one catches the "Hit," a player in the field is allowed to take three steps toward the hole from the spot where the stick landed. The field player then throws the short stick towards the hole, attempting to get within one length of the long stick from the hole. If successful, the player is out. But the player is allowed to guard the hole with the long stick to prevent this from hap-pening. This move could be somewhat hazardous, especially if the three strides mentioned above brings the field player almost on top of the hole.

Step 3. Assuming the player survives step 2, the player moves to this final step called "Pinkle." This is the toughest step of all. Player pres-tige was developed or not depending on how well this step was carried out. The object is to gently hit or loft the short stick with the long stick into the air as many times as possible, with the last hit going for distance. A minimum of two hits was required to avoid being out. The number of hits was important because it determined the number of points earned from the Pinkle step. Where the small stick landed in the field from the hole was measured with the long stick. Two lengths, three lengths, whatever the distance happened to be. If the small stick had been hit twice, the minimum number, the distance was counted by fives; if three times, by tens; if four times by twenty-fives, if five times by fifties, and if six times, a rare occurrence, by hundreds.

For example, if the small stick landed five long stick lengths from the hole, and the small stick had been struck three times, the score earned was fifty points (ten x five).

South Natwick School, Vernon County, 1948-1949. Children in upper grades. Robert Erickson, teacher.

Those in the field tried to catch the Pinkle before the short stick hit the ground, which was worth 500 points and the player was out.

A player surviving step 3 started over with step one, and continued until eventually out. When there were three outs, or when each player had been up, the teams changed sides. The game continued indefinitely, taking up all of recess and noon hour, picking up where it had left off at the last break, and sometimes on for days.

One of the unusual features of this game was both the side that was up and the side in the field could earn points at the same time. This fact influenced greatly the game strategy, even when choosing players for the teams. It was just as important to choose someone who could catch or throw accurately as one who was good on offense.

Another benefit of this game, besides the team effort, eye hand development and the like, was its emphasis on arithmetic skill.

Fox and Geese

A favorite winter game, especially after a fresh snow fall. A large circle is tramped in the snow. Then, like spokes in a wheel, two cross paths are constructed, forming a hub in the center of the circle. One player is designated the fox, all the others are the geese. The object of the game is for the fox to tag the geese, until there are no geese left. The center of the circle is "safe," but only one player can be there at a time. Everyone must stay on the circle or on one of the spokes. The game continues until the fox has tagged all the geese. The last person tagged becomes the fox.

Hide and Seek

One player is selected "It." With eyes covered, "It" counts to 100 and then tries to find the other children. "It" starts from home base. As "It" attempts to seek the other children, they try to return to home base without being tagged by "It."

Hide The Chalk

An inside game, for a rainy day recess. One player is sent from the room. While the player is out, someone hides a piece of chalk, or some other small object which is previously shown to the absent player. After the object is hidden, the absent player is called back and proceeds to search for the hidden object. While he or she is doing this, the others clap their hands, very softly when the player is far from the object, and more loudly when the player is close to finding it.

A variation of the game is for the players to call out hot or cold, depending on how close the person is to finding the object. Cold when the person is far away, hot when close. Various modifiers are used, freezing cold, when very far away; boiling hot when quite close and so on.

Keep Away

Players form a circle with one chosen as "It" who stands in the center. The other players bounce or throw a ball around or across the circle to each other. They try to keep the ball away from "It." When "It" catches the ball, he or she changes places with the last player who threw it and the game continues.

Kick the Can

A form of Hide and Seek, a tin can is placed at home base. Someone is selected as "It." Another player kicks the can and while "It" goes to retrieve it, the other players hide. "It" places the can back at home base, and begins searching for the other players. If a player, who has been hiding, can successfully return to home base without being caught, and is able to kick the can again, players find new hiding places and "It" continues as in the beginning. The last one caught becomes "It" for the next game.

London Bridge

The game requires at least six children. Two children are chosen to be a bridge. They grasp each other's hands and raise their arms in the air so the other children can walk underneath. At the beginning of the game, the children form a line and march under the bridge singing:

> London Bridge is falling down,
> Falling down, falling down,
> London Bridge is falling down,
>   My fair lady.

The following are penmanship exercises:

All temptations attack the idle.

After dinner sit awhile, after supper walk a mile.

Marry in haste, repent in leisure.

A friend in need is a friend indeed.

Keep your face to the sun and the shadows will fall behind.

Upon singing the words "My fair lady," the children forming the bridge drop their arms and capture the child who is walking underneath. The captured child then replaces one of the children in the bridge. Another variation of the game is to take the prisoner to a corner of the room, singing "Off to prison you must go, you must go, off to prison you must go, my fair lady." In this version, the game continues until all of the children are caught.

Musical Chairs

Another rainy day game for inside the school building. A record player is needed, or someone to play the piano. Many schools had wind-up record players with a few records of march music which worked well for this game. Chairs are placed in a circle, one less than the number of children playing. Everyone marches around the chairs as the music plays. When the music stops, everyone quickly searches for a chair. The person who doesn't find a chair is out. Another chair is removed and the game continues until only one person is left marching and is declared the winner. This game works well with all ages; even parents enjoy it.

Pom-Pom-Pull-Away

One player is selected to be "It" and stands in the center of the field. All the other players gather back of a line drawn on the ground, about fifty feet away. A similar line is drawn on the opposite end of the playing field. The player who is "It" yells "Pom-pom-pull-away, come away or I'll pull you away." All of the players now run for the opposite end of the field, attempting to arrive safely behind the line. "It" tries to tag as many players as possible. Those who are tagged join "It" and the game continues, except this time everyone in the center tries to tag those who attempt to run across the field. The last person caught is "It" for the next game.

Rachel and Jacob

All of the players except two form a circle, holding hands. The two remaining players go to the center of the circle. One of them, "Jacob," is blindfolded. The object of the game is for Jacob to catch the other player, "Rachel," by listening for the sound of her voice. Rachel must answer Jacob's questions, but she may answer, and then move quickly to another place inside the circle, leaving Jacob befuddled. Rachel may bend down, dash from one side of the circle to another, and otherwise do what is necessary to avoid Jacob catching her.

When Rachel is caught, Jacob returns to the ring. Rachel chooses a new Jacob, is blindfolded and the game continues, except this time Rachel attempts to catch Jacob.

Red Light, Green Light

Two lines about twenty-five feet apart are marked on the ground—one is a goal line, the other a starting line. One player is designated "It" and he or she stands on the goal line. The rest of the players stand behind the starting line. "It" stands with his or her back to the players, counts to ten and then quickly turns around, announcing "Red Light." While "It" is counting, the other players walk or run as far as they can toward the goal line. But the players must be careful to stop before "It" turns around. When "It" turns around and catches a player moving, that player is called by name and must go back to the starting line. The winner of the game is the player who reaches the goal line while "It" is still counting. The last person to reach the goal line becomes "It" for the next game.

Take a Giant Step

"It" stands about fifty feet from the other players who are in place at the starting line. "It" asks the first person in line to follow a series of directions: "take a baby step," "take a giant step," etc. When the player makes a mistake, he or she is out of the game. The first player to reach "It" is the winner.

Red Rover

Parallel lines are drawn about fifty feet apart. One player is chosen to be "It" and stands in the center of the field. All the other players gather behind one of the lines. "It" calls out, "Red Rover, Red Rover, let (names a child) come over." This child then attempts to run to the opposite line without being tagged by "It." If tagged, this child then becomes "It's" assistant and helps to tag the next person called to come over. The last person tagged becomes "It" for the next game.

Ring Around The Rosy

Younger children especially enjoy this game. At least four children are needed. The children walk or skip in a circle, holding hands and singing:

Ring around the rosy,
A pocketful of posies,
Ashes, ashes,
We all fall down.

And down on the ground they go. The game may be repeated indefinitely.

Notes

1. From Marguerite Kohl and Frederica Young, *Games for Children*. New York: Cornerstone Library, 1953, 1971; John B. Kline, Ed. *Rural Recreation*. Denver, PA: Saul Printing, 1990; Rural Schools Research Committee, *Good Old Golden Rule Days: A History of Sauk County Wisconsin Country Schools*. Baraboo, WI: Sauk County Historical Society, 1994; J.T. Giles. *A Manual of Physical Education for the Public Schools of Wisconsin*. Madison: Wisconsin State Department of Public Instruction, 1925, 1931, and the Author's memory.

2. Material from Burton Olson, Foley, MN and his brother, Clarence Olson, Madison, WI, who fondly remember playing this game when they attended a country school in Vernon County.

Appendix B

School Museums

*Bethel School. 1868.
Now a museum
school in Monroe.*

Photo by Steve Apps.

Balsam Lake. Located a block south and a block west of old courthouse museum on Main Street. Open Memorial Day weekend through Labor Day.

Beloit. Daisy Chapin School Museum at 2149 St. Lawrence, Beloit. The school was built before 1873 and used until 1920. It is operated by the Beloit Historical Society and is a part of the Hanchett-Bartlett Homestead museum site which includes several other buildings.

Berlin. Clark School Museum, 254 Water Street, Riverside Park. Open June to September, first Sunday of the month.

Brown Deer. Village Park, 4800 W. Green Brook Drive, Brown Deer. This school was built in 1884 and is listed on the National Register of Historic places. It operated until 1922 and later served as a church, a factory and a warehouse before it was moved in 1972 and restored by the Brown Deer Historical Society. Includes a "living schoolhouse" program for fourth graders each year, where teachers conduct classes as they were conducted in the early years of the school.

Burlington. Whitman School in Schmaling Park. Open by request for tours, and school classes.

Cadott. On Hwy 27, approximately one mile north of Hwy 29, east of Chippewa Falls. The Cadott Women's Club operates this 110-year-old school museum, which was the former Baker School. Open Sundays from June through Labor Day or by appointment.

Coon Valley. The Erickson School is part of Norskedalen Nature and Heritage Center, located one-fourth mile west of Coon Valley, off Hwys 14 and 61. It was built in the mid-1870s, and was moved from South Ridge to the Skumsrud-Thrune Farmstead to become part of the heritage exhibit. Open May first through October and as requested by groups.

Dodgeville. Located on County Hwy BB, east of Dodgeville, the Old Wakefield School is now part of Folklore Village.

In the 1830s white settlers came to this area to work in the lead mines. The Wakefield Mine was located on the same forty acres as the school, thus the name for the school. The Cutler Mine was also located nearby. Families associated with this mine formed a village they called Frogtown. Thirty children from this little village attended the Wakefield School, boosting the total enrollment to sixty-five when both mines were active in the last half of the 1800s.

In 1893, the community met to discuss building a new school as the old one had been condemned. After much debate, they finally decided to borrow money to build, with interest no more than eight percent. They agreed to pay Fred Farwell $15.00 for a half acre of land. The finished building cost $750, not including the pantry and entry which were built later.

In 1967, after the school closed, Jane Farwell, an internationally known folk dance instructor and recreational leader, bought the century-old building and created Folklore Village. She began weekly Saturday evening potluck suppers and dances, and restored the school as a center of community activities. Ms. Farwell died in April, 1993, but the Folklore Village continues.

A "life in a one-room school" presentation offers children a taste of earlier school days with slates, slate pencils and McGuffy Readers. [1]

Eagle. The Raspberry School is part of the State Historical Society's Old World Wisconsin complex located near here. Originally built by Scandinavians in Bayfield County in 1896, it has been restored to a 1906 appearance.

Eau Claire. The Sunnyview School, built in 1881, is located in Carson Park. It was moved to the park in 1964 from its original location at the junction of Eau Claire Cty F and II, in the Town of Washington. The original name of the school was Happy Jack. It closed in 1961 when the school district consolidated. With the help of school children's pennies, nickels, and dimes, the school was moved to Carson Park. Operated by the Chippewa Valley Museum.

Edgerton. Sheepskin School, Albion Academy Historical Museum, two miles north of Edgerton. The school closed in 1959 and was moved to its present site in 1969. Originally the school was located about two miles west of Edgerton in

Log School, Door County. Built 1866, closed 1881. Now a visitor center for Sister Bay.

the Sheepskin District, where the story goes, the farmers, after butchering their sheep, hung the skins on fences to dry. The museum has records back to 1861.

Fond du Lac. On the grounds of Galloway House and Village, 336 Old Pioneer Road. Moved to this site in 1963 when the building was purchased by the Fond du Lac Historical Society. Includes a collection of textbooks that date to the 1840s, lunch buckets, and children's straw hats. It was originally known as the Willow Lawn School and located on Hickory Street Road, southwest of Fond du Lac. Open from Memorial Day until Labor Day.

Galesville. One-room school museum at Trempealeau County Fairgrounds. Open for the county fair, and by request. Operated by Trempealeau County Historical Society.

Horicon. The 1884 Oak Park School, originally located on Birch Road south of Hustisford, was moved to Horicon, and placed on the grounds of the Satterlee Clark House. This brick school had replaced a log structure where classes were held beginning in 1852. In those days, each family with children in school was asked to furnish a half cord of wood cut to fit the wood stove. Teacher's salary was $25 for three months in winter, and $10 per month for the summer term. With school consolidation, the Oak Park School closed in 1953, and used as storage. The school is open the second and fourth Sundays, from 1-4. It is operated by the Horicon Historical Society.

Iola. A reproduction of a one-room country school is located at the Iola Historical Society complex, on Oak Street. The school was dedicated in 1994, and is used as a meeting place for the Iola Historical Society as well as a museum.

Janesville. The Francis Willard Schoolhouse located on the Rock County 4-H Fairgrounds, was built in 1853. The building is 18 x 24 feet, with two entry doors, one for boys and one for girls. It was closed as a district school in 1920. The Rock County Women's Christian Temperance Union purchased the building in 1921. It was used briefly as a classroom during the early 1950s, when area schools were overcrowded.

In 1969 the WCTU donated the school and property to the Rock County Historical Society, where it was eventually moved to the Rock County Fairgrounds in 1972. Listed on the National Register of Historic Places. Available to third grade students for half-day classes for three weeks in the spring and fall. Open during Rock County Fair, and by appointment.

Jefferson. Bakertown School Museum. 303 East Ogden St.. Open May to September, third Sunday of the month. Jefferson Historical Society.

Ladysmith. Little Red Schoolhouse. Located on Rusk County Fairgrounds, Ladysmith. Open weekends during summer. Operated by Rusk County Historical Society.

Lake Mills. Aztalan State Park. Lake Mills-Aztalan Historical society purchased the Aztalan School across the road from their museum in 1958, restored, and dedicated it in 1979. The school is of red brick and replaced an earlier one that burned in 1918. With school consolidation, it closed in 1956. It is furnished as a typical one-room schoolhouse. Open May through September.

La Pointe. On Madeline Island, the Lake View School was moved from the north end of the island in 1987 to the village of La Pointe, twelve miles from its original site, to become a museum. It was built in 1905 and became a center for community life on the north end of the island. Church services were even held there during the summer months. Two other schools also once operated on the island. One is still in operation, La Pointe School, where one teacher meets with K-7 grade students in one room.

Loganville. Friendship rural school museum located three miles south of Loganville on Hwy 23, then one-half mile west on Friendship Road. Open June to September and by appointment.

Manitowoc. The Shadyside School is now a part of Pinecrest Historical Village (3 miles west of I-43, Exit 152, Cty Hwy JJ to Pine Crest Lane). The school, which operated from 1872-1956, was originally located on Highway 151 about two miles west of Silver Lake College in the Town of Manitowoc Rapids. It was built at a cost of $500 following a fire which destroyed the log school in operation since the 1850s. In the early days, students attended a five-month winter term or a three-month summer term—older students attending in the winter, younger ones in the summer. The building was moved to the Pinecrest Historical Village in 1976 at a cost of $5,645 and is operated by the Manitowoc County Historical Society.

Mazomanie. East, at the intersection of State Hwy 19 and Cty F. The Old Halfway Prairie School is Dane County's first country school. It was originally a log building constructed in 1844 and donated by Mary Fowler, a member of the British Temperance Immigration Society. The name, Halfway Prairie, relates to the school grounds serving as a camping place for lead miners who traveled from Mineral Point to Portage, and found the place to be about midpoint on their journey. The word "Old" was added in 1915, to avoid confusion with a later school. In the early days, the school operated according to the seasons of the year. The fall term closed with the first heavy snowfall, and the spring term began when the roads opened. A more standard eight-month school term was adopted in 1895. The school and the grounds are now a Dane County park. The building is open to visitors at selected times.

Menomonee Falls. An 1851 school is located in Old Falls Village on the corner of Pilgrim Road and County Line Q. It was built at a reported cost of $55.00. Initials and names from bygone days carved into the original wood dado walls can be seen today. Open Sundays May through September. Operated by the Menomonee Falls Historical Society.

Menomonie. Schoolhouse located at Dunn County Recreation Park, Menomonie. Open during fair time and by appointment.

Merrill. Brickyard School Museum, 4-H Fairgrounds, Sales Street. Tours by appointment.

Monroe. Little Red Schoolhouse (old Bethel School) Museum. Adjacent to Green County Historical Museum, 1617 9th Street, Monroe. Open late May to September, Saturdays and Sundays, 2-5.

Muskego. Mill Valley School at Muskego's Old Settlement Center at W184-So 8092, Racine Ave. Originally the school was located on Milwaukee-Beloit Road, now called Hillendale Drive. The school was named Mill Valley because three mills once operated in the valley. The school was restored and opened in 1984. The school is open May to September, third Sunday of the month and by appointment.

New Glarus. A one-room school is part of the Swiss Historical Museum, 612 7th Avenue. The building is over a hundred years old and was moved to the museum complex in 1963. In May, the fourth graders visit the museum and tour the other museum buildings. Then for the next two days, each fourth grade class spends a day attending school in the school museum. The museum is very popular and has had visitors from every state and many foreign countries.

New London. An 1857 one-room school. New London Heritage Historical Society museum complex.

New Richmond. Camp Nine School (1902) located at New Richmond Heritage Center, 1100 Heritage Drive, Hwy 65 South. The school was built in 1902 and restored to look as it did in the early days. It was moved to the Heritage Center in 1993. Camp Nine school was built to accommodate the children of logging families who worked at the nearby logging camp. Francis Bittle taught at the school in the 1920s, walked to school in winter with snowshoes, and was paid $35.00 per month. A wind-up phonograph provided music for the children until a piano was purchased for $15.00. The school closed in 1957 when it was consolidated with Glenwood City. In the fall, the school sponsors a "living his-

Camp Nine School. St. Croix County. Built in 1902. Currently in the New Richmond Heritage Center where it is a museum.

tory" classroom for elementary students in grades one through four. Operated by the New Richmond Preservation Society.

Pardeeville School Museum. The Portage Prairie School, located near Friesland and built in 1872, was moved to the museum site in Pardeeville in 1994. It is open five days a week, 1-4, starting in early June until early fall.

Plover. Hie Corners School Museum is located in Heritage Park, Washington Avenue. It was built in 1894 and formerly located on Cty T, Amherst Township, Portage County. The museum is operated by the Portage County Historical Society.

Racine. An 1888 Bohemian Schoolhouse is located at the Living History Museum, Five Mile Road and Hwy 31 in Caledonia Township, Racine County. The school was built to teach the Bohemian language and culture on weekends to children who also attended the regular public schools during the week. As the Bohemians married members of other ethnic groups, and became more comfortable with their new country, there was less interest in the school. It became a meeting place for the Bohemian Society and other social events. The building was deeded to the Racine County Historical Museum in 1974.

Reedsburg. An 1865 school is located at Pioneer Log Village and Museum on Hwy 23 and 33, three miles east of Reedsburg. First used as a church, then as a school. It was moved to the Pioneer Village from its original location three miles south of Reedsburg.

Rhinelander. Adjacent to the Logging Museum. Known first as the Neuhaus School and later as the Tom Doyle School, the building was constructed in 1908 or 1909. In 1953, the school was purchased by the Pine Lake School Board for $700 and moved to River Road where it became an extra classroom for the Pine Lake School while a new building was being constructed. By 1955 the building was vacant.

In 1976, the Rhinelander Kiwanians bought the building for $100 and gave it to the Rhinelander PTA Council. Moving costs were $900 plus $775 to build a new foundation. The building was refurbished in 1977 and early 1978, and opened to the public on July 15, 1978. It is operated by the Rhinelander Area PTA Council and the Rhinelander Area Retired Teachers Association.

Richland County. The Akey School Museum School is located three miles south of Twin Bluffs on County TB. The building has been completely restored as a rural school and is open on Sundays, from 2-4 Memorial Day to Labor Day. Operated by Richland County Historical Society.

Ripon. Little White School House on grounds of the Republican House.[2] Probably the most famous one-room school in Wisconsin as it is the birthplace for the Republican Party on March 20, 1854. During a time of intense debates over the issue of slavery, a meeting was held at the Congregational Church in Ripon, on March 1, 1854. At that meeting a resolution was passed which read: "Resolved, that the passage of this bill, if pass it should, will be the call to arms of a great Northern party, such a one as the country has not hitherto seen, composed of Whigs, Democrats and Free Soilers; every man with a heart in him united under the single banner cry of 'Repeal! Repeal!'" The resolution was in response to the 1854 Kansas-Nebraska bill which would negate the Missouri Compromise of 1820 and allow slavery north of a line once agreed on by everyone.

On March 20, a public meeting was held at the schoolhouse in Ripon. At this meeting 54 people signed a statement creating the first Republican committee which would lead to the consolidation of antislavery opinion under the name Republication.

The schoolhouse closed in 1860 when a larger brick school building was constructed. After that it was a home for a time. In 1908 it was moved to the Ripon College Campus, and then later moved to the grounds of the Republican House. A special celebration was held at the school in 1954 to mark the centennial of the party. At the event, President Eisenhower lit a gas torch by remote control from Washington, D.C.

St. Croix Falls. County Fairgrounds, St. Croix Falls. As part of the Amery summer school program, two Amery elementary school teachers conduct two-week classes here each summer. They have a waiting list of students who want to attend.

Museum School, Rhinelander. Formerly Neuhaus School. Built c. 1908, closed 1955. Moved to museum site 1976.

Red School. Walworth County. Built 1876, closed 1963. Now operates as a school museum.

From Nora Walnoha.

Sharon. Red School Museum, Sharon Township, Walworth County, corner of Town Hall and Peters Road. The first red school was built on this site in 1846; the present building was built in 1876 and was open until 1963 when the district became part of the Sharon Community School. Operates as a museum and gift shop.

Shawano. One-room school, North Franklin Street on Wolf River Pond, Shawano. Open Mid-June through August, Wednesdays and Sundays, 1:30-4. Operated by Shawano County Historical Society.

Tomah. Called the Little Red School House, this museum school is located in Gillette Park in the 1300 block of Superior Avenue. It was the former Water Mill School, in rural Tomah. The last teacher was Margeurite Griffin. The museum is operated by the Retired Teacher's Association of Monroe County.

Former Water Mill School in rural Tomah, now a museum school in Gillette Park, Tomah.

Viroqua. The Foreacker School Museum is found at 606 W. Broadway. It is used in the month of May for area third graders where a teacher conducts classes as she did in the 1940s. Operated by Vernon County Historical Society.

Watertown. Octagon House and America's first kindergarten, 919 Charles Street, Watertown. Open daily.

Wausau. Little Red Schoolhouse museum located in Marathon Park, Wausau. Open Saturday and Sunday afternoons during the summer months. This was the former Spooner School that was located six miles west of Wausau in the town of Stettin. It was built in 1894 and closed in 1962. The Altrusa Club of Wausau owns the school, and the Marathon County Historical Society runs a living history program there for fourth and fifth grade children.

West Bend. Old Oak Knoll School, now a part of Cedar Lake Home Campus (three miles south of Hwy 33 on Hwy Z). In this 1917 school, schooling in the late 1800s and early 1900s is recaptured through intergenerational programming for first through eighth graders along with adults.

Westfield. The Cochrane-Nelson House Museum, 213 Lawrence Street, includes a school room on the second floor furnished with desks, library, water bubbler, globe, school clock, teacher's desk, blackboard, dunce stool, etc. Also includes teachers' record books and minute books from the school clerks. Open Wednesday afternoons from last Wednesday in May until first Wednesday in September.

Wild Rose. Within the museum complex is the former Progressive School, also known as the Swamp School which was built in 1874. The building was moved to the museum site in 1982, a project of the Waushara County Retired Teachers Association. After purchase of the building, they constructed a new foundation, replaced interior walls, repaired window casings, constructed a new chimney, reinstalled the blackboards, and put on a new roof. Meanwhile, they purchased desks, and gathered books, samples of seatwork, historic pictures, a stone drinking fountain and other interior fixtures. The original bell was located and the owner donated it to the school. Total costs for the project: purchase of building, $600, moving building, $750, repairs, paint and renovation, $2200.

The first teacher who taught at the Progressive School in 1874 received $20 per month during the winter term (four months) and $16 per month for the summer term (two months). Tours of the school are available on Wednesday and Saturday afternoons during the summer months.

Notes

1. Margaret Metcalf, Violet Williams, and Marion Pustina. *Schools of Iowa County*. Blanchardville: Iowa County Bicentennial Education Committee, 1976, pp. 119-120.

2. Ruth Shaw Worthing. *The History of Fond du Lac County*. Fond du Lac: Privately published, 1976, pp. 12-13.

Index of Schools

A

Akey School 214
Audubon School 180
Aztalan School 212

B

Badger School 36, 67
Baker School 210
Bakertown School 212
Bay View School 167
Bell School 80
Bethel School 209, 213
Blooming Prairie School 117
Blue Mounds School 32
Bohemian School 214
Boice Creek School 103
Brickyard School 213
Bryon School 59, 66
Burritt School 157

C

Camp Nine School 213, 214
Campbell School 150
Chain O' Lake School . . 2, 3, 57, 66, 104, 114,
        123, 131, 139, 141, 144, 146, 148, 175
Chapp Creek School 135
Christensen School 167
Clark School 209
Coher School 112
County Line School 149, 150

D

Daisy Chapin School 118, 209
Dalton School 62
Dodd School 37, 160
Dopp School 125, 126
Downsville School 155
Dyer School 39

E

Eagle Valley School 129
Erickson School 210

F

Fairview School 90
Fauver Hill School 150
Ferndale School 39
Fernside School 10
Finch School 129
Flora Fountain School 158
Foreacker School 217
Francis Creek School 17, 150
Francis Willard School 211

G

Gard's Corner School 86
Government Indian School 151

H

Happy Jack School 210
Hie Corners School 214
Hillside School 38, 157
Hochungra Indian Mission School . . . 151, 152
Hope School 101, 143, 144
Hugunin School 153

J

James Otis School 99, 101, 104, 106

K

Kaminski School 27
Kathan Lake School 143

L

LaFollette School 112, 136, 144, 177
Lake View School 167, 212
La Pointe School 165, 166, 170
Larkin School 157
Linrud School 35
Little White School 215
Louisville School 38, 67, 153, 155, 201
Lower Wilson Creek School 155, 156
Lynxville School 139

M

Maple Grove School 175
Maple Valley School 33
Meadow View School 58
Mill Valley School 213
Mt. Moriah School 35, 70

N

Nelson Dewey School 131
Neuhaus School 214, 215
North Bend School 156
North Bright School 61

O

Oak Dale School 50
Oak Knoll School 217
Oak Park School 211
Oasis School 139
Old Halfway Prairie School 212

P

Pine Lake School 214
Pioneer School 30
Pleasant Ridge School 147, 158
Pleasant Valley School 162
Polk Dairy School 58, 85, 86, 100
Popular Grove School 33
Portage Prairie School 214
Prairie View School 58
Progressive School 25, 116, 217

Q

Quarry School 9, 159

R

Raspberry School 210
Red School 216
Reynald School 62, 64
Richfield School 154
Richmond Island School 159
River View School 101
Riverview School 111
Rock School 38
Rogers School 141, 161, 184
Roosevelt School 28
Round Lake School 66, 162, 191
Russell Flats School 199

S

Sentinal Ash School 130
Shadow Lawn School 118
Shadyside School 212
Sheepskin School 210
South Bright School 61, 73, 122, 130
South Natwick School . . . 31, 58, 116, 123, 205
Spooner School 217
Squaw Lake School 30, 58, 94, 141
Stone School 26, 193
Sunnyview School 137, 210
Swamp School 25, 217

T

Tom Doyle School 214

U

Union No. 1 School 57, 132
Union Valley School 65, 121, 134

W

Wakefield School 160, 210
Water Mill School 216
White Rapids School 102
White School 117
Whitman School 210
Willow Grove School 139
Willow Lawn School 211
Wilson School 118
Wiota School 146, 160, 163
Wisconsin Point School 35, 39
Woodprairie School 163
Woodrow Wilson School 35

Index

A

Acott, Mrs. Norma. 53
Adams, Henry B. 36
Afield With Ranger Mac 80, 90
Albion Academy Historical Museum 210
Alcott, Louisa May. 73
Aldrich, George I. 88
American Association of
    School Administrators 192
American Country Life Association 181
American Spelling Book 71
Amherst Township, Portage County 214
Amish 165
Anti-I-Over 6, 115, 162, 202
Antigo 36, 67
Apostle Islands 167
Apps, Marcie Kirk 193
Arbor Day 28, 144
arithmetic 17, 70
Audubon, John James 73
Aurora, Illinois. 118
Aztalan State Park 212

B

Bailey, L. H. 83
Bakken, Phoebe 143
Balsam Lake. 209
Baraboo News, The 155
Baraga, Frederick 167
Barber, George W. 86
Barker, Bruce O. 196, 200
Barnard, Henry 19
Barnum, Nettie 154
Barron County 112, 131, 136, 144, 177
Bartell, Jerry. 97
battery operated radios 90
Bayfield 166, 168, 169, 171
Bayfield County 186, 210
Bear in the Pit 202
Beecher 5, 168
Beetown Township, Grant County 158
Beloit. 118, 209
Bennett Law of 1889 20
Berger, Richard 52
Berlin 209
Bible study. 19

Bill of Rights 13
Bisegger, Lucile. 23, 119, 164
Bittle, Francis. 213
Black Hawk District. 164
Black River Falls School District 151
Black Stallion, The 96
Blanchardville 176
Bloom, Allan 51
Bohemian Society. 214
Bondele, Marjean 23, 119, 164
Bonheur. 150
Boscobel 62
box socials 142, 143
Boxrucker, Rosemary 102
Bray, Mary. 129
British Temperance Immigration Society . . . 212
Brodie, Fawn M. 28
Brosnan, Anna 53
Brown Deer 209
Brown Deer Historical Society 209
Bruce. 27, 130
Bruso, Lelah 39, 140
Bryhn, Estella Krohn 56, 189, 190
Buffalo County 129
Burlington 210
Burnett County 66, 162, 191
Burroughs, John. 83
Buslaff, Joy. 9, 164
Button, Button,
    Who's Got the Button 117, 202

C

Cadott. 210
Cadott Women's Club 210
Caledonia Township. 214
Captain Midnight 79
Carey, Alice 88, 158
Cedar Lake Home Campus. 217
Chapman, Mabel 164
Charter of Education for Rural Children . . . 182
Chicago Northwestern 135
Chippewa County 135
Chippewa Falls. 210
Chippewa Valley Museum. 210
Christmas program(s) . . . 27, 99, 101, 102, 196
Christmas program, values from 109
Christmas seals. 103

Churchill, Winston 70
Cincinnati College 72
Civil War 17, 159
Clark County 61, 73, 122, 130, 136
classes 61
Cochrane-Nelson House Museum 217
colonial schools 12
Committee on Rural Education 181
Common School Diploma 48
community activities 140
community center 197
compulsory attendance law 20, 23
Connecticut 19
consolidation 8, 11, 16, 23, 179,
180, 182, 184, 186, 196
constitutional convention 15
Coon Valley 210
Cooper, James Fenimore 73
Cooperative Educational Agencies 53
cops and robbers 117
Cotts, Myrtle 154
country school teachers 25
county superintendent of schools . . 16, 22, 51, 53
county examinations 83
County Line Lutheran Church 149
county nurses 53
county school committees 189
Crawford County 30, 62, 64, 112, 139
Creaser, Janet 111, 164, 201
Cubbage, George 163
Cubberley, Ellwood P. 178, 183, 190
Culter, Horace M. 40, 190
cursive writing 77
Cutler mine 210
Czechoslovakia 36

D

Dahl, Eleanor 144
Dahlberg, August 48
Daluge, Gwen 164
Dane County 32, 58, 65, 101,
143, 144, 157, 177, 186
Darlington 146
Darlington district 164
Dayton, Town of, Waupaca County 161
Davidson, Ed 131
defense stamps 145
demonstration room 45, 46
Department of Interior 153
Depression *see Great Depression*

Dick and Jane 77
Dickens, Charles 73
Dietz, Arthur 84
diploma, Common School 48
diploma, eighth grade 85, 87
distance education 98
district taxes 16
Dodge Ball 202
Dodge County 66, 149, 177
Dodgeville 210
Door County 36, 211
Douglas County 33, 135
Drop the Handkerchief 115, 202
Dunn County 38, 67, 111, 153, 201
Dunn County Recreation Park 213
Dunn, Elizabeth 48
Dunn, Town of, Dunn County 153
Dupuis, Kateri 28
Duzynski, Nancy 86

E

Eagle 210
Eau Claire 210
Edgerton 210
education, importance of 199
educational reformers 183
eighth grade diploma 85, 87
eighth grade graduation 84
Einstein, Albert 107
Elefson, Jean 172, 173
Elefson, Vern 172, 173
Elk Mound 30
Ellarson, Robert 92
Ellsworth 90
Elson, William H. 88
Elson-Gray Basic Reader, Book Two 76
Emerson 63, 188
end of year picnic 141
end of school souvenir 21
Engle, Hildegarde 99
English grammar 17
Epstein, Betty 152, 164
Erickson, Robert 31, 32, 58, 205
Erickson, Walter 48
Everts, Jim 180

F

4-H 145, 163
Faribault County, Minnesota 112
Farmer in the Dell 203

Farmers Union 163
Farwell, Fred 210
Farwell, Jane. 210
Fauver, David. 150
federal land grant money 16
Festge, Otto. 65
Fetch the Bacon 203
first year teaching. 33
flash cards 81
Flipstick. 116, 203
Florence County. 177
Flugstad, Naomi. 44, 45, 46
Folkers, Gail Olson. 159
Folklore Village 160, 210
Fond du Lac County 34, 37, 49, 59,
                        80, 99, 101, 104, 160
Fond du Lac. 211
Foote, Mary A. 52
Forbes, Alexander. 88
Forest County 186
Fort Atkinson. 92
Fowler, Mary 212
Fox and Geese 119, 162, 205
Fox, Lloyd 132
Fox River. 11
Francis Creek Sportsman's Club 151
Frank, Michael. 18
Frederic. 29
Frederic Common School District. 163
free public education 17, 22
Frees, Jennie. 193
French, Joseph 150
French traders 166
French trading days 9
French trading posts 11
Froebel, Fredrich 18
Fyksen, Jane. 200

G
Galesville 211
Galesville Republican 156
Galloway House and Village 211
Ganter, Shirley. 164
Gardner, Teresa 55
Gays Mills 30, 144
geography 17
George Foster Peabody Radio Award 92
Gillette Park. 216
Gipple, Bert. 156
Glenwood City 213
goiter pills 58

Golden Book of Favorite Songs, The 60, 61
gophers 111
Gordon, Edgar B. "Pop" 90, 93, 94
Gorhn, Palma 53
Gorske, Wilmer 35, 70, 186
graduation, eighth grade 84
grammar, English 17
grammar schools 12
Grant County 12, 27, 38, 39, 103,
                        135, 143, 147, 158, 177
Gray, William S. 88
Great Depression. 35, 143, 177, 199
Green Bay 11, 12, 22
Green County Historical Museum. 213
Green Lake 70, 149, 187
Green Lake County 35, 58, 62,
                        70, 137, 186, 187
Green Lake County Board 186
Greene, Agnes Lynch 35, 39
Greig, Edvard. 95
Griffin, Margeurite. 216
Grignon, Pierre 11
Grover, Edwin Osgood 40
Gulliford, Andrew. 24, 63, 68, 87, 200

H
Haferbecker, Henry 145
Halloran, Harriet 23, 119, 164
Halloween party. 140
Halstead, Ellouise. 62
Handrich, Arlin 175
handwriting 77
Hanley, Mary 99, 101, 104, 106
Hansen, Sigrid Jensen. 44
Harper's Fourth Reader 74
Haugen, Selmer 32
Hawley, Inez Thompson 25, 44, 116
Hawthorne, Nathaniel 143
Hayes, Mrs. Miriam 30
Heagle, Dorthea. 163
hectographs 81
Heger, Jeff 86
Heritage Park. 214
Hide and Seek 162, 206
Hide The Chalk. 206
high school teacher training 47
hiring procedures 30
Holland, Magdalen (Flanagan) 146
Holman 35
home credits 18
home schooling 172

Horicon 211
Horicon Historical Society 211
Hornby, Hal 187
Horne, Harley 70
Humburg, Wilfred 112
Hunt, J. N. 88
Hustisford 211

I

If I Were Going 77
Illinois 177
Indian Agency 153
integrated school 158
integrated district 186
iodine pills 55
Iola 211
Iola Historical Society 211
Iowa County 12, 22, 121, 134
Iowa 177
Irving, Washington 73

J

Jablonic, Randy 61, 122
Jackson County 151, 152, 156, 186
Janesville 153, 211
Jefferson 212
Jefferson Historical Society 212
Jefferson, Thomas 13
Jenks, Faith 60
Johnson, Morris 159
Johnson, Pearl 35
Jorgenson, Lloyd P. 23, 40, 56
Junior Forest Rangers 91
Junior Red Cross 145
Justiss, Zona Schwandt 149

K

Kapok 145
Keeney, Mary 86
Keep Away 206
Kenosha 18, 22, 41
Keskimaki, Vieno 136
Kick the Can 115, 206
Kieffer, Twyla Hart 118
Kindergarten 18
Kjelland, Arnold 32
Klein, Kathy 168, 170
Kline, John B. 208
Klingbeil, George 50
Klug, Mary 100

Knoff, Mildred Larsen 30
Knutson, Marilyn 121, 134
Kohl, Marguerite 208
Komenski, Town of, Jackson County 151
Kreitlow, Burton 184, 192
Krogstad, Roland 90

L

La Baye 11
La Crosse 47
La Crosse County 35, 52, 150, 186
Ladysmith 27, 33, 212
LaFayette County 146, 160, 163, 176
Lake Mills 212
Lake Mills-Aztalan Historical Society 212
Lake Superior 22, 166, 169, 171
Lancaster 158
Langlade County 36
La Pointe 167, 168, 169, 212
LaPrairie & Rock Townships 153
LaPrairie District 153
Larsen, Carl 33
Larsen, Mabel Grundahl 58
Larson, Norman 188
Lawson, Vera 62
Lehner, Philip 186
Leicht, Hazel 52
LeSueuer, Pierre 166
Let's Draw 94, 98
Let's Sing 92, 94
Lewis, Loren 66
life vests 145
literary society 140
Living History Museum 214
Locke, John 19
Logan, Ben 191, 200
Loganville 212
London Bridge 116, 206
Lone Ranger 79
Longfellow, Henry Wadsworth 73
Longfellow's "The Village Blacksmith" 76
Luening, Diederich 38
lunch time 63
Lund, Doris J. 102, 103, 110, 143, 146

M

Mabon, Ruby Waldon 38, 67
Mackinac Island 167
Madden, Shirley Bennett 35, 41, 102
Madeline Island 22, 23, 165,
166, 167, 169, 170, 212

Manawa. 86
Manitowoc. 212
Manitowoc County 17, 150
Manitowoc County Historical Society 212
Mann, Horace 19, 20
Mann, Thomas 21
Mantor, Elta. 28, 40
Marathon County Historical Society 217
Marathon Park. 217
Marinette County 28, 35, 102, 186
Marinette County Normal School. 41
Marion 30
Markesan. 187
Marquette County 50, 199
Marquette County School Directory 49
Marth, Elmer 58, 85, 100
Massachusetts Bay Colony 12, 22
Mattson-Port, Carol . . . : 135
Mawhinney, Jan Otten 117
Mazomanie 212
McCarty, Harold 92
McCombe, Charlotte Boyd. 164
McGuffey Reader. 72
McGuffey, William Holmes 72
McKnight, Ada. 62, 64, 112
McLane Grade School 86
McNeel, Wakelin 90, 91
Medary, Town of, LaCrosse County. 150
Meiller, Larry 101, 144
Menomonee Falls. 213
Menomonee Falls Historical Society 213
Menomonie. 213
mentor system 63
Merrill 100, 213
Metcalf, Margaret. 23, 217
Michigan 17
Michigan law. 11
Michigan territory 11, 22
Midweek Lakeshore Chronicle, The 164
Milfred, Jeffrey. 174
milkweed pods 145
Millet 150
Mineral Point 12, 22, 212
Mining Region Teacher's Association 41
mischief. 65
Monico 39
Monroe 209, 213
Montessori, Maria 39
Moorefield, Story. 24
Mott, Alva 33, 135
Mueller, Erhart. 40

music participation. 93
Musical Chairs 117, 207
Muskego 213
Muskego's Old Settlement Center 213

N

Nagel, Paul. 65, 164
National Committee on Rural Education . . 182
national patriotism 13
national school reforms. 19
nature corner 80
Natzke, Myrtle 100, 101
Nelson, Judy 66
Nelson, Raymond 27
Nesbit, Robert C. 23
New England 12, 18
New England Primer. 71
New Glarus 213
New Jersey. 17
New London 213
New London Heritage Historical Society. . . 213
New Richmond 213
New Richmond Heritage Center. 213
New Richmond Preservation Society 214
New York. 17
Nicolet, Jean 11, 22
Niedzwiecki, Esther Luke 130
normal schools 10, 42
North Bend 156
Northwest Ordinances 22
Northwest Ordinances of 1785, 1787 13
Norwegian Ball 116

O

O'Donnell, Mabel 88
Odanah 167
Ojibway. 166, 167
Old Falls Village. 213
Old World Wisconsin. 210
Olsen, Lola 101
Olson, Burton 116, 123, 208
Olson, Clarence 208
Olson, Dewey 159
Olson, Ella. 32
Olson, Lizzie Holloway. 161
Olson, Mrs. Lawrence. 151, 152
Onalaska School District 150
Oneida County. 39, 82, 85, 186
Oneida County Normal School 45

opening exercises 60
orthography 17
Outagamie County Normal School 30
Ozaukee County 52

P

Palmer, John. 118, 178
Palmer's Guide to Business Writing 78
Pardeeville 214
Parent Teachers Association 163
passenger pigeon 73
Patzer, Conrad E. 24, 29, 40, 56, 190
Pennsylvania 17
petty schools 12
Phillips 44
Phillips Elementary school 43
Phillips Times, The 53
phonics 71
picnic, end of year 141
Piechowski, Theresa 2, 70
Pierce County. 57, 90, 132
Pinecrest Historical Village 212
Pittsburgh Coal Dock. 39
Plato 144
Platteville. 42
Platteville Normal School 42
Plautz, Ruth. 137
pledge of allegiance. 60
Plover 214
Polk County 29
Pom-Pom-Pull-Away. 115, 207
Porlier, Jacques 11, 22
Port Washington 52
Portage. 11, 212
Portage County 214
Portage County Historical Society 214
Prairie du Chien. 11, 22
Prescott 172
Price County. 43, 48, 53, 55, 157
Price County Training School 43, 44
Priem, Linde Lee 33
Prisoner's Goal 162
Progressive Course in Reading, The 75
Progressive Course in Spelling Complete 79
prohibition law 28
Public School Methods 82
Pulliam, Roscoe 181, 190
purposes for the schools 20, 21
Pustina, Marion 23, 217

R

Rachel and Jacob 207
Racine. 214
Racine County. 214
Racine County Historical Museum 214
radios, battery operated 90
Rahn, Jane. 164
Ranger Mac 80
Raphael 150
Rasmussen, Lillie Ann 141, 161, 164
rate-bill tax. 15, 22
Reader's Circle Certificate. 78
reading and arithmetic 17, 70
recess 111, 119
recess games. 201
recipe for making a hectograph 82
Red Banks 11, 22
Red Cliff 167
Red Light, Green Light. 207
Red Rover 208
Reedsburg 43, 214
Refior, Everett 113
Reinders, Marlene 154
report card, 1940 4
report card, 1945 7
Republican House 215
Republican Party 215
Retired Teachers Association
    of Monroe County 216
Rezek, Clarence 17
Rhern, Charles. 59
Rhinelander 28, 102, 140, 143, 169, 214
Rhinelander Area PTA Council. 214
Rhinelander Area
    Retired Teachers Association. 214
Rhode Island 17, 19
Richland County 214
Richland County Historical Society. 214
Riley, Martha. 9, 23
Ring Around the Rosy 115, 208
Ripon 215
River Valley District 156
Rock County 118, 153
Rock County 4-H Fairgrounds 211
Rock County Historical Society 212
Rock County Women's
    Christian Temperance Union 211
Rooney, Elizabeth. 32
Rose, Town of, Waushara County 148
rules for teachers 29

Run Sheep Run 116
Runquist, Edna 57, 132
rural district school system 181
rural-urban differences 177
rural values. 185
Rusk County 27, 130, 175
Rusk County Fairgrounds. 212
Rusk County Historical Society. 212
Rusk County Normal 33
Ruskin, John 77

S

safety patrol 60
Satterlee Clark House 211
Sauk County 10, 26, 38, 53,
145, 155, 157, 189
Sauk County Training School 43
Sauk polio vaccine 52, 55
Schatzmann, Iman Elsie 181, 190
Schedel, Mrs. Gerhard R. 157
scholastic assessment test scores 197
school aids 182
school consolidation law 186
school district(s) 13, 16
school committees 185
School Law of 1848 15
School of the Air 96, 98
school reformers 192
school's purpose 12
Schueffner, Ray 34
Schuette, William C. 10, 26, 43, 155, 157
Schultz, Ruby. 36, 48
Schurz, Carl. 18
Schurz, Margarethe Meyer 18
Schwalbach, Jim. 94
science 79
Sears Roebuck catalog. 81
Seerley, Homer H. 29, 40, 179, 190
Servin, Sandra 86
Shakespeare, William 73
Sharon. 216
Sharon Township, Walworth County. 216
Shawano 216
Shawano County 100
Shawano County Historical Society. 216
Shepard, Isaac 147
Siedenglanz, Mrs. Georgia 28
Sister Bay. 211
Slamer, Caroline. 134
slaves 158
Smith, Alice E. 23

Smith, Sally 65
snowball fights 119, 201
Soderland, Doris 140
softball game. 121, 141, 162, 201
Solon Springs. 33
Soo Line Railroad. 135
South Lancaster Township 38
Southport. 18, 22
souvenir, end of school 21
spelling 79
spelling book 69
Spencerian approach. 78
Spors, Florence Heineck 158, 164
Spring Green 156
St. Croix County. 30, 58, 94, 141, 214
St. Croix Falls. 215
state superintendent of schools 15, 16,
17, 20, 182
State Department of Public Instruction 153
Staton, Marcia 27, 130
Stettler, Hulda 129
Stevenson Training School 41
Stokes, Bill 112, 136, 137, 144, 177, 178
Stone, Julia M. 40, 190
Straseski, Aileen 37, 49, 80, 160
strengths of one-room country schools 199
subscription schools 12
Suderland, Doris 82
Sugar Camp. 143
sugar rationing. 52
Superior. 35, 39
Superior Bay 39
superintendent of schools
county. 16, 22, 51, 53
state. 15, 16, 17, 20, 182
township 16, 51, 179
supervisory teachers 47
Sveda, Joe. 36, 67
Swiss Historical Museum 213
Sylvander, Carolyn Wedin. 68

T

Take a Giant Step. 208
Tarbox, Judy Lee 30, 144
Tarry, Peggy 86
Taylor County 163
teacher 25, 194
characteristics 28
contract. 32, 34, 52, 54
creed. 26
duties 27

high school training 47
preparation 41
rules for 29
teacher's association 41
teaching aids 81
territorial legislature 15
Terry and The Pirates 79
textbooks 70
Thanksgiving 99, 140
Thompson, Isabel Clark 58
Thompson, William F. 23
Thompson, William 190
Tomah 92, 151, 216
township government 13
township school superintendent 16, 51, 179
Trade Lake, Town of, Burnett County 162
Trempealeau County 186
Trempealeau County Fairgrounds 211
Trempealeau County Historical Society 211
Trimbelle Town Hall 172, 173
Troy Township, Sauk County 155
truancy 20
Trudell, Bonnie 30, 58, 63, 94, 98, 141
Twain, Mark 53

U

Udelhoven, Hazel . . 38, 39, 135, 143, 158, 164
Uminski, Phyllis 27, 103
United States Office of Education 177
United States Constitution 13
University of Wisconsin 20, 97

V

Valentine's day 140
values 196
Vernon County 35, 58, 116, 123, 177, 205
Vernon County Historical Society 217
Vernon County Normal School . . 31, 44, 45, 47
Victrola record player 61
Vilas County 186
"Village Blacksmith, The" 76
Viroqua 217

W

Wabiszewski, Andrew 188
Wakefield mine 210
Walnoha, Nora 175
Walter, George 86
Walworth County 117, 118, 129, 159, 216
war bonds 145

Washington County . . 32, 52, 58, 85, 100, 154
water cooler 58
Watertown 217
Waukesha County 9, 10, 159
Waupaca County 87, 141, 161, 184
Waupaca County graduation exercises 86
Waupaca County
   Superintendent of Schools 30
Wausau 217
Waushara Argus 146
Waushara County 3, 27, 35, 66, 84, 102,
      114, 116, 131, 145, 148, 175, 177, 186
Waushara County Normal School . . . 44, 46, 83
Waushara County Retired
   Teachers Association 217
Wautoma 46, 83, 85
Weber, Leona 164
Webster, Noah 71
*Webster's American
   Spelling Book,* 1831 . . . . . 12, 31, 136, 151
Webster's Blue Back Speller 13, 71
Wedin, Carolyn 66, 164, 191
Welch, Mildred 190
West Bend 86, 217
West Salem 189
Westby 31, 123
Westfield 217
Weyerhauser 33
WHA radio 61, 90
Wheelock, J. H. 31
White House conference
   on rural education 182
Whitewater 42, 113
Whitewater Normal School 42
Whittier, John Greenleaf 2, 73
Wild Rose 1, 25, 217
Williams, Violet 23, 217
Wilson Creek 156
Winnebago County 193
Winnebago students 151
winter 130
Wiota Handy Helpers 4-H Club 146
Wiota Recreation Park 160
Wisconsin High 95
Wisconsin Idea 97
Wisconsin legislature 180, 182
Wisconsin Public Radio 101
Wisconsin River 11
Wisconsin School of the Air
   (WHA radio in Madison) . . 4, 69, 89, 96, 98
Wisconsin State Teachers Association 41

Wisconsin territorial law, 1840 15
Wood County 65, 180
Woolsey, Jean. 86
work-up 162
Works Project Administration (WPA) 150
World War I. 145
World War II 21, 35, 65, 90,
                      145, 177, 183, 186, 199
Worthing, Ruth Shaw. 217
writing. 17

Y

Yellow River. 144
Young, Frederica. 208

To order

One-Room Country Schools:
History and Recollections from Wisconsin

or for a free catalog
of other Amherst Press Books-To-Go titles,
call toll free 1-800-333-8122.

Amherst Press
PO Box 296
318 N Main Street
Amherst, Wisconsin 54406